Compensatory Education for the Disadvantaged

Programs and Practices: Preschool through College

by Edmund W. Gordon
Professor of Psychology and Education
Ferkauf Graduate School of Humanities and Social Sciences, Yeshiva University

Doxey A. Wilkerson
Associate Professor of Education
Ferkauf Graduate School of Humanities and Social Sciences, Yeshiva University

College Entrance Examination Board, New York, 1966

Inquiries regarding this publication should be addressed to Editorial Office, College Entrance Examination Board, 475 Riverside Drive, New York, New York 10027.

Copies of this publication may be ordered from the College Entrance Examination Board, Publications Order Office, Box 592, Princeton, New Jersey 08540. The price is $4.50 per copy.

Library of Congress Catalog Card Number: 66-28250

Printed in the United States of America

Dedication

This book is dedicated with love to Susan and Yolanda, our respective partners in life.

Acknowledgments

To write a book while one does too many other things requires more than usual dependence upon colleagues and friends. In the conduct of the study which is reported in this book I have had to depend on the assistance of many people. From the initial stages of this study I have had the cooperation and help of my dear friend of many years, Doxey Wilkerson, who shares the authorship of this work with me. As senior research associate in the department that I chair, he carried major responsibility for all data collection and for the analysis and summary of the data on programs in higher education. In addition he has been a constant source of advice and support in the development of all sections of the report. Richard Plaut, who originally had the idea for developing a directory of programs of compensatory education, has supported this project from its beginning. Through the organization that he heads, the National Scholarship Service and Fund for Negro Students, he arranged for the grant from the Old Dominion Foundation which enabled us to initiate this study. It was through the generous support of the College Entrance Examination Board and the kind assistance of S. A. Kendrick that the study was expanded and completed. In the conduct of various stages of the survey of programs and practices Mrs. Stella Lubetsky, Mrs. Gertrude Goldberg, Mrs. Ruby Puryear, Mr. Lawrence Perkins, and Dr. Julian Roberts have made helpful contributions.

The yeoman work in the completion of this report has been performed by my editorial assistant, Mrs. Joan Gussow, who spent endless hours poring over correspondence, questionnaires, field observer reports, descriptions of programs, newspaper reports, and my own notes in the production of an integrated description of the fast-moving developments in this field. In addition she and Mrs. Ann Kaufman, College Board editor, had the difficult task of taking my often ponderous prose and translating it into readable copy. While work progressed on this front, there were other fronts to cover. I am indebted to my fellow faculty members and to my two cherished and devoted administrative assistants, Mrs. Effie Bynum and Miss Frances Green for helping me to keep these several fronts covered.

It is a pleasure to express my appreciation to all of these friends, but it should be made clear that they bear no responsibility for the limitations of the product. They have made it possible for me to complete this study, but cannot be held responsible if I have not done my work well.

A final word of thanks and apology is due the many persons who took the time to complete questionnaires, to receive members of my field staff, or to answer questions put by telephone and letter. The information supplied by their efforts is the primary data upon which this study is based. I deeply appreciate the cooperation thus provided and as deeply regret that the time lapse between data collection and the publication of this report may have made it impossible for the published report to do justice to some programs and developments in the field.

Edmund W. Gordon

Foreword

It is fitting that the College Entrance Examination Board and the National Scholarship Service and Fund for Negro Students (NSSFNS) should join in publishing a compendium, analysis, and evaluation of compensatory education across the nation. Ten years ago, these two organizations, and the New York City Board of Education, cosponsored the first program in what later came to be known as compensatory education—the Demonstration Guidance Project at Junior High School 43 and George Washington High School. The Demonstration Guidance Project later expanded into the Higher Horizons program. For the uninitiated, the term compensatory education is used for programs of special and extra services intended to compensate for a complex of social, economic, and educational handicaps suffered by disadvantaged children.

The National Scholarship Service and Fund for Negro Students continued to carry the message of compensatory education to all parts of the country through its Community Talent Search program. The program was supported by the Old Dominion Foundation. The foundation also provided funds for the NSSFNS share of this study and publication. The project was initiated through a NSSFNS approach to Dr. Gordon for a study of compensatory education on the elementary and secondary school level. It was enriched by a subsequent decision by the College Board to ask Dr. Gordon to expand the study to include programs of higher education, and a more intensive analysis of elementary and secondary school programs.

From these beginnings sprang the programs discussed and listed in this volume. Many of the programs are local, supported by both public and private funds. There are also statewide programs, like the ones in New York and California. More recently the federal government has entered the field in a rather handsome way. The Office of Economic Opportunity appears at both ends of the spectrum: Project Head Start for preschool children and Upward Bound for students planning to attend college. The United States Office of Education came in through the Elementary and Secondary Education Act.

The College Board and NSSFNS are hopeful that this publication will lead to a greater understanding of the current nature, extent, and value of compensatory education. Both organizations are grateful to Dr. Gordon and his associates for the professional competence and high degree of commitment they have brought to the undertaking.

Richard Pearson
President
College Entrance Examination Board

Richard L. Plaut
President
National Scholarship Service and
Fund for Negro Students

Contents

1. The socially disadvantaged – a challenge for education

Over the last two decades a number of economic, political, and social factors have combined to bring to the forefront of public attention the condition of underdevelopment among human beings in all parts of the world. Although the American people have become increasingly aware of the economic and social disparities which exist everywhere on the globe, nowhere are the handicaps imposed by deliberate and accidental underdevelopment of human resources a greater source of embarrassment and concern than in the United States in the second half of the twentieth century. Faced with an embarrassing situation, public opinion has performed as it is wont to perform – it has looked for a scapegoat – and, in this situation, no one has seemed more available to bear the blame than the professional educator. The choice is not without justification. Granted that the school has not created the conditions that make for social disadvantage and economic deprivation. It is, nevertheless, quite clear that neither have professional educators done much to help significantly the children who are products of these conditions – and this in spite of the fact that there have been tremendous gains in educational technology and educational resources during the first half of this century.

The Panel of Education Research and Development has reported:

"By all known criteria, the majority of urban and rural slum schools are failures. In neighborhood after neighborhood across the country, more than half of each age group fails to complete high school, and 5 percent or fewer go on to some form of higher education. In many schools the average measured IQ is under 85, and it drops steadily as the children grow older. Adolescents depart from these schools ill-prepared to lead a satisfying, useful life or to participate successfully in the community." (Zacharias, 1964)

Who are the children so poorly served by this, the most affluent nation in history?

The term socially disadvantaged refers to a group of populations which differ from each other in a number of ways, but have in common such characteristics as low economic status, low social status, low educational achievement, tenuous or no employment, limited participation in community organizations, and limited ready potential for upward mobility. Variously referred to as the "culturally deprived," the "socioeconomically deprived," the "socially and culturally disadvantaged," the "chronically poor," the "poverty-stricken," the "culturally alienated," and so on, these are people who are handicapped by depressed social and economic status. In many instances, they are further handicapped by ethnic and cultural *caste* status. For a number of interrelated reasons more and more of these families are concentrated in the decaying hearts of our great metropolitan centers. Predominantly Negro, Puerto Rican, Mexican, and southern rural or mountain whites, these people are the bearers of cultural attitudes alien to those which are dominant in the broader communities they now inhabit, and their children come to the school disadvantaged to the degree that their culture has failed to provide them with the experiences that are "normal" to the kinds of children the schools are used to teaching.

As a consequence, in school these children show disproportionately high rates of social maladjustment, behavioral disturbance, physical disability, academic retardation, and mental subnormality. Such problems are acute wherever they are found, but they have been exacerbated and brought to the focal point of public attention because of the recent increasing concentration of this population in the center-city areas.

Now the fact is that the presence in our schools of children whose background of experience and whose readiness for the traditional demands of the school differ from those of white, middle-class United States nationals is not a new phenomenon. We have had large numbers of such children in the past, particularly during the period of great migrations to this country. History reveals that the schools were challenged at that time just as they are today, and it further reveals that they failed in their attempt at providing for the educational needs of many of these children. But the schools' failures in previous years had far less serious consequences for the children and for society than do our failures today.

Unlike the industrializing economy of the nineteenth and early twentieth centuries, our automating economy has little need for the talents the uneducated have to offer, strong backs and clever hands, simple manual strength and manual skill. Instead, we have a growing need for trained minds, educated judgments, and conceptual skills. We have arrived at a period in human history in which man is increasingly required to manage vast categories of knowledge, to identify and solve highly complicated interdisciplinary problems, and to arrive at infinitely complex concepts and judgments in order to maintain, control, and advance the technological and social organization by which we live. The quality of intellect, the adequacy of conceptual competence, and the depth of human understanding and compassion required of those who must man that organization are not routinely produced in today's schools. And our failure to train the best qualified to the maximum extent is but an extension of our failure to provide even the minimum survival skills for this complex age to those whom we call the socially disadvantaged. Obviously, the highest level of intellectual competence will not be required of everyone, but educators are increasingly embarrassed by the large numbers of young people whom they have failed to prepare for much less complex intellectual, academic, vocational, and social functioning. In fact, they are quite properly under attack, from a number of quarters, for their failure to provide adequate preparation even to many of the young people who seem to succeed in our system. Witness the large number of high school and college graduates who have difficulty in recognizing a concept and who are practically incapable of producing a clear one. Professional education has a long history, and is not without its successes, but its failures are many. In its present state it is hardly ready to meet the demands of the latter half of the twentieth century — this time of crisis in the management of knowledge and technology.

While the explosive expansion of knowledge and the technological revolution would, in any case, have increased the pressure for educational change, other pressures have also been brought to bear on the nation's educational establishment. The growing crisis in intellectual resources and the management of knowledge has been paralleled by a social crisis involving civil, or more properly, human rights. A social revolution is in progress, led by the Negroes, other poverty-stricken people, and their allies — a revolution in which these dispossessed members of our affluent society are demanding total and meaningful integration into the mainstream and an opportunity to share in the wealth of the nation. More than any other single factor, equality of educational opportunity and, ultimately of educational achievement, is viewed as crucial in achieving this end.

Herein lies the challenge to the school. In the early thirties, under the pressure of the great Depression and the demands of workers organizing to claim their rights, new concepts, new techniques, and new approaches to political, social, and economic organization were introduced, and our nation as a whole was led into accepting a greater degree of responsibility for the promotion of the general welfare. The civil or human rights revolution will inevitably require of society in general – and of the educational establishment in particular – that they assume responsibilities for true universal education to a degree heretofore unknown. For we have never actually achieved universal education in this country although the notion of universal education as the goal to strive for is by no means a new one. It is not only contemporary society that has failed. There has never been a time in human history when certain groups of people were not cut off from the educational mainstream.

In this country, though the term "disadvantaged" is new, a concern for the kinds of people the term designates goes back at least as far as the Civil War. During the short-lived period of the Reconstruction following the Civil War, considerable attention was given to the problems of the disadvantaged in this country. The Freedmen's Bureau recognized as one of its major responsibilities the development of educational facilities for former slaves. Religious groups, foundations, and state governments became active in the establishment of training academies and fledgling colleges. Poor whites and freed Negroes, who were then represented in state legislatures, established free public education for their children in states where it had not previously existed. But these efforts were greatly reduced and retarded when the Reconstructionists were betrayed by a political sellout to the forces of reaction. The Reconstruction had moved forward in part as a result of Northern support and because the presence of federal troops in the South had controlled Ku Klux Klan resistance movements. The election of Rutherford B. Hayes marked the end of the Reconstruction. Northern support was cut off; all federal troops were withdrawn. The result was the establishment of more conventionally stable governments and the introduction of serfdom as a substitute for slavery for most Negroes and for many poor whites in the South.

Despite the change in the popular mood, educational concern for the disadvantaged, still primarily Negroes, continued. In the latter years of the nineteenth and the early years of this century the effort was marked largely by the struggles within the Negro community itself. Struggles between those who would emphasize mechanical and vocational training – represented by Booker T. Washington – and those who recognized the need for a liberating education, one that would train the minds of at least a leadership group. The latter point of view was most prominently represented by W. E. B. DuBois. Ultimately, it was those who advocated the training of hands in vocational skills who gained impetus from the accelerating industrialization of the national economy.

This same industrial growth brought about a change in the composition of the population that was the object of special efforts in education. The great immigrations that began around 1880 and continued through 1924 brought to the United States a new disadvantaged population of Caucasian Europeans. Where the uneducated masses of Negroes had been largely confined to rural areas, the immigrants congregated in the growing industrial centers that were to become our great cities. The principle of free public education having been established, the children of these new citizens were drawn into the schools. But for those who could not or would not stay in school, there was a ready place in the nation's burgeoning labor force. The major problems of compensatory education for these children of foreign parents appear to have been born of language differences. Problems of differences in learning patterns, cognitive style, aspiration, or level of intellect were of less significance; of greater significance was the fact that the society could absorb the school's failures.

During the thirties, three forces began to draw the attention of the nation's schools to the problems of young people who were not succeeding. With the coming of the great Depression, the students rejected by the school found themselves less and less welcome in the labor force. At the same time a newly developing concern with mental health and human welfare forced on society a new view of its responsibilities for serving the needs of the handicapped. And finally, the never-extinguished embers of the Negroes' civil rights struggle flared anew with a demand for equal though then separate educational opportunities.

This equal though separate approach was first focused on the question of teacher salaries. Little concern was openly expressed at the time over the existence in many school districts of two school systems, one for whites and another for Negroes, and court battles in the thirties and early forties turned on the question of whether two teachers with equal preparation and equal responsibility could be paid different salaries simply because one teacher happened to be white and the other teacher Negro. Similar attacks were mounted against differing budgets for Negro and white schools and differing quality in school programs and plants. Under the impact of these attacks, schools, particularly in the South, but also in the North and West, began to make major improvements in the facilities, staffs, and programs of schools which served predominantly Negro populations. In a few instances where it proved too costly to provide equal *and* separate facilities, Negroes were even admitted to facilities previously reserved for whites. Southern legislators strained state budgets to make available record sums of money for the improvement of Negro education, largely to insure against the forced mixing of the races in public schools. So effective were their efforts that many of the children coming out of these improved segregated schools surpassed those of the less clearly segregated but predominantly Negro schools in the North.

The "separate but equal" struggles had served as a catalyst in the improvement of educational opportunity for children who were disadvantaged by their racially segregated status. But the logical and ultimate outcome of these struggles, the rejection of "separate" as inherently unequal, temporarily neutralized their catalytic effect. Pragmatic experience, social history, and constitutional clarification combined to remove the legal sanctions for alleged separate but equal public educational facilities. Without the hope of continued segregation even if Negro schools were improved, and faced with directives to desegregate in any event, the legislators' enthusiasm for improving education for Negroes quickly diminished. The 1954 Supreme Court school desegregation decision having killed the "separate but equal" position also temporarily stifled school improvement for Negro pupils in the South.

But progressive social forces are not so easily destroyed. A rapidly changing world situation, significant changes in our own economy, and the momentum of the civil rights struggle—massively supported by the 1954 and other Supreme Court decisions—gradually supplanted the negativism of a school improvement program based on maintaining Negro segregation. It was replaced with a more general and a more positive concern—that of providing adequate education for a variety of disadvantaged children whom the public school had not adequately served in the past. And while the civil rights struggle was bringing pressures to bear on the educational system from one direction, there was evidence from elsewhere that everything was not as it should be in the schools. During World War II the nation was suddenly made aware of the large numbers of young men who were ineligible for military service or were of reduced value to the war effort because of their limited intellectual development.

So it was that after the war serious national attention began to be given to the problems of education for the disadvantaged. Some pilot projects date back to the mid-forties when New York City's Harlem Project was initiated. And in New Mexico, work was begun with Mexican-American and American Indian children. The Harlem Project provided for greater teacher stability, increased auxiliary services—primarily in the field of mental health—and an attempt at improved pupil and parent motivation. The Harlem Project appears to have met with modest success. The New Mexico project focused on remedial reading and language usage and on inculcation of middle-class values—an approach which seems to have met with little success.

The landmark effort directed at the rehabilitation of disadvantaged youth was the Demonstration Guidance Project of Junior High School 43, continued the following year in George Washington High School in New York City. This project was proposed by the New York City Board of Education's Commission on Integration and was cosponsored by the Board of Education, the National Scholarship Service and Fund for Negro Students (NSSFNS), and the College Entrance Examination Board. The major objective of this project was the early identification and stimulation of able students from low socioeconomic status homes. Its program included multi-focus identification procedures, intensive individual and group counseling, special training for teachers, and follow-up through senior high school and college. It required an increased investment per pupil in educational materials, additional and specialized personnel, and schoolwide organization around the procedures and goals of the project. The Demonstration Guidance Project not only succeeded in greatly increasing the pursuit of training and higher education beyond high school, but also reduced the dropout rate and incidence of behavior problems below what would have been anticipated for such a population if left untreated. Expanded in coverage, though reduced in substance, the successful Demonstration Guidance Project was incorporated into the regular structure of the New York City Public Schools as the Higher Horizons Program and became the model for much of the work across the country directed toward the rehabilitation of disadvantaged youth.

The movement was materially furthered by Community Talent Search, an activity of the NSSFNS. Community Talent Search carried the message of what was learned in Project 43 to cities across the country and to two states—New York and California—through a program of consultation and technical assistance. This work was financed by grants from the Old Dominion Foundation.

Three additional developments that have had a profound influence on programs of compensatory education deserve mention. The National Defense Education Act, passed under pressure of international competition and concern for national security, made special provision for the discovery and encouragement of youth with latent or unrecognized talent. With funds made available through the legislation, state departments of education and local school districts were able to initiate programs providing increased opportunities and services for this part of the population.

The second contribution was developed entirely outside the public schools as an outgrowth of the research programs of the Peabody College for Teachers and the Institute for Developmental Studies at New York Medical College. There, experimental programs emphasizing language enrichment at the preschool level provided evidence that early intervention was one of the more promising approaches to overcoming educational disadvantages. As a result of these programs, a number of private agencies and public school systems began to institute special nursery school projects as a supplement to, and in some instances as a part of the public school program. The summer 1965 Project Head Start provided dramatic evidence of awareness on a national level of the possibilities of early intervention. The evaluation of the results of this eight-week program will, it is hoped, provide further leads to the kinds of techniques and approaches that may prove to be most effective in overcoming the handicaps with which disadvantaged children start to school.

One of the most influential growth forces in programs for the disadvantaged has been the Ford Foundation's Great Cities Project. By providing grants as large as $500,000 to a number of the larger cities, the foundation has encouraged massive and integrated attacks upon the problems of education in urban depressed areas. Typically, these projects have mobilized a wide range of school and community resources, but they have placed no emphasis on a single approach. What they have had in common is a concern for disadvantaged children and their families.

It is, then, a constellation of forces—the struggle of the disadvantaged and segregated for improvement in their life chances; society's growing demand for competence in the development of concepts and use of knowledge; and the new insights growing out of research projects, pilot demonstrations, and research programs—that have raised to the level of national concern the issue of providing special educational and social projects for disadvantaged children and their families. This national concern has been reflected in the establishment by Congress of the Office of Economic Opportunity whose principal focus is an attack on the problems, including the school problems, of the disadvantaged. In addition, Congress has passed legislation providing increased support, through the United States Office of Education, for research and innovation in the improvement of education for disadvantaged children. In this respect, it is encouraging to note that during the same year in which a number of our local military establishments were shut down, Congress passed legislation funneling $1.5 billion into education—a sum which may well be doubled in the next year. It is indicative and provocative. It may be that we have finally come to a time in our nation's history when we shall begin to look for our ultimate national security not to our defense establishment, but to our schools.

Sensitive to the emergence of education for the disadvantaged as a major national concern, NSSFNS and Yeshiva University through its Ferkauf Graduate School of Education (FGSE) embarked upon a nationwide study of programs directed at improved education for socially disadvantaged children and youth. The study was initiated by the National Scholarship Service and Fund for Negro Students through a grant from the Old Dominion Foundation. Additional support for the expansion and continuation of the study was provided through a grant to the university from the College Entrance Examination Board. The investigation began in the fall of 1963. The bulk of the data reported here was compiled before June 1964, but includes supplementary materials that continued to arrive as late as March 1966.

The investigation of compensatory educational programs and practices was designed to identify and describe the status of such activity in the United States; to identify and discuss the pragmatic and theoretical bases of such programs; and to evaluate major trends in these programs against the background of existing knowledge concerning the nature of the problem and the teaching-learning process. The study was conducted in two parts. Attention was first directed to a survey of programs and practices in the public schools of this country. Inquiries were sent to the chief education officers of the 50 states, to all cities with populations of more than 50,000, and to each person or project listed in the combined files of the NSSFNS and FGSE. The combined files were based upon extensive bibliographic review and personal visits. Part two of the study was directed to a survey of practices in higher education. Questionnaires were mailed to 2,000 institutions of higher learning in the United States and to several noncollege-based programs whose focus was on increased opportunity in higher education for youth from disadvantaged backgrounds.

2. Pupil characteristics and theoretical bases for compensatory education

It is quite evident that in order to provide equality of education for disadvantaged children we must identify the children and characterize the specific nature of their disadvantage. We need to know exactly how these youngsters differ from those with whom our traditional educational system has been successful; for even though the existence of academic deficiency among a high percentage of this population is well documented, the specific character of the deficiency is not. Psycho-educational appraisal has more often been directed at establishing the fact and quantity of deficit than at evaluating its quality and nature. In attempting to characterize disadvantaged populations, the California Advisory Committee on Compensatory Education concluded that these children could generally be identified among those who are "below average in school achievement as measured by standardized tests," and who, in addition, have some combination of one or more of the following problems:

1. economic deprivation attributable to an absent, nonproducing, or marginally producing breadwinner;

2. social alienation caused by racial or ethnic discrimination with all its accompanying deprivations in housing, employment, and education, or by membership in a different or non-English-speaking subcultural group; and

3. geographic isolation because of transiency, or residence in an area far removed from adequate educational facilities.

If these are the social factors which correlate most highly with disadvantage, what are the personal qualities which appear to be common to children who are the products of such socially handicapping backgrounds? The California report suggests:

"They tend to lack in the social experiences which our present school curriculums assume to be common to all students. This means that their experiences in the society are marked by sharp differences from the 'normal' or 'regular' pattern assumed by the middle-class oriented school.

"Their motivation may be inappropriate to normal school achievement or success. That is, they may display a sense of failure or lack of drive.

"They often have been subjected to values and expectations which tend to generate conflict between themselves and the school."

Intellectual, social, and environmental characteristics

Valuable as this classification of traits may be in identifying children who should be included in specially designed educational programs, it can hardly serve as an adequate theoretical basis for the structure of these programs. To say that a disadvantaged child lacks readiness, motivation, and a learning-oriented value system is not so much a description of what a disadvantaged child is as it is a description of the way he appears to be when he is faced with a traditional school environment. In order to determine whether or not the disadvantaged child is, indeed, what he appears to be, the serious attention of research workers in the behavioral sciences is required. The questionable genesis of identified conditions always presents the scientist with the challenge of discovering the sources and mechanisms whereby these conditions arise and are modified. Although there has been a considerable delay in the serious undertaking of investigations related to the education of the disadvantaged, increased research efforts are finally being directed at these problems. These efforts have had three principal focuses: the child, the environment (school, family, and community), and the teaching-learning process. Of these three factors, the disadvantaged child has by all measures been the subject of greater research attention than either environments or processes.

Available research data permit the identification of several categories of behavior which are encountered with great frequency among socially disadvantaged children. First, there are the language studies. Several of these studies suggest that children from disadvantaged backgrounds, in comparison with middle-class children, are less able to make use of standard English in representing and interpreting their feelings, their experiences, and the objects in their environment. It is important to note that the apparent deficiency which has been observed is in the use of standard English —there is no definitive evidence that these children suffer from an underlying deficiency in the use of language and other symbols.

Differences in the use of language can be the result of a variety of circumstances, some of which make for disadvantaged status. Differences on all quantitative measures of language function were found in a group of children of the same age, sex, intellectual quotient, and economic level. The observed differences consistently favored those children who were raised in their own homes when compared to children who were raised in institutions (Pringle and Tanner, 1958). In the interpretation of these findings the investigators suggested that the children raised in institutions had been adversely affected by inadequate exposure to language which resulted in restricted language development. Other investigators have been concerned with the relationship between economic group status and language development. For example, more children with retarded speech development have been found among lower socioeconomic groups than in the upper classes (Beckey, 1942; Irwin, 1948). Templin (1953) found that speech articulation test scores were higher for children from an upper economic group than they were for children from a lower economic group. Her data indicate that children of the lower socioeconomic group took about a year longer to reach essentially mature forms of articulation than did children from the upper economic group. After age one-and-a-half years, children show differences in their mastery of speech sounds.

Other evidence indicates that it is not only speech articulation but general language usage that may be influenced by social and economic status. In studies by Thomas (1962) and Templin (1957), in which the variable studied was the number of words used per remark, lower socioeconomic group children showed a mean of 5.6 words used per remark and the middle-class children showed a mean of 6.9 words per remark. In a comparison of the speech of Negro and white children, Anastasi (1952) found a higher frequency of mature sentence types, more complex sentence construction, and better detailed concepts among the white children. The language of lower-class youth has been described as restricted in form, as serving to communicate signals and directions, and as tending to confine thinking to a relatively low level of repetitiveness (Bernstein, 1961). The language of middle- and upper-class youth is described by the same investigator as elaborated in form, serving to communicate ideas, relationships, feelings, and attitudes. These findings suggest that while complex language systems are present in children from all socioeconomic groups, important qualitative differences exist in the form and use of the language systems. These differences may have important implications for learning. However, since the investigations upon which these findings rest have not included the analysis of learning facility or lack of it in the context of language forms and vernaculars peculiar to the disadvantaged, the finding of differences does not enable us to specify the nature of the learning problems involved.

The conclusion that learning problems among disadvantaged children are somehow related to differences in language development gains some support from studies of concept development in this population. It has been noted that differences in language associated with social class tend to increase with the age of the child (Deutsch, 1963; Hilliard, 1957). As lower-class children grow older, they fall further and further behind middle-class children on the language variables measured. Several investigators have observed these differences and the cumulative deficits reflected in the functioning of lower-class children. They have suggested that if the acquisition of language is a prerequisite to concept formation and problem solving, then the presence of this language deficiency would indicate a tremendous lower-class deficit in conceptual function. In his study of this problem, Deutsch (1963) found that children from socially disadvantaged backgrounds were relatively good on motor tasks, on tasks which required a short time span, and on tasks which could be most easily related to concrete objects and services. Children from similar backgrounds were found to be generally inferior in abstract thinking and placing pictures and objects in appropriate categories. It appears that a delay in the acquisition of certain elements of language may make the transition from concrete to abstract modes of thought more difficult (Ausubel, 1964). Concept formation, the development of ideas and generalizations about experiences and relationships, has been described in the disadvantaged child as an emphasis on content rather than on form. Reasoning in socially disadvantaged children is thought to be dominated by inductive rather than deductive processes (Riessman, 1962). This way of thinking may limit the child's ability to make accurate generalizations and to transfer knowledge through the utilization of previously learned concepts (Gordon, 1964).

In a cross-cultural inventory of the arithmetic concepts of kindergartners, Montague (1964) found significant differences between social classes in favor of the higher socioeconomic status group; but Deutsch (1960) found that arithmetic scores were higher than reading scores among a population of lower-class children, even though both scores were depressed below national norms. In interpreting this finding, it is possible that the difference might be accounted for by the view that reading involves motivations arising from specific value systems which may not be fully shared by the disadvantaged segment of society. On the other hand, arithmetic may involve concrete acts, such as marketing and other natural counting situations, which are common to the entire society. In a report of work in Prince Edward County, Virginia (Gordon, 1965), arithmetic scores were similarly found to be less depressed than reading scores in the 7- to 10-year age groups. These children, who had been deprived of formal education for four years, are thought to have developed simple arithmetic skills in their everyday chore experiences. These experiences did not, however, provide a basis for the casual or incidental acquisition of reading skills.

If these assumptions are correct, that reading and arithmetic skills vary in the degree to which their acquisition is dependent upon experience, then the Montague, Deutsch, and Gordon data would seem to support the observation that disadvantaged children tend to depend more on real life encounters than on symbolic experience in developing ideas and skills. In a study by Siller (1957), however, this view is subjected to closer examination. Studying 181 white sixth-graders he found that higher status children scored higher than lower status children on all tests of conceptual ability; showed a greater tendency toward abstraction in making choices between types of definitions than lower status children; and when matched with lower status children on nonverbal tests, scored higher than their counterparts on verbal tests. Had Siller stopped there, his findings would confirm the impressions of others. When, however, the groups were matched on the basis of IQ scores, none of the differences remained. Thus, while there is a considerable body of evidence to support the statement that lower status children tend to prefer concrete to abstract frames of reference in dealing with concepts and mastering certain skills, the origin and nature of this preference and its relationship to intelligence and the teaching-learning process are yet to be established.

Among other characteristics, disadvantaged children have been noted by several investigators and observers to demonstrate perceptual styles and perceptual habits which are either inadequate or irrelevant to the demands of academic efficiency. Although high levels of perceptual awareness and discrimination are often present, these skills tend to be better developed in physical behavior than in visual behavior and in visual behavior than in aural behavior (Riessman, 1962). Probably the most significant characteristic in this area is the extent to which these children fail to develop a high degree of dependence on the standard verbal and written language forms for learning. Many of the children simply have not adopted the modes of listening and speaking which are traditional to and necessary for success in school.

The extent to which patterns of perception and expression differ among children of different backgrounds is well documented. In his study of retarded, average, and gifted children, Jensen (1963) concluded that many children viewed as retarded have merely failed to learn to use the language in a manner which facilitates school learning. Earlier, Carson (1960) found white children superior to Negroes and northern Negroes superior to southern Negroes when it came to understanding the meanings of words used in communication. In a study of children's use of time, in which the children told their own stories, LeShan (1952) found that time orientation varies with social class and that middle- and upper-class children told stories involving a more prolonged period of time than did lower-class children. Riessman (1962) includes slowness as a feature of the cognitive functioning of disadvantaged youngsters. This conclusion was arrived at by Davidson about 10 years earlier (1950) on finding differences in speed of response to be primarily responsible for racial differences in IQ scores estimated by timed performance tests. Deutsch (1965) found lower-class children relatively poorer in recognizing similarities and differences between things seen and heard, and in the formation of phrases and sentences. Earlier (1960), he had found these children inferior to a middle-class control group on tasks requiring concentration and persistence.

Many of the children with whom we are concerned show a marked lack of involvement with, attention to, and concentration on the content of their academic experiences. There are few academic tasks which commit them to deep involvement. Their work habits are frequently poor. Because of the high interest demands of their nonacademic experiences and the relatively low interest demands of academic experiences, they frequently are limited in their ability to control their responses to those things in the environment which are extraneous to academic learning and less inclined to respond to those which are pertinent to academic learning. Deutsch reported that lower-class children tend to ignore difficult problems with a "so what" attitude, and as a result they learn less.

Moreover, several investigators have found that socially disadvantaged children are less highly motivated and have lower aspirations for academic and vocational achievement than do their middle- and upper-class school peers. Not only is motivation likely to be lower but it is likely to be directed toward goals inconsistent with the demands and the goals of formal education. This depressed level of aspiration is usually consistent with the child's perceptions of the opportunities and rewards available to him. Symbolic rewards and postponements of gratification appear to have little value as motivators of achievement. For disadvantaged children goals tend to be self-centered, immediate, and utilitarian, just as they are for the dominant culture. However, children growing up under more privileged circumstances have many sources of immediate satisfaction and immediate feedback available as well as evidences of the utilitarian value of academic effort. The differences between the privileged and the disadvantaged in this area are not so much in values as in the circumstances under which the values are called into play. Although the values from which motivation is derived in the disadvantaged child seem to reflect the dominant-culture concern with status, material possessions, ingroup morality, Judeo-Christian ethics, and competition, there is usually a lack of concern with the aesthetics of knowledge, symbolism as an art form, introspection, and competition with one's self. In other words, dominant societal goals and values exist among the disadvantaged but the direction taken and the context in which they operate may not be complementary to academic achievement.

Rosen (1956), observing a relationship between high motivation and high grades, concluded that middle-class children are more likely to be taught the motives and values which make achievement possible. Similarly, in Gould's study (1941), only the sons who fully adopted their parents' values of aspiration were sufficiently motivated to overcome obstacles which faced them in school. Bernstein (1960) found concern with achievement resulting from parental demands for success to be a more important motivational factor among middle-class than among lower-class children.

Attitudinal factors are closely related to these motivational factors, and these too are often a source of problems in educational planning for disadvantaged children. Hieronymus (1951) found that higher socioeconomic status was correlated with a high level of aspiration and positive attitudes toward school, while negative attitudes toward school and lower levels of aspiration were more frequently encountered in lower socioeconomic status groups. Sewell's (1957) finding that class values tend to greatly influence educational aspirations in a manner favoring the middle and upper classes is consistent with the earlier work in this field.

A number of observers have noted utilitarian attitudes toward knowledge in this population and negative attitudes toward the pure pursuit of knowledge. Many of these children and their parents view education primarily in terms of its job market value and their orientation is pointed toward achieving the minimum level of education commensurate with employability. Carroll (1945) sees the lower-class ideal self as characterized by personal beauty and fame, in contrast to the moral and intellectual qualities which are thought to characterize the ideal self of middle-class children.

As important as these attitudes toward school and learning may be, it is in the area of attitude toward self and others that the crucial determinants of achievement and upward mobility may lie, and it is in these areas that our data are least clear. It has been observed by some investigators that disadvantaged children show an affinity for ingroup members and demonstrate distaste for or even hostility toward representatives of outgroups, whether in peer or nonpeer relationships. By contrast, other observers have noted the high degree of respect and awe in which these children hold selected outgroup status persons or idealized models. Tendencies toward self-depreciation and depressed self-concepts have been noted by several observers (Dreger, 1960; Keller, 1963; Silverman, 1963). Goff (1954) found that lower-class children have more feelings of inadequacy in school than do children from the middle class. On the other hand, some recent findings (Gordon, 1965) suggest that depressed self-concept is not so prevalent a condition, and that even where it is present it may have little negative bearing on achievement. In fact, it is entirely possible that positive or negative feelings of self-worth may operate respectively to depress or accelerate achievement. Furthermore, it is in this area that rapidly changing national and world situations involving underdeveloped peoples are likely to be most influential, and it is difficult to predict the ultimate effect of these altered situations on self-perception and behavioral change. Our knowledge and even our hunches are as yet limited. But it is around these changing situations that the school may yet find a support on which to lever up motivation, aspiration, and involvement. There is growing empirical evidence that young people actively associated with the current civil rights movement draw from their involvement in that struggle a new source of motivation and an enhanced view of themselves (Coles, 1963). The impression is gained that these experiences are reflected in greater application of effort to and greater achievement in academic endeavors. The evidence for this improvement is less clear, yet there can be little doubt that attitudes toward self and toward the environment in relation to self are crucial variables in academic as well as in social and emotional learning situations.

It is noteworthy that much of the work done on the characteristics of disadvantaged children has focused on their weaknesses, deficits, or limitations. With the notable exception of Riessman (1962), attempts at identification of positive characteristics or strengths in this population are hard to find. However, even in Riessman's treatment there is a tendency to romanticize these characteristics. This may be a more serious error than to ignore them. It is essential that we begin to identify as assets those behaviors and conditions which can be utilized and built upon for the purposes of educational improvement. It is extremely important to recognize that selective motivation, creativity, and proficiency are present in this population, and, as Riessman has consistently stressed, if we look for these characteristics in their traditional form and along traditionally academic dimensions, we shall merely insure that they not be found. These children, like others, *are* motivated by *some* factors. They show creativity in *some* situations. They are proficient at *some* tasks and under *some* conditions.

In contrast to the generally accepted idea that language is inadequate in disadvantaged populations is the fact that there exist in these populations quite complex languages. The form in which the language is expressed may not be verbal nor may the specific symbols be consistent with those normally used by the dominant culture. But the presence of a language adequate to the needs of the culture in which it has developed should not be ignored. The important question then becomes one of not whether language exists, but to what extent a given language system may be utilized in understanding and managing complex technical problems. If the facts, relationships, and ideas of science and philosophy cannot be expressed in forms capable of incorporation into the language system in question, then that language is inadequate to the demands of contemporary educational processes. To date, investigations into the utilitarian dimensions of divergent language patterns have not been conducted.

Our research has established the fact of language differences (Deutsch, 1963, 1965; Jensen, 1963; John and Goldstein, 1964), and in addition we know something of the nature of these differences. The Bernstein work (1961, 1962), referred to earlier, characterized lower-class language as restricted and middle-class language as elaborated. Strodtbeck (1964) has described circumstances under which such language patterns may develop and be perpetuated. He attributes the elaborated language style of the middle-class family to the fact that there is greater sharing in the family decision making process by both parents in these families than in lower-class families. Restricted language, on the other hand, develops as a product of unilateral decision making in the lower-class home. In a situation involving equality and conflict of ideas in family decision making, the child learns at an early age to be sensitive to language as a vehicle for the elaboration of ideas. Where the opposite situation exists, the child develops a sensitivity to language as a vehicle for the communication of signals or directions.

The findings of C. Deutsch (1964), that there are significant class differences in the time spent in parent-child communication, are also related to the differences in language usage between social classes. Her data indicate that the length of such communication is considerably shorter for lower-class than for middle-class subjects. This difference has been viewed as a handicap, but it may be that given a different instructional method this tendency toward brief verbal exchanges could be turned to the advantage of the learner.

Much of our knowledge concerning children from socially disadvantaged backgrounds has been drawn by inference from the wide literature on juvenile delinquency. Sensitive analysis of this literature leads to an awareness of several other characteristics of this population. One cannot study the literature on boys' gangs or juvenile offenders without coming to the conclusion that these youngsters are ingenious and resourceful in pursuing self-selected goals and in coping with very difficult and complex conditions of life. This kind of behavior reflects accuracy of perception and generalization around a variety of social, psychological, and physical phenomena. It is at once obvious that these children are capable of meaningful and loyal personal relationships, and they operate with an ingroup morality that surpasses that of some of the more privileged segments of society. In many situations where the learning task flows from familiar experiences and is important for the pupils' self-selected goal, operations like memory, recall, generalization, computation, and symbolic representation have been demonstrated to be functionally adequate.

Now all of these studies concerned with disadvantaged children have stressed the delineation of characteristics thought to be peculiar to this group. Considerable attention has been given to the projection of "needed" changes in this population with the research effort more often directed at the question of whether the change can be made and measured rather than to such questions as: Is a change needed? If needed, what is the nature of that change? What is its relevance to the learning process? By what mechanisms are such changes achieved?

In an earlier period, our studies of disadvantaged children followed the example of much of the research relating to children in general—that of emphasizing emotional or personal social development. This work has been replaced by studies emphasizing intellectual development. In both cases less attention is given to developmental sequence than is devoted to comparing the status of emotional or intellectual development in the disadvantaged child with that in more privileged children. But the nature of these functions, their idiosyncratic patterns, and the courses and mechanisms by which they develop have largely been ignored. This research is also limited by the absence of concern for the study of the emotional and intellectual dimensions of learning as a single process. Noteworthy exceptions to this are the investigations of the academic performance of Negro students under varying conditions by Katz (1964) and the very sensitive description of education in an American Indian community by M. and R. Wax and R. V. Dumont (1964).

The second area to which research attention has been directed is the environment. Studies of environmental influences have consisted largely of a cataloging of the factors in homes and communities from which disadvantaged children come that may interfere with normal school achievement. These studies have often been conducted with the ultimate aim of incorporating knowledge obtained from them into the training of school personnel so that they may "understand" the culture and values of their pupils. The simultaneous occurrence of certain conditions of life, certain population characteristics, and poor school adjustment has been interpreted as indicating a causal relationship between these factors. The evidence, however, supports only the conclusion that these phenomena are correlated. These studies, while they may have social-anthropological value, are of questionable use in planning educational programs for these children. It is probably true that adverse conditions of life do not facilitate academic achievement in most children, but we have no firm evidence that such conditions preclude academic success. In fact, there are sufficient cases of success despite adverse conditions to make untenable the conclusion that difficult life circumstances prevent success in school. Insufficient attention has been given to the fact that many "normal" and well-functioning individuals have equally adverse circumstances in their lives. There are many good reasons for improving the living conditions of the disadvantaged, and there is certainly no good excuse for an affluent society to fail to do so. But a concern on the part of the school for improved conditions of life for its pupils should not be substituted for a primary concern with the teaching-learning process as it relates to the individual. It is the individual, his potential for learning, and the sources of his behavior as a learner that represent the third focus of research attention.

Models from special education and interactionist theory

Serious concern with the problems of individual differences in intelligence and learning ability is a relatively recent phenomenon. Around the turn of the century Binet advanced the position that several aspects of intellectual function could be trained. His concern with the ability to train intelligence led him to argue for special instructional procedures designed to strengthen certain aspects of intellectual function that seemed less well developed than others. An interest in the need for classification procedures by which children could be grouped in school and, later, men could be selected and grouped for military training, led to the subversion or neglect of Binet's earlier concern for modifying intellectual development. Following World War I, psychologists in the United States became so preoccupied with problems of the quantification of intellectual function, diagnostic classification, and treatment within the narrow confines of psychoanalytic theory that this earlier concern with the ability to train intelligence was ignored. Despite the parallel and prophetic model reflected in Montessori's work with slum children, these ideas, born more of optimistic and humanitarian attitudes than of scientific knowledge, lay almost dormant until very recent years.

Resurgence of interest in the ability to train the intellect and in the graduated step-by-step development of intellectual functions grew out of serious concern with the educational problems of mentally, physically, or neurologically handicapped people. With the strongest push coming from the works of Strauss and Kephart (1955), Kirk (1958), Gallagher (1958), Haeusserman (1958), and Birch (1964), educators began to be sensitive to the possibility that subnormal intellectual function did not necessarily reflect subnormal intellectual potential. In fact, these special educational efforts with handicapped children produced results which in large measure began to change some of our concepts of intellectual function and the role of educational experience.

Given the special education model, and some success in its application to children with brain injuries and cerebral palsy, some educators have begun to build compensatory education programs for the disadvantaged child based on learning experiences designed to compensate for or circumvent certain identifiable or alleged deficiences in function. Educators utilizing this model have not bothered to argue the origins of the functional state but have set about developing experiences by which that state may be improved. Still others, sensitive to the political implications of accepting a theory based upon alleged deficiences, have made a major point of placing emphasis on the deficiencies which exist in the schools. This latter group insists that differential achievement is only a reflection of these school-based inadequacies. Both of these positions are reflected in the programs and practices which represent the major contemporary efforts at modifying the teaching-learning process.

Behind all these efforts and, indeed, implicit to the process of education itself, particularly of compensatory education for special groups, is the assumption that the form taken by behavioral organization, including intellectual function, can be predicted, can be directed, and can be modified. Much of our educational practice however has reflected a commitment to the assumption that behavior is predetermined and generally limited in its form and quality by the intrinsic characteristics of the learner. The prevalence of such an assumption may account for some of the emphases in traditional educational practice that have left large numbers of disadvantaged children undereducated. Belief in the importance of intrinsic determinants of development could account for a prevailing laissez-faire attitude toward the training and development of intelligence which has prevailed in traditional approaches to education. This belief, combined with the view that the quality of intellectual function is fixed, may account for the exaggerated emphasis on the predictive value of tests, and for a monitoring approach as opposed to a stimulating approach to academic and social readiness. Commitment to these ideas and practices has tended to restrict the teaching-learning process and has led to a humanistic exhortation approach to the training of teachers as opposed to the development and teaching of a science of pedagogy.

Although educational practice is dominated by the influence of these earlier views of the origin and nature of intelligence, few scholars are anxious to defend the classical instinct theory from which these views have developed. Theoretical support for assumptions based on theories of instinctive behavior and genetic limitations is less often found in contemporary writings than in those of an earlier period. It is encouraging to note the increasing influence of the interactionist views of behavioral and intellectual development as advanced by Turkewitz, Gordon, and Birch (1965), Hunt (1961), and Sells (1963) on the current effort being directed toward the education of the disadvantaged.

Theories of behavior may be divided between those which advance a projective view and those which are based upon a reflectional or interactive view of the mechanisms underlying behavioral organization. In the projective view, predetermined patterns within the individual are thought to be released by certain forms of stimulation and are projected into the behavior of the individual where their specific form is facilitated or inhibited by environmental factors. Among persons adhering to this position, emphasis is given to hypotheses which assume the presence in the individual of intrinsic drives which existed prior to and independently of life experiences. These drives are seen as the basic forces in the determination of behavior. Certain behavioral patterns are seen as pre-formed, stored, and waiting for the proper time and condition for emergence. Capacities and traits are seen as determined by these intrinsic factors which can be only somewhat modified by the environment. The fundamental character of patterned behavior then is seen as genetically established and bound. Environmental forces are believed to influence the organization of behavior by determining the directions taken by the primary energies and drives; the environmental objects to which they become attached; and the specific time and form in which they will emerge.

On the other hand, the interactionist or reflectional position holds that all organized patterned behaviors are reflections of the interaction between living things and their environment. Encounters with the environment are seen as the crucial determinants and molders of the patterned behavior of the individual. Specific events and circumstances are thought to cause behavior or to mediate behavioral expression rather than to cause the release of certain behavior patterns. All organized patterned behaviors are seen to exist only as a result of sensory input flowing from encounters of the individual and the environment. Behavioral potentials are said to be genetically seeded in the sense that the individual's physical characteristics provide the basis for certain types of responses. These biological characteristics are largely determined by the nature of the genes, but the behavioral patterns, behavioral characteristics, and quality of functions are determined by interactions between the individual and his environment. The nature of these interactions are critical for the form and pattern that behavior will take.

Implicit to the interactionist position is the assumption that change is possible. It follows that educational intervention functions as more than a catalyst for the stimulation and release of latent potentials. Without rejecting the maieutic character of many good learning experiences, this position suggests that learning experience appropriate to given characteristics of the individual can produce certain potentials. An interactionist position with respect to the organization of behavior leads one to view the developmental process as malleable, to regard intelligence as nonstatic and variable, to see motives and attitudes as determined and modifiable by experience, and to recognize all achievement as the product of the individual's characteristics in continuous and dynamic interaction with those elements of the environment which are effective at a given time. Unfortunately this view lends itself to colloquial interpretations which reflect vulgar environmentalism. Too often the basic concept is interpreted to mean that through the manipulation of the environment infinite modifications are possible. But as significant as are these experiences in the environment, it must be remembered that development, according to this view, is the result of the interaction between these two forces. Behavioral products may be enhanced or limited by either, or by the interference with or compensation for one by the other of the two forces.

Given the problems inherent in manipulation of the human organism, the most available evidence on the impact of intervention in the developmental process comes from studies involving environmental manipulation. The Klineberg (1963) studies support the view that intelligence test scores can be changed by changes in the environment such as migration, acculturation, and adequate educational programs. In a study of Negro children migrating from states in the South to Philadelphia, Lee (1961) found that intelligence test scores improved significantly and steadily with length of residence in that northern city, where the quality of education was superior to that previously experienced. Clark (1954) reports the reverse of these findings when Negro children moved from schools in the South to a northern city where de facto segregation and other problems resulted in their exposure to educational experiences of poorer quality in the North than those which had been available to them in the South. Davis (1963) attributed a 10-point increase in the measured IQ of Negro children in Chicago and Philadelphia over a period of five years simply to acculturation. The intelligence and reading readiness scores of a group of Negro children in Tennessee are reported by Brazziel and Terrell (1962) to have been raised to national norms as a result of a six-week enrichment program consisting of exposure to reading readiness materials, training in perceptual discrimination, vocabulary building, verbal reasoning, and training in following directions for the children, together with a series of informational and supportive conferences with parents. A limited number of systematic evaluations of programs of compensatory education show that many forms of environmental and educational intervention appear to be accompanied by improved functioning for large numbers of the children served.

The work of Pasamanick and Knobloch (1958) suggests further that environmental conditions less conducive to wholesome physical development are not only reflected in impaired health, but in behavioral sequelae as well. It is not unexpected that they find that where maternal health and prenatal care are poor, where obstetrical service is inadequate, where postnatal care is deficient, and provision for child care is precarious, the incidence of neurologic defects, of childhood illnesses and disorders, of behavior disorders, and of learning disabilities or inefficiencies is high. Implicit to these findings is the assumption that if the social and physical conditions of life were improved, intellectual and social function would improve as well. Interventions directed at changing the environment and the experience of the individual can result in changed behavior. These changes in life conditions result in changes in function which could not have been predicted by the assumption that the quality of the individual's function is intrinsically determined and bound.

Lest we become too optimistic and mechanical in our approach, it is important to recognize that there are a few studies and numerous programs which seem to result in no demonstrable change in behavior or achievement as a result of what may appear to have been massive interventions. It is likely that many of these efforts do not apply to the crucial determinants of behavior, are applied in insufficient concentrations, or represent inappropriate combinations of remedial services. Evidence mounts to support the view that in many situations in which necessary or essential behavioral determinants are present and available, these determinants may not produce conditions that are sufficient for the achievement of certain behavioral results.

It is anticipated that several changes will result from improved educational facilities and equal educational opportunity. Among these changes will be improved school achievement, improved social development, and greater upward mobility. For these and other reasons the civil rights struggle has focused so sharply on education. Keppel (1964) has pointed to the contribution to the advancement of education made by the national human rights effort. Although Negro children do not constitute the largest segment of the poverty-stricken population in this country, they have come to represent one of the major focuses of attention in the antipoverty and compensatory education efforts. It is from our experience with educational efforts directed at Negro children, particularly in recently desegregated settings, that we also get encouraging but sobering findings that face us with some of the most challenging problems in compensatory education. Systematic study of the impact of desegregation and improved educational opportunity is limited. While one is encouraged by reported gains on the part of Negro students with no loss on the part of white students (*Southern School News*, 1960), it is in these improved situations that the difference between conditions which are desirable, necessary, and even essential, and those which are sufficient is highlighted.

In the few available studies it is clear that improved opportunities for education which have paralleled school desegregation efforts have resulted in improved school achievement for Negro pupils. In his study of school achievement in the Louisville public schools, Stallings (1959) found gains in median scores for all grades tested. The degree of improvement in achievement levels over the year prior to school desegregation was greater for Negro pupils than for white pupils. However, the Negro pupils level of achievement did not equal that of the white pupils. The analysis of academic progress in schools in the District of Columbia following desegregation (Hansen, 1960) shows consistent gains for the Negro pupils. This analysis also shows some initial decline for white pupils, followed by a return to previous rates of academic achievement. The achievement level for white pupils, however, remained somewhat in advance of that for Negro pupils. Reporting on experiences in a North Carolina school system, Day (1963) indicated that Negro pupils in the desegregated schools of that system had failed to keep pace with their white classmates. The picture is one of achievement gain following improved opportunity. But it is not at all clear that these gains result from the simple act of desegregation, since in most instances covered by these reports, Negro pupils remained in largely segregated settings. In fact, Stallings (1959) found greater gains when Negro pupils remained with Negro teachers and, incidentally, in segregated class groupings. Of even greater significance to those concerned with equality of educational achievement is the fact that, as groups, Negro pupils continue to be academically outdistanced by their white counterparts despite improvements in educational opportunities and desegregation efforts.

When selected populations are studied, results of improved opportunity are more encouraging. The Demonstration Guidance Project (1956–62) findings suggest that improved educational opportunity, even under conditions of de facto segregation, result in substantial gains for Negro pupils chosen from the upper fiftieth percentile. Similarly, the beneficiaries of services from the National Scholarship Service and Fund for Negro Students were found to far exceed norms for completion of college and were effective in competition with other students in predominantly white institutions. If one is willing to accept success (completion of high school or college) rather than excellence as the criterion, it is clear that, given improved opportunity, many disadvantaged youth can make the grade in academic achievement.

There are two parallel demands being made of the public school. One is the increasing demand for the development of academic excellence in large numbers of pupils. The second and more pervasive demand is for academic competence in all pupils. As we have indicated, the civil rights focus on racial integration in education and equality of educational achievement is part of this dual demand. In response to this demand communities and school systems across the country have begun to develop programs designed to meet the needs of the heretofore undereducated. In many instances they are identifying important and necessary ingredients for that effort. In the descriptions of programs and practices that follow, it will be observed that a wide variety of innovations and adjustments are being undertaken. The talents and energies of school people are being directed at this problem with a vengeance. That their efforts include desirable, necessary, and even essential changes is not questioned. However, many of the fundamental questions involving ideal educational programs for the disadvantaged remain unanswered, for there has been an urgency in the situation that could not wait for definitive answers. The translation of these efforts into procedures and programs which are sufficient to meet the needs of disadvantaged populations in a rapidly advancing society is one of the central educational problems of the current period.

3. The status of compensatory education

As the most casual perusal of the daily newspapers makes clear, the newly aroused concern about providing adequate educational opportunity for the disadvantaged is generating compensatory programs at an ever accelerating rate. The increasing availability of federal government financing, and the increasing, though reluctant, awareness on the part of tax-paying property owners that stinting on school budgets is ultimately a poor economy, is encouraging more and more local school boards to take a fresh look at those pupils whom they have, until now, too often dealt with as a problem rather than as a challenge.

Number, distribution, and nature of programs

The summer 1965 Project Head Start operation that provided an introduction to learning to 560,000 children in 13,000 centers in over 2,500 communities across the country, focused national attention on the need to reevaluate an assumption implicit in most conventional school programs — that we can afford to deal with all children as if they were equally prepared to begin school. And, at the other end of the educational track, the recent alarming figures on joblessness among teen-agers, particularly Negro teenagers, has brought into focus the extent of the school's failure to prepare for work those whom it has the responsibility for educating.

In response to the pressure to do something, educators have mounted a great variety of special educational programs — generally classified as compensatory. In this study, the initial survey turned up programs of compensatory education in 108 communities. With the exception of the large midwestern cities, these programs were heavily concentrated in the middle Atlantic and the far western regions, and notably sparse in the extreme Northwest and in the South. But figures on the number of participating cities, on the numbers of programs, and even on geographical distribution are subject to a high degree of error. The first source of error is the speed with which programs are being generated, even as this book goes to press. Of the 76 programs for which starting dates were available after responses to the first survey, 95 percent were begun since 1960 and 43 percent had been initiated in the school year 1963–64. Data subsequently received have doubled the number of cities participating and have generally related to programs of even more recent vintage. Moreover, the pace is accelerating.

The heavy concentration of programs in the middle Atlantic and far western states is influenced by statewide programs in New York and California, as well as by outstanding programs in Pennsylvania, Maryland, Connecticut, and Washington, D.C. In New York, the State Education Department has sponsored and helped to finance four separate types of programs, designated as Project Able, Talent Search, STEP, and Re-entry. These programs currently function in more than 100 communities, both small and large, throughout the state. In California, the state legislature passed a compensatory education bill familiarly known as the McAteer Act. The Act helped 24 communities mount two-year pilot programs of compensatory education, and the results have been used to plan a comprehensive statewide attack on the school problems of the disadvantaged children in that state. Geographic distribution is also affected by the populations involved. The heavy concentration of programs on the East Coast and West Coast, with pockets of big-city activity in between, reflects national population distribution with fair accuracy, and it further reflects some special population problems of these areas with their high proportion of minority groups, recent in-migrants, or both. This is not to say that problems of disadvantage do not exist everywhere, but rather that in some areas they have seemed less urgent, or, because they are less concentrated, they have been less readily observed.

As for the relative quiescence of the South, that may well be a deception. Aside from the work of the Southern Association of Colleges and Secondary Schools, the Appalachian Volunteers, and the North Carolina Fund which are sponsoring a number of projects to improve education and educational opportunity in various areas of the South, there is some evidence that in a number of communities in the South, efforts are quietly being made to improve the educational lot of Negroes and the less privileged whites. For reasons of political expediency, school administrators in the South are often reluctant to publicize these efforts.

Even if it were possible to determine at any given moment, just how many cities were engaged in some kind of compensatory activity, it would still be impossible to determine the precise number of programs that are functioning. In many cities, particularly in large metropolitan school districts, there are at this moment numbers of innovations and modifications, trial and error experiments, and specifically experimental interventions, going on simultaneously in one or more classrooms, schools, or districts. In a city like Boston, where a variety of school and community projects have been linked under a single titular umbrella—Action for Boston Community Development (ABCD)—it is possible to speak of a "compensatory program." In Wilmington, Delaware, on the other hand, an already completed three-year project on Schools in Changing Neighborhoods has left results of compensatory activity in various areas throughout the city, most of which are not definable as specific programs. It therefore becomes misleading to talk of programs, for these programs represent only a part of the extensive experimentation which is actually going on. Indeed, there are several large cities to which one could apply Havighurst's[1] description of compensatory education in Chicago: "There is probably not a single suggestion made anywhere in the country for the improvement of the educational program for such children that is not being tried out, *within the limits of available resources*, in some Chicago school."

In some places everything is being tried. It does not necessarily follow that in every place something is being tried. However, given the current emphasis on educational compensation, there is probably no community of any size with a substantial population of socially disadvantaged children that is not giving at least lip service to the provision of some special services to that population. But it is well to keep in mind that changes planned or put into effect in a school district under the name of compensatory education, may represent nothing more than an equalization of services for a population that had previously been stinted, often because of budgeting practices which discriminated against schools in the poorer sections of the community. Consequently, while it is misleading to speak only of pro-

---

1. Robert J. Havighurst, *The Public Schools of Chicago; a Survey.* Chicago: The Board of Education of the City of Chicago, 1964, 499 pp.

grams, it is equally misleading to accept at face value every modification in local practice which a community may itself define as compensatory.

While this is, then, a survey of programs, it is also a compendium of practices. It is an attempt to cover the ground at least once—to examine the variety of practices, whether they are combined into programs or not, that are being explored in various areas of the country. What all these programs and practices have in common is a dual goal—remedial work and prevention. They are remedial in that they attempt to fill gaps, whether social, cultural, or academic, in a child's total experience; they are preventive in that by doing so they aim to forestall either an initial or a continuing failure in school, and, by extension, in later life.

In size and scope the programs vary widely from place to place throughout the country. This is to some extent a reflection of population variety—problems of disadvantage are different qualitatively as well as quantitatively in a Maine hamlet and in a midwestern metropolis. But even when populations—and presumably problems—are somewhat comparable, the approaches toward altering an unsatisfactory status quo show wide variation. This is partly because any program is always limited by the resources, both human and financial, available to the community, and—no less significant—partly because program direction and emphasis are always subject to the judgments of those responsible for the best utilization of these resources. In some projects every suitable school in a district is involved and resources are so thinly spread as to severely restrict the likelihood of measurable student change. In other school districts, available resources have been heavily concentrated to serve, in depth, a smaller number of students.

Comparisons of overall program costs, as well as per pupil costs have proved difficult to make. Basic per pupil allotments vary widely from community to community so that no fundamental preprogram equivalence can be established. Where a program is clearly based on a grant from the federal or state government or a private foundation, with or without matching funds from the school district, it is possible to speak of a $20,000 program or a per pupil cost of $30. But even under these circumstances one must reckon with the fact that in a number of metropolitan school districts extra funds for equipment, or staffing, or both, are available to certain schools on the basis of special formulas which take population differences into account. New York City's Special Service Schools and Minneapolis' practice of staffing on the basis of the socioeconomic index are examples of these. Whether or not the additional funds represented by these practices should be included in calculating program costs at one of these schools is one of the questions which makes financial comparisons so difficult. On the basis of per pupil costs reported, there are programs, such as the St. Louis (Mo.) Banneker District program that have utilized no funds in excess of normal school board expenditures and there are others who have reported per pupil costs in excess of $250. In general, the fewer the students the higher the per pupil costs. The validity of such a statement is, of course, dependent on similarity in the services provided. Where a large number of services are added, costs will inevitably rise, but usually, a large city school system will have personnel available, particularly in the areas of counseling, testing, and evaluation, who can perform functions for which a small rural school will require the services of an outside consultant.

Most communities, in attempting to equalize educational opportunity, have acknowledged that the less than equal current status of the disadvantaged pupil requires a more than equal quota of staff and services; and the addition of extra personnel is an almost universal practice in compensatory programs of any size. The extra personnel employed in project schools have generally fallen into one of three categories: special instructional staff, special service staff, and nonprofessional staff. While classroom teachers are not, strictly speaking, special instructional personnel, the addition of extra teachers to the staff to reduce class size is a fundamental way in which additional personnel have been used in compensatory programs. It is a fundamental way, and also an expensive way. As the California McAteer figures show, in schools where teachers are paid $7,000 annually, it costs $42 per pupil to reduce class size from 30 to 25. In many cases it has proved more economical, in money and qualified personnel, to free experienced teachers from specific classroom assignments and use them in a project school to perform a variety of coordinative, supervisory, resource, remedial, or other functions. These teachers, designated in various programs as master teachers, coaching teachers, program teachers, helping teachers, and so on, are used to backstop a number of less expert classroom teachers. The reorganization of existing personnel into teaching teams or other instructional groups under the guidance of an expert teacher as team leader is another way of making maximum use of inexperienced and experienced personnel. One New York City program makes double use of its experienced personnel. During school days seven full-time teachers assigned to a Higher Horizons school are available to help classroom teachers with curriculum and guidance activities. They then take charge of an All-Day Neighborhood School program for two hours after school.

Curriculum specialists have been employed in a number of larger programs as a means of upgrading instruction in a particular subject area, predominantly in the language arts. The familiar remedial reading teacher has given way in many instances to a reading specialist whose function is to improve generally the teaching of reading; or to a language arts specialist who may provide additional services to teachers and pupils in the areas of oral language, literature, and creative writing. Speech therapists may be used, as they are in Buffalo, to provide oral language assistance to all pupils in a project school, rather than just to those with obvious speech defects. Bilingual teachers are usually employed where there is a large population of non-English-speaking children. In Merced (Calif.) a special language teacher teaches Spanish to Mexican-American children. A librarian may be added to a staff to provide literature enrichment and to enable a project school to keep its library open for longer hours.

Subject-matter specialists, particularly in the area of reading, often serve as teacher trainers, conducting demonstration classes and providing information on new materials and techniques in the area of their specialty. But specialists may also conduct classes themselves, particularly in the areas of mathematics instruction and remedial mathematics, art, music, and science. Special teachers in these areas have been added to the staffs of a number of schools involved in compensatory programs. Specialized supervisory or administrative personnel are used as coordinators where a program in a large city involves groups of teachers, groups of classes, or even groups of schools. Music and art consultants, subject supervisors, and curriculum coordinators are used to unify various project areas. New York City has special coordinators who serve as curriculum assistants for teachers of non-English-speaking children. Philadelphia has a "new-teacher" consultant who aids in the orientation and support of newly appointed staff members. On a still higher administrative level are the project consultants, project directors, assistant principals, and other personnel who are specially hired, promoted, or released from other duties in order to oversee all activities in a project school or district.

The principal services for which nonteaching professional personnel are added to a staff are in the areas of guidance and health, both physical and mental. Guidance counselors have been more frequently employed in compensatory programs than any other single classification of personnel. Many projects also have available the services of a psychologist, a psychiatrist, or both, although this kind of professional personnel is rarely employed full-time by any but the largest school programs. Hartford (Conn.) has a special worker concerned with pupil adjustment, and there are several communities in which a county welfare officer serves a project school in a guidance capacity. Pittsburgh, which has made extensive use of the team approach in a variety of areas has a mental health team oriented toward preventive care, consisting of a child psychiatrist, a psychiatric social worker, a clinical psychologist, community case aides, and a mental health coordinator. St. Louis formed mobile "combat teams" of administrative assistants, a guidance counselor, and a social worker to reduce high school absence and tardiness. These functions are usually the prerogative of the attendance officer — often himself a new addition in project schools. Social workers are often hired to work with children, their families, or both, and in many projects special personnel designated as home visitors, visiting teachers, family workers, and so forth, are engaged for school-home liaison work. Where health and dental services have not been available, or where they have been inadequate for the special needs of disadvantaged children, many programs have added full-time school nurses to the staff and arranged to have available the services of a physician, a dental hygienist, or both, when needed.

Other specialized personnel are utilized where employment outside of the school is part of a compensatory program. In many dropout projects, personnel designated as job development specialists, job placement supervisors, or work supervisors are employed both to find outside employment for the students and to oversee them on the job. Other projects have employed specialists in communication. In Syracuse, the Madison Area Project hired a public information coordinator to help tell its story to the neighborhood and the larger community. In another Syracuse project a writer was hired to improve intrastaff communications.

The increasing seriousness of the personnel shortage, particularly in schools serving disadvantaged areas, and the continuing concern for developing employment opportunities for persons of relatively limited training, has led to a strong movement in the direction of using nonprofessionals or preprofessionals in project schools. Philadelphia uses lay people as school-community coordinators. Many other communities have made use of class mothers or other volunteer personnel as home visitors. Teachers in pre-service training, student teachers, preteaching student assistants, and teaching interns have been used as teacher assistants in many programs. The Kings County (Calif.) compensatory program has made use of social welfare students from a local college to make home visits and develop project-student social histories. The increasing interest in preschool programs has exacerbated a chronic shortage of qualified teachers in this specialty and led to the extensive use of volunteer mothers, college students, or, as in Fresno, California, junior high school students from the same project, in the staffing of such programs. Pittsburgh pays project mothers as team aides in its team teaching program. College students, paid or volunteer, have been used in a variety of tutoring and study hall programs, along with high school students, parents, and other community adults. Lay persons have taught classes for adults in the evenings in Detroit. In a number of communities they have supervised after-school clubs and social and recreational activities. Berkeley, Washington, D.C., and New York City all have extensive programs utilizing the services of volunteers in supplementing and augmenting the school program. Layman specialists in every kind of field have served as guest speakers or as consultants in special educational or inspirational programs.

The increasing popularity of volunteer personnel could easily be explained in financial terms alone. Extra professional personnel cost money. Indeed, in most projects, personnel costs represent the largest single item in the budget. In the data reported for many of the programs there are obvious discrepancies between the personnel listed as involved in a special program and the reported per pupil costs. There are two reasons for this. In the first place, personnel may be listed who are simply available to the program when needed, but whose salaries are not reflected in the project budget because they are already on the school staff. In the second place, newly hired personnel may be hired for varying amounts of time. A psychologist serving in a large program may be serving full time. A psychologist listed as serving a small program may be giving only one-fifth of his time. Consequently, personnel lists should always be looked on as indicating the kinds of services offered rather than their extent.

The amount of personnel time optimally required in a program — or, indeed, even the minimum personnel requirements — are clearly related to program size. Many of the programs reported serve well under 100 pupils. Jay (Maine) has a Practical Arts Course for Potential Dropouts, with an enrollment of 13. New York State sponsors programs that operate in a number of small communities. In South New Berlin (N.Y.), a Talent Search Program served 38 pupils and a STEP project served 7. On the other hand, Detroit's expanded Great Cities Project for School Improvement now serves 32,250 youngsters. New York City, with its great variety of problems, meets them with an equal variety of programs.

As an approach to discussing the various practices which have been utilized in meeting the educational problems of disadvantaged youngsters, we have found it most useful to group these under seven categories: teacher recruitment and training, curricular innovation, reading and language development, counseling and guidance, extracurricular innovation, parental involvement, and community involvement. These are the common strands from which the fabric of compensatory education is woven. Though there are a number of programs which have focused on one or two of these approaches to the exclusion of the others, it should be understood that the specific practices described in the following chapters often function as interrelated parts of larger programs covering many phases of the relationship between the school, the child, and the community. In the remainder of this chapter we shall examine two types of programs that do not yield so readily to dissection: the dropout and the preschool programs.

School dropout programs

In one sense, all compensatory programs, because their aim is to provide a successful school life for their participants, have dropout prevention as their goal, and for all of them the motto might well be, "The earlier the better." By the time a student has experienced consistent failure through nine or ten grades of school, any program designed to help him is bound to be an emergency measure. Nevertheless, as the unemployment statistics for dropouts clearly demonstrate, emergency measures would seem to be necessary as long as there are youths reaching high school for whom the school has as yet provided no incentive to graduate. The most immediately practical of these emergency measures are the summer contact campaigns, aimed at assuring the return to school in the fall of potential and recent dropouts.

In the summer of 1963, President Kennedy set into motion a large-scale program of this sort under the auspices of the United States Office of Education. Aided by nationwide publicity, the campaign focused on 63 of the larger cities through whose local guidance machinery 59,301 young people were contacted. Following the identification through school records of recent dropouts or students considered likely to become dropouts, school personnel (usually guidance counselors) phoned, wrote, or personally visited the homes of these students urging a return to school in the fall and enlisting the parents in a cooperative effort to achieve that end. In addition to returning 51.5 percent of the students who were contacted to a school affiliation, the program also succeeded in focusing the attention of the communities involved on the dimensions of the dropout problem and on the factors which lead to dropping out. In fact, one of the by-products of the campaign was the increased awareness on the part of the schools of their own past failure to offer programs of sufficient flexibility and personal relevance to prevent dropouts.

In Baltimore, the local campaign utilized the services of 35 counselors to contact the dropouts, and the school administration, by altering a number of organizational procedures, attempted to make school a more useful and attractive place to those who indicated an interest in returning. The goal was not always return to a regular school program, but rather to encourage the dropout to return to some kind of school affiliation where he would be accessible to the personal concern of the school staff. In some cases there were alterations in the curriculums offered; in other cases, students were transferred to schools offering more suitable programs or permitted to make subject choices within the standard curriculum even though such choices would not necessarily lead to graduation. For slower learners the schools provided some employment in the school itself, policing the school grounds, stockroom work, and so forth. Other communities found that by adjusting time schedules to allow for employment or other outside activity, young mothers as well as already employed youths could be returned to active school affiliation. In some cases, students were allowed to devote their full school time to a single subject, for example, remedial reading or mathematics. In general, there was an increased emphasis in the modified school program on remedial help through special classes, tutoring, and after-school study sessions.

Pittsburgh's program at the Fifth Avenue High School, a direct outgrowth of the summer 1963 campaign, provides for basic academic work in the mornings and shop activities in the afternoon and is oriented toward preparing 16- to 18-year-old former dropouts for employment rather than pushing them toward graduation. Several local communities have continued with programs of summer or early fall guidance and counseling for dropouts. In 1964, a state-sponsored program of the same kind operated in eight New York communities. The program, called Re-entry, was expanded into 22 communities in the summer of 1965.

Most dropout programs that offer more than counseling add varying proportions of three other ingredients: job experience, job training, and academic work. Frequently the proportion of each ingredient is determined by the ages of the youth involved. There is an indeterminate break-off point, of course, where a dropout ceases to be a dropout and becomes simply an unemployed and unemployable young adult for whom the task becomes one of acquiring sufficient basic competence and job skills to permit him to find employment. Various manpower training programs, financed through the Office of Manpower, Automation, and Training of the United States Department of Labor; through the United States Department of Health, Education, and Welfare; or, more recently, through the United States Office of Economic Opportunity, are concerned with precisely this population. While these programs are certainly providing compensatory education, they do not really fall within the purview of this study. But there are a number of school-based dropout programs, particularly those aimed at the 16- to 21-year age bracket, which share this emphasis on immediate job placement.

Philadelphia's Manpower Defense Training Act-Youth Project provides 16- to 22-year-old youths with basic academic work and shop for 12 weeks, followed by a maximum of 40 weeks of vocational training. Its goal is to train out-of-work, out-of-school youth for immediate employment. In such a program academic work is pursued in terms only of its relevance to employability.

Houston's Multi-Occupational Youth Project, another Manpower Defense Training Act (MDTA) program has a similar orientation, combining counseling and vocational training with such academic subjects as mathematics and science added, only to the degree that they are specifically related to the occupation being pursued. The MDTA projects and similar programs are aimed at what some educators have called the "determined" dropout, the youth for whom any return to school is out of the question. In recognition of the fact that such a youth exists, but that he is by no means the only kind of dropout, a number of programs use a combined approach that permits them, in a sense, to give in gracefully if a student is determined to leave school, while maintaining their own orientation toward urging further education. The Urban Youth Program in Chicago, financed by the MDTA, offers the alternatives of a training and transition program that concentrates on providing short-term training followed by full-time employment in various low-skill occupations, or a work-study program in which the youth spends approximately one-third of his time in school and two-thirds in a merchandising or clerical job. New York's Project III included both a job education program—a short-term pre-employment course followed by job placement and follow-up supervision—and an evening high school study program that offered job placement services but also provided credit for evening school attendance as a substitute for part-time day school attendance.

Since no single approach to the dropout problem has yet demonstrated its superiority, large metropolitan areas like New York and Chicago tend to have not just one, but several dropout programs—preventive, remedial, work-oriented, and school-oriented—operating simultaneously, as a means of offering what they hope will be appropriate assistance to the diverse problems represented among the dropouts. The distinctions among the programs are matters of educational emphasis, of organizational detail, or of shades of difference between the goals they strive for. One program may lean more heavily in the direction of preparation for work, another, toward returning the dropout full-time to school. In Cleveland, for example, a pre-employment Work-Study Program involves supervised work experience for four hours a day and a school program emphasizing remedial work and basic job-holding skills. The Program, designed for self-recruited dropouts who are under 21 years of age and have been out of school for six months or more, begins with a six-week orientation course that terminates just as a new school semester begins. New York City's job counseling centers, on the other hand, have as their stated goal a return to school for the dropout either full-time or part-time with a job. These centers provide counseling, tutoring, prevocational orientation, and vocational experience in "try-out" shops. Whatever the differences in stated goals, most of the programs designed for the already dropped-out student have a similar three-part purpose: to contact the dropout and make him accessible to some kind of training; to provide him with the maximum amount of academic education he will sit still for; and finally, whether he does or does not return to formal schooling, to provide him with sufficient job-holding skills to make him employable.

Frequently, the kinds of programs organized to attract dropouts back into school vary little from the kinds of programs which are organized to keep them there in the first place. A number of dropout prevention programs have an introduction to, and preparation for, the world of work as their primary focus. Many disadvantaged pupils abandon school not only because they have failed there, but because its content seems to have no relevance to their present or future lives. The work-study type of program is intended to cope with this sense of irrelevance. New Haven's Work-Study Program is one of this kind. It provides ninth-grade pupils with a morning school session followed by a period of counseling and two hours of supervised work in the afternoons. New York State's STEP project serves potential dropouts who are at least 15 years of age with a similar program in 29 communities. A morning session involving two to four regular classes and at least one period with a teacher coordinator is followed by an afternoon of supervised work. The teacher coordinator who provides work orientation in the mornings is also responsible for job placement. In order to assure STEP students of employment where there are insufficient jobs in private industry, the state provides stipends to pay them for work in tax-supported agencies. The Youth Conservation Corps in Philadelphia combines full-time summer work in the city parks with a school-year work-study program. Participants receive school credit for their work. In Oklahoma City, students at one high school who want to work may participate in a cooperative training program in which the school work is fitted to their employment schedule. They may attend adult day or night school, or regular high school in order to continue their education while working.

Kansas City has a specialized work-study program, now in its fifth year of operation, which is designed to test the effectiveness of an early work experience as a delinquency preventive. The students begin half-day work in groups in the seventh grade, progress through a second work-study stage involving individual work, and finally between the age of 16 to 18 move into either full-time work or the regular school program. Work-experience programs for slow learners, like those in Jay (Maine) and Livermore Falls (Maine), and other communities are often designed with a special academic track which will give the slower learner every opportunity to reinstate himself in the regular school program. Failing that, he is provided with sufficient job skills and work experience to make him employable.

To meet the need of the desperately poor, many of whom have tended to drop out of school in order to help support their families, or because they could not meet even the minimal school expenses, the Economic Opportunity Act of 1964 authorized the establishment of the Neighborhood Youth Corps projects which are now in operation in 639 communities. These projects are designed to permit 16- to 21-year-olds to stay in school, full- or part-time, by providing them with remuneration for doing useful community work in such capacities as teachers' aides, playground attendants, park maintenance people, or nurses' aides.

In addition to programs that provide paid work for potential dropouts, there are others which emphasize vocational training while maintaining the youth in a full-time school program. These programs are difficult to distinguish from traditional vocational education programs. Indeed, some of the programs now being called compensatory education or dropout prevention programs are nothing more than updated (or not so updated) vocational education. They serve, under the least appropriate circumstances, as a dumping ground for students who are not rated bright enough for the academic track. These programs are unlikely either to prepare the student for real work or to prevent his dropping out. However, under the education acts of 1963–64, financial provision was made for updating and expanding vocational education, and there are currently in operation a number of research, demonstration, and training programs whose effect should shortly be felt in the field.

Meanwhile, some communities have already made efforts in the direction of modernizing vocational education programs to provide more effective and up-to-date training. Pittsburgh's public schools are developing a new occupational-vocational-technical program that provides training for various levels of ability and includes a technical curriculum extending into the thirteenth and fourteenth grades in the area of computer technology. Boston has a diversified shop program that allows potential dropouts to devote 80 percent of their school time to shop and 20 percent to marginally academic subjects like citizenship, health, and basic English.

The pupil who has fallen two or three grades behind in school is always a likely candidate for dropout status. New York City has made special provision for vocational high school students who wish to make up subject failures. Since their school day is so organized as to allow no free period for make-up during the regular school year, a summer vocational high school provides make-up courses, thus permitting students who have failed in one or two subjects to graduate on time.

Chicago has approached the problem of the student who is overage for his grade through vocational Education and Guidance centers. Overage pupils still in elementary school are enrolled in these centers and, in special ungraded classes of no more than 20 pupils, are grouped on the basis of reading and arithmetic achievement, tested ability, and chronological age. They receive a concentrated and personalized program of instruction plus extensive counseling and guidance to enable them to complete elementary school work and move on as rapidly as possible to a regular high school program. Those unable to do so are given the opportunity to develop occupational skills that will make them employable when they leave school.

The Wood School in Indianapolis has organized its entire school program to provide a chance for success to even the slowest learner. Retarded learners are routed through various areas, for example, art, music, industrial arts, and so forth, in order to discover a niche in which they might succeed. The school also offers training in seven service occupational courses developed cooperatively with local businesses. Ideally, this sort of program provides a flexibility that does not doom the late starter or the apparently slow learner to either an unsuitable occupational track or to perennial failure.

Several communities have organized special programs for nonconformist junior high school students who are potential dropouts. New Haven's joint education and training project was this kind of program for students in the seventh and eighth grades who were frustrated and uninterested in school, but of sufficiently high IQ to succeed if motivated. They were given an individualized program based on their own interests and abilities, field trips, and a good deal of counseling and guidance. The program's aim was to regenerate students who had a history of social or academic failure, or both. When students in the special classes seemed ready, they were reintroduced class by class into the regular school program.

As the emphasis in dropout programs moves downward from tenth-, eleventh-, and twelfth-graders to seventh-, eighth-, and ninth-graders, the distinctions between dropout programs and other kinds of compensatory education become matters of what a community chooses to call its program, rather than matters of special program content.

In South Norwalk (Conn.), an overall Ford Foundation-sponsored school improvement program is called Potential Dropouts. This program serves seventh-, eighth-, and ninth-graders. It includes special academic classes emphasizing special projects, a variety of cultural, occupational, and recreational field trips, guidance, and social worker involvement with the boys and their families.

Fort Worth has a similar program for pupils who are at least 13 years old by the time they reach the seventh grade. They are dropout programs in name, but in approach they are like programs not so designated.

Columbus, Ohio, instituted a similar general school-improvement program for all pupils in the school district as a means of reducing its dropout rate. But the program, a broad-spectrum approach involving teacher re-training, classroom reorganization, new instructional materials and tech-niques, guidance, and other alterations of the traditional program, is really a general attack on the educational problems in the city. The dropout rate was only a symptom. While programs aimed at the junior high or senior high school student who is viewed as ready to drop out, and soon legally able to do so, have proved useful in dealing with an urgent problem in a short-range manner, the most effective long-range programs to prevent dropouts are clearly those aimed at the preschool child. There is overt rec-ognition of this in the fact that Pennsylvania's long-range, statewide Pro-gram to Prevent Dropouts has been initiated with an extensive Preschool and Primary Education Project.

Preschool programs

During the past few years, both laymen and professional educators have become increasingly aware that chronic school failure begins early, and that there are numbers of children to whom school life offers nothing but defeat almost from its beginning. These are the children whose life experi-ences prior to entering school have not prepared them to meet the demands of a curriculum designed with other, more privileged, children in mind. Accumulating experimental evidence and pragmatic experience have both suggested that such a state of affairs is not inevitable. A period of pre-schooling, designed to develop in disadvantaged children those specific skills with which middle-class children come ready equipped to kinder-garten, can compensate for a good deal of the gap in background experi-ences they bring to the school. Thus the new preschool programs are not meant to be simply nursery schools for the poor. The best of them add to the nursery school's traditional concern for social and emotional develop-ment, activities that are designed to develop, as well, the other skills, selec-tive auditory and visual attention, problem solving, and other cognitive functions that are necessary for academic success.

The prekindergarten programs are in one sense all very similar. Under the best of circumstances there is only so much one can do with a three- or four-year-old child, and what these programs set out to do is to get him ready for school. The fact is that the very experiments designed to de-termine the kinds of intervention which are most effective in accomplish-ing this end are still in progress.

In Murfreesboro (Tenn.), an Early Training Program was designed to determine the minimum duration of a program of effective intervention. In New York City, the Deutsch therapeutic curriculum is still being de-veloped at the Institute for Developmental Studies. In a number of other experimental programs in Chicago, Boston, Syracuse, Long Beach, and elsewhere, investigators are still working to determine just which proce-dures, applied for how long, and under what circumstances, are effective in increasing the subsequent school success of disadvantaged children. Given the fact that the optimum situation is as yet undetermined, the assumption has been that for many a disadvantaged child even the minimum preschool situation will offer more than he is getting at home.

What most preschool programs have tried to provide is a warm accepting atmosphere in which a child may achieve his own maximum social and physical development, and an ordered atmosphere in which selected equip-ment and activities are offered in sufficient variety to meet each child's own level of interest and ability. Other than differences of quality, the principal differences between them have to do with their duration. Are they eight-week summer programs of the kind generated throughout the country by Project Head Start? Or are they five-year programs like Pennsylvania's? Do they function two or three mornings a week like a number of the pre-school programs set up by the local sections of the National Council of Jewish Women in various communities? Or are they five days a week, five hours a day programs like the Pilot Kindergarten Program in Racine and like many Head Start programs are doing in year-round programs now? A second distinction has to do with personnel and, by extension, with cost. Many preschool programs are staffed almost entirely by volunteers — indeed, together with tutoring and study hall programs, preschool projects draw more heavily on volunteers than any other compensatory programs, and are often financed by volunteer contributions for materials and other incidental expenses. On the other hand, foundation- or government-sponsored intensive research-oriented programs like the one in Ypsilanti, Michigan, use a concentration of paid professional personnel and are, as a consequence, very expensive. The Ypsilanti program, with perhaps the most ponderous title in all compensatory education, Intervention in the Cognitive Development of the Culturally Deprived and Functionally Retarded Negro Preschool Child, and project HELP, the early school admissions program in Baltimore, Maryland, both initiated in 1962, are among the better known and, in the field of preschool education, among the earlier of the major school-connected projects. The Baltimore project operated four centers. Each center served about 30 children, and was located in a way that provided variety in the populations served. Two centers were in predominantly Negro neighborhoods, one was in an integrated neighborhood, and one was in a predominantly white neighborhood. The children were selected from families showing evidence of multiple social, economic, physical, or psychological problems. The daily program was centered around various subject areas: art, music, literature, science, and so forth, with activities in each area designed both to encourage the child's self-expression and to widen his experience of the world. Like other preschool programs, the early school admissions project focused on language skills and provided constant practice in both speaking and listening.

If the preschool programs can be said to have an academic emphasis, it is in this area of verbal expression that such an emphasis lies, because a lack of high quality verbal self-expression is one of the most consistent observable characteristics of children from homes with limited advantages. Consequently many preschool programs consider improvement in the quantity and quality of children's speech production a major goal in itself. Activities such as reading aloud, discussing books, cooperative storytelling, naming of objects, rhyming games, and other activities have been utilized to encourage more elaborate verbal expression. The Ypsilanti project shares this emphasis on stimulating language usage and, as they do in other projects, makes use of field trips to community places of interest as another way of broadening the child's base of experience and encouraging the naming of activities, as well as questions and conversation about what he is seeing.

The Ypsilanti project is most notable, however, for its method of extending the school program into the home. During a two-hour afternoon period each week, a classroom teacher goes into each child's home, bringing along any equipment she thinks is useful and is able to carry. There, in a kind of private demonstration lesson, she continues the education of the child on a one-to-one basis with the cooperation and participation of the mother.

A similar in-the-home approach is one significant aspect of Pennsylvania's preschool and primary education project which initiates the learning situation with a preschool summer nursery program for three-and-a-half-year-olds. During the following school year the same teacher works in the family's home with both children and parents. She continues into the summer with a prekindergarten program and then becomes the children's kindergarten teacher for the following school year. A third summer of postkindergarten classes precedes the entrance of the children into first grade, and the children remain in the project through grade 3. This prolonged and intensive program includes parent counseling and an effort at overall improvement in community services to the families involved.

The family emphasis in preschool programs is not an incidental one. The involvement of parents in the goals of any kind of compensatory educational programs is a generally recognized asset in the success of this kind of program. But the greater vulnerability of the very young to the effects of the home environment, and the greater possibilities of effecting changes in young children through alterations in that environment, have led to an overwhelming emphasis on parental involvement in preschool programs. With few exceptions the majority of preschool programs have made significant efforts not only to inform the mothers of project goals, but to involve them as teacher aides, as participants in field trips, and as observers of preschool techniques in action in the classroom. A new program for American Indian children at Fort Totten, North Dakota, utilizes mothers to prepare lunch for the children. Detroit's preschool program brought in mothers to read aloud to the class. Many programs also provide for parent discussion groups, parent education on matters of child guidance, and individual parent meetings with professional psychiatric personnel for consultation on behavior or other emotional problems. In New Haven, no child is accepted in the public school prekindergarten program unless a parent will consent to participate in a parallel but separate program. This program is a two-and-a-half hour weekly discussion of the preschool program, community resources, suggested family activities, and child rearing practices.

But some projects have gone even further in demonstrating a conviction that effective preschool education is also parent education. In Chicago, the Parents' School Readiness Program at Firman House and the Tutoring Project for Mothers, are oriented toward providing child care and child guidance information, and toward educating the parents in reading, mathematics, and other academic skills, both for their own sakes, and to better equip them to provide readiness experiences for their preschoolers. In Sacramento, parent-child observation classes provide a mutual learning experience.

The primary motivation for involving parents in preschool programs is that the involvement seems to benefit both parent and child. The benefit to the preschool program itself in terms of staffing is incidental, and the goal has not generally been to reproduce among the culturally disadvantaged the middle-class cooperative nursery school situation. The problem of staffing the growing number of preschool programs has had to be met in other ways. One of the ways that has been utilized to develop qualified professional personnel is the summer teacher training institute, operated in conjunction with an experimental nursery school program. Philadelphia has an ongoing project of this sort, designed to develop both techniques and personnel for educating disadvantaged preschoolers. But there is little hope, in the face of an overall shortage of qualified teachers at every level, that the supply of professionals will ever catch up with the demand, particularly at the preschool level where the pupil-teacher ratio should ideally be low. Consequently, a growing number of preschool programs are looking to trained volunteers, backed up by at least one professional teacher in a classroom, as the mainstays of their staffs. These volunteers are often former teachers or people otherwise trained in education, and in many of the programs they are given specific courses of instruction before they go into a classroom. The National Council of Jewish Women, through their various local sections, have helped to sponsor a number of volunteer preschool programs in cities like New Orleans, Cincinnati, Central Parkway (N.J.), Cleveland, and New York City. In several of these cities professional personnel are used to conduct organized training courses for the volunteers. In Cleveland, for example, volunteers receive training and orientation for a total of eight sessions and regular on-the-job workshop training after they begin work.

Another approach to the staffing of schools that has been used with some success is what might be called the "mutual benefit" program. Recently, in Miami (Fla.), 993 children participated in a preschool program conducted by trained high school graduates. John F. Kennedy Community Service Awards, providing free junior college tuition and $500 cash, were made to 60 high school graduates from the same disadvantaged neighborhoods as the preschoolers. In return, the awardees, trained for their jobs by college psychology and education faculty and local public school personnel, have conducted daily two-and-one-half hour preschool classes. In Fresno (Calif.), the preschool program, a part of a larger compensatory education effort, is conducted by parents, Fresno State College students, and disadvantaged junior high school pupils from a project school. The arrangement resulted immediately in improved grades for the teen-agers. Fresno also provides health services for its preschoolers. This is a frequent practice where preschool programs are part of a public school project.

In a number of communities preschool programs have been developed under school board auspices as a downward extension of the regular school program or as an addition to services already offered in an ongoing compensatory project. The preschool programs in Detroit, Oakland, Providence, and Mount Kisco (N.Y.), are a part of larger programs of compensatory education. New York City now has prekindergarten classes operating in 151 city schools. Pittsburgh is developing an ungraded preschool through primary sequence, suggesting a direction in which early school education would seem to be moving. School-based preschool programs are often conducted within the school buildings, but many of the volunteer-staffed programs are housed in whatever facilities are available in the area being served. Preschool classes have been held in churches, community centers, perambulator rooms, auditoriums, and even in apartments in housing developments.

There are several programs for preschoolers which are unclassifiable, but are worth mentioning, either because they are so sizable or because they are unusual enough to suggest ideas for others. In San Francisco a special program for parents and children with special needs provides cultural orientation and English language classes for mothers and preschoolers who are recent immigrants to the Bay area from the Far East, Latin America, or other non-English-speaking areas.

A similar although a much more extensive program is conducted yearly in Texas. The statewide preschool program for non-English-speaking children is designed to meet a statewide problem and provides training in word recognition and oral English to thousands of Mexican-American preschoolers each summer.

While preschool programs provide the earliest intervention into the lives of disadvantaged children, and therefore offer the most hopeful long-range solution to their school problems, the majority of the present generation of disadvantaged children are already in school. For these children the preschool programs come too late, and it is for these children that the great bulk of special educational programs must provide help.

4. Innovations in school program and staffing patterns

It is no secret among educators that special efforts have been required to staff effectively those schools that draw students largely from "disadvantaged" or slum populations. Not only is recruitment difficult, but teacher turnover and dissatisfaction often tend to be high in schools that have a history of relative failure within the system. Some school boards have attempted to meet these staffing problems by quota systems which guarantee that a high percentage of experienced teachers will be assigned to inner-city schools, or by regulations that require experience in these schools as a prerequisite for advancement within the system. However, these methods leave unresolved the problems of teacher attitude toward such assignments or teacher resignation in the face of them. One dispirited teacher teaching 20 pupils is no more likely to be effective than the same teacher teaching 40 pupils. Numbers alone are not enough, and an inspired and competent staff has usually proved to be the sine qua non of any successful program for the disadvantaged. No attempt at reaching and teaching disadvantaged children can hope to be successful unless the attitude of the teaching staff and the administration is both optimistic and enlightened, and unless new approaches are not only accepted but welcomed.

Teacher recruitment and training

It is, of course, of inestimable value to begin with a staff which *wants* to be where it is; and perhaps the most effective long-range approach to this achievement lies in making preservice teacher trainees acquainted with the problems of teaching the disadvantaged before they ever take charge of a classroom. An experimental project at Hunter College in New York City clearly demonstrated that placing preservice trainees in difficult schools for a period of supervised practice teaching would not only develop their competence to deal with disadvantaged pupils, but would also encourage them to choose a "difficult" school to teach in. Teacher training programs, per se, have not fallen within the scope of our study, but it is worth noting that the preservice orientation approach is being utilized in a number of these programs.

Project Beacon at Yeshiva University exposes students in preservice training to a curriculum emphasizing the social, developmental, and learning problems of the disadvantaged. This is coupled with field experience and practice teaching in the Mobilization for Youth project and its affiliated schools. The Newark Teaching in Central Urban Areas program, the Cardozo project in Washington, D.C., that uses returning Peace Corps volunteers, the University of Missouri's Junior Practicum, and the training institutes at the Bank Street College of Education represent some of the current efforts to prepare teachers for the challenge of educating disadvantaged children. There are also less extensive programs which provide for future-teacher, future-pupil contact. In Cleveland, for example, education majors at a local women's college spend one morning a week during their junior year working at an inner-city school. In Boston, students from local teacher-training institutions are trained as tutors for individual project students, and, as is the case with a number of college student tutoring programs, the relationship is looked on as providing teacher orientation experience for the tutors as well as remedial assistance for the children who are being tutored. The Mundelein College Work-Scholarship Program in Chicago provided college students with summer jobs at various agencies in the inner-city area as a means of acquainting them with the problems of local families and their children.

For the future, the projected teacher-training program sponsored by the Research Council of the Great Cities Program for School Improvement will establish 10 centers specifically oriented toward the training of teachers for depressed areas. And in a short-range program, the extension of the NDEA summer training institutes to include programs of training for teachers of the disadvantaged should help to assure a supply of better qualified personnel for these schools.

In the meantime, the schools have had to find ways of dealing with the insecurities and problems of teachers who have, more frequently than not, had no preservice orientation and training, and whose initial attitude on being assigned to a school with a bad reputation may range from dismay to actual fear. At one Cleveland junior high school, a one- to three-day preschool institute for incoming teachers combined talks about school organization with visits to local settlement houses as well as at least one afternoon spent in the homes of students. Home visits early in the school year are often a first step in providing a teacher whose previous experience has been limited to middle-class children and parents, with a realistic and, it is hoped, affirmative view of her new pupils. In one so-called bad neighborhood, extra police protection was provided at the urging of the administration, for teachers' safety during home visits. When this precautionary measure proved unnecessary, morale immediately improved.

Obviously, special concern for the successful adjustment of the new teacher extends far beyond basic orientation programs. In Philadelphia, for example, there is a special teacher in each project school who is responsible for helping new teachers with classroom management, suggesting and demonstrating instructional techniques, and rendering any other needed assistance. New York City has operated a Student Teacher and Newly-Appointed-Teacher-Training Program since 1959. Teacher-training consultants, usually one consultant to three schools, provide a variety of supportive services to student teachers, substitutes, and teaching personnel newly appointed to special service schools. In Buffalo (N.Y.), a center-city elementary school, which has been the beneficiary of an extensive pilot program of educational improvement, has become a demonstration school in an expanded compensatory program. New teachers (defined as those with less than three years of experience in the Buffalo schools) are brought to the pilot school in groups of 12 to work for four days with experienced teachers at their grade level while their own classes are being handled by experienced substitutes.

But in most project schools it is not only the new, the inexperienced, or the less able teachers who need assistance. It is possible to bring into a compensatory program the best teachers in the system, those who have been rated most able in their work in other schools, only to have them fail in their new situation. Because the problem is not simply one of teaching, but of teaching the disadvantaged. Many teachers, very often those with years of experience in schools where projects are being initiated, have attitudes toward their pupils which insure defeat of any program of upgrading. Because the child's learning is affected by his motivation, his motivation is affected by his attitudes toward himself and the learning situation, these attitudes are to a large extent in the hands of the teacher. As Niemeyer has put it, "When teachers have a low expectation level for their children's learning, the children seldom exceed that expectation."[1]

Where achievement levels and expectation levels have been low, an honest appraisal of the problem, together with a determination to do better, may effect a considerable improvement, as it did in the Banneker School District program in St. Louis. Teachers in the district elementary schools were told to ignore IQ scores and to teach as if all the children had superior ability. This advice, combined with pupil and parent motivational techniques, effected some changes in a deteriorating situation. However, most schools have found that inspiration produces more results when combined with a strong program of inservice training and workshop experience. As the administrator of one large and successful program stated, the training program had not only given the teachers faith in the pupils, it had "given them the means to translate that faith into reality."

Much of the inservice teacher training in compensatory programs puts emphasis on increasing the teachers' knowledge of the lives of the disadvantaged and on increasing teacher sensitivity to the hopes and anxieties, the particular strengths and weaknesses lying behind the classroom behavior of the disadvantaged. When a teacher understands how the disadvantaged differ from herself and from the children she may have previously taught, she often becomes aware of the degree to which her own middle-class values inhibit her positive perceptions of and relations with these children. This awareness may help to develop the teacher's skill in recognizing ability and learning behavior which she might otherwise overlook.

In New York City, Mobilization for Youth (MFY), conducts this kind of sensitization course for public school teachers. Teachers who attend the Lower East Side Community Course of 12 lecture workshops and 13 field trips get a stipend and inservice credits for attending, and, it is hoped, come away with a better understanding of the community in which they teach

---

1. John Niemeyer, "Some Guidelines to Desirable Elementary School Reorganization," in *Programs for the Educationally Disadvantaged*. U.S. Office of Education Bulletin 1963, No. 17 (OE-35044). Washington, D.C.: U.S. Department of Health, Education, and Welfare, 1963, pp. 80–85.

and of its children. A similar MFY-sponsored course that includes visits to pupil homes, also emphasizes understanding of the culture, the personal characteristics, and the learning attitudes of disadvantaged families.

Other inservice programs have been conducted as summer workshops, or on television. In Oakland, 28 half-hour TV showings dealing with the teaching of disadvantaged children were offered for course credit. In the Mc-Ateer program in Stockton, teachers were offered informal instruction in the cultural background of their pupils. In Redwood City (Calif.), the Sequoia McAteer project devoted its entire first year to a program of teacher reorientation, providing weekly discussion groups under the leadership of a consultant, and teacher meetings with small groups of students as a way of acquainting the teachers with the needs of their pupils.

But understanding, it appears, is only the beginning. Most of the inservice training programs are devoted not only to promoting understanding but to helping teachers to acquire the specific skills, the techniques, and the coping strategies for teaching pupils who cannot benefit from the traditional curriculum. In a White Plains (N.Y.) project, teacher inservice training is provided by faculty meetings, conferences, and a weekly information sheet giving tips from experienced teachers on methods that have worked in the classroom. In Detroit, teachers are paid for attendance at Saturday and summer workshops, concerned with modifying curriculums as well as attitudes. A Model School System in Washington (D.C.) includes plans for special inservice training programs in such areas as the new mathematics, the new remedial reading programs, and in programed instruction. This training will permit a greater flexibility in teacher selection, because personnel not qualified can be given training on the job.

Faced with the problem of luring already busy teachers to inservice education courses, many projects have provided time for this training within the school day. In New Haven, for example, 12 days on the school calendar are set apart for half-day, teacher inservice programs. In Chicago, the children in one program are shown a movie while their classroom teachers attend regularly scheduled grade-level workshops dealing with such topics as diagnostic testing, teaching techniques, and special educational materials. As part of Philadelphia's language enrichment project, a language arts teacher conducts a literature program for the children one morning a week, freeing the regular teachers to attend grade-group inservice workshops where language arts consultants conduct a graduate course in pedagogic theory and methods.

The insights, methods, and materials developed in the workshops are not theoretical. They are meant to be applied immediately in the classroom and are tested in action research designed to explore their effectiveness. While the content of training programs varies from project to project, depending on the needs of a particular school or group of schools, improvement in the teaching of reading is an area of major concern. New York City has offered courses on the Negro in America and on Latin American culture in order to enable teachers to incorporate materials that are personally relevant to minority group children into their curricular offerings. Workshops are often utilized for the introduction of new textbooks. In other cases, they have focused on introducing or producing new teaching materials more related to the backgrounds of the children. In at least one project, teachers were offered a writing workshop in which to prepare original reading matter of immediate interest to the disadvantaged child.

All these methods of providing for teacher orientation and teacher training have a common goal: to upgrade the quality of instruction in schools serving the disadvantaged. But regardless of the degree to which attitudes and techniques may be improved, it is improvement in the teaching *situation* which often has the most salutary effect on teacher effectiveness, and so, by extension, on teacher morale. For the teacher, the size of the class she is asked to handle, the availability or nonavailability of help when she needs it, the structure within which she teaches, and the materials with which she has to teach—are all major factors in her success or lack of success. The traditional methods of approach to both the conduct and the content of the classroom have not worked with disadvantaged pupils. Methods that *do* work benefit teacher and pupil alike.

Curriculum innovations

Among the approaches that have been utilized for more effective teaching and learning are various alterations of the traditional one-teacher, one-class relationship. And one of the more currently popular of these alterations is team teaching—a rearrangement of staff which provides support to less effective or less experienced personnel, as well as allowing for the fuller utilization of each teacher's talents. Combining teachers with varying degrees of experience on a team for planning, as well as for instructional activities, ideally allows the less able teacher to benefit from the advice and guidance of the more able teacher. It also permits teachers with special areas of competence to share their knowledge with a larger group of students.

In a program like New York City's newly instituted More Effective Schools, a team of four teachers is assigned to three elementary school classes, numbering not more than 22 pupils each. In Pittsburgh, as many as 120 students may be grouped for instruction under a team of four teachers and a team leader, augmented by a teacher intern and a paid team mother or aide trained in handling audiovisual equipment, duplicating equipment, and classroom supplies. Early primary grade teams in Pittsburgh are assembled on the basis of grade level. Intermediate teams are composed of teachers of different subjects: language, arts, social studies, science, arithmetic, and library. Junior high school teams are organized by subject matter. In practice, the total group of students, whether it is 60 or 120, is rarely taught as a unit. While one or more team teachers are instructing a large group in one room, other members of the team work with groups as small as five or six (or even with a single pupil), to provide special work, remedial help, or—in the case of pupils with outstanding ability—enrichment. Within the team-teaching structure, pupil groupings will be influenced by the specific learning tasks and will vary in size according to the nature of the subject and the ability and achievement level of the students. Where the subject matter contains technical content, smaller groups may be necessary. Where the subject matter contains less technical material and the emphasis is on social learning, larger groups may be preferable.

Children involved in a team-teaching project may be grouped in homerooms, heterogeneously, as in the More Effective Schools project, or, more commonly, homogeneously on the basis of reading ability. They may spend as much as 85 percent or as little as 10 percent of their week in team-teaching structured activities. In Tucson's seventh- and eighth-grade Safford Exploratory Program, for example, each grade-level team devotes a four-hour block of time daily to group work. This arrangement permits much flexibility in the scheduling of large- and small-group instruction periods, field trips, and special programs. On the other hand, team teaching occupies only one afternoon a week in Project Able in Albany. During that time no bells are rung and elementary school pupils spend two hours exploring a particular area of interest with the aid of teachers particularly qualified in that field along with numerous outside consultants. Each semester the pupil group shifts to a new interest area and new teachers so that by the end of four years each pupil has explored eight areas such as arts and crafts, science, music, and so forth, in these special sessions. A team-teaching demonstration project in a New Rochelle junior high school used a four-teacher team at each grade level solely for social studies instruction. The pupils, who were grouped homogeneously in their regular school program, were grouped in heterogeneous teams for their social studies classes in an experiment designed to determine the effect of this sort of grouping on their achievement and their attitudes.

Some of what is loosely called team teaching in compensatory programs really involves the use of supplementary personnel. Teacher aides or volunteer mothers are used in the classroom, instead of the genuine organizational change represented by a team-teaching program. This is particularly true at the preschool level where what is described as team teaching often merely means that a number of persons work in the classroom under the guidance of one certified teacher in order to provide the more individualized attention required by preschool-age children.

Relaxation of the one-teacher, one-class structure has been paralleled by modification of the one-grade, one-year relationship. Two major avenues of approach have been utilized in attacking the traditional year-by-year, grade-by-grade progression which has so often offered nothing but defeat to the disadvantaged pupils. The first of these approaches has to do with grouping. Where it has not previously been employed, the practice of tracking students by ability (homogeneous grouping) has often been looked upon as a compensatory practice. It provides each student with an opportunity to be with other students of similar ability, thus doing away with what is often a defeating competitive situation. Students in a track *do* progress through the usual grades, but they have also, theoretically, the possibility of horizontal movement from one track to another when their achievement, or lack of it, so dictates. Where no disgrace is attached to occupying the lowest track, tracking may offer one method of solving the grade progression lockstep. In actual fact, the effect of tracking is often to consign permanently to the lowest tracks the disadvantaged children the system is supposed to help. In many communities with large minority populations, it has become obvious that tracking results in segregation. As a result, there has recently been a good deal of experimentation with heterogeneous classroom assignments and flexible ability-level subgroupings within the classroom. The Project Able programs in White Plains (N.Y.) and Hartsdale (N.Y.) have made use of heterogeneous homeroom groupings in primary school programs that emphasize genuine racial integration in the classroom. Through flexible groupings and subgroupings of children within the classroom, ability levels are brought within a range which permits effective teaching of various academic subjects. The upper-grade centers in Chicago group seventh- and eighth-graders heterogeneously for homeroom study, group counseling, art, music, physical education, and club activities, while providing for ability-level instruction in the tool subjects.

As another alternative to tracking, a number of projects serving disadvantaged children have made use of a nongraded form of organization. Norfolk (Va.), for example, has developed a nongraded block in three elementary schools for the primary grades, in which placement is determined by reading levels. Children are moved from class to class or from group to group within a class according to their readiness for any one of nine predetermined reading levels, but classes are distinguished only by a teacher's name and the designation, "Primary." In this kind of an arrangement children are not stigmatized by failing to maintain a year-by-year, grade-by-grade progression but rather are moved through the various academic areas at the speed of which they are capable. Baltimore is now operating nongraded programs, primarily in what would have been grades 1 to 3, in 26 schools. A number of other large communities are experimenting with the ungraded structure as a part of ongoing programs of compensatory education in the school system. The idea of ungraded sequences of learning, rather than single age-grade steps, which in Pittsburgh is being extended to a preprimary through grade 3 sequence, is an attempt to correlate school organization with the way children really learn. In Chicago, the continuous development plan has been introduced into grades 1 to 3 in a number of elementary schools. The plan provides for an eight- or nine-level progression and permits the child to reach the end of grade 3 without being stigmatized by failure. Any child not ready to proceed into fourth grade at the end of three years is retained for a fourth year in the program.

Although ungraded primary classes are the most familiar pattern, Chicago has also made use of an ungraded class structure in a program for average pupils from age 11 to 15. Milwaukee has incorporated into its regular school program ungraded transitional classes for in-migrant and transient children from the primary grades through high school. Elementary school classes are self-contained; at the secondary school level pupils take nonacademic subjects with students in the regular program and academic subjects in ungraded classes taught by orientation-center teachers. Special remedial classes, from which pupils eventually move back into their regular classrooms, have been used in a number of programs, particularly in schools where high transiency rates make for little continuity in classroom experience. In Denver (Colo.), for example, four elementary schools have orientation rooms in which pupil registry is held to 15 in order to provide intensive reading and mathematics instruction for pupils moving into the school district. For the perennially transient, the children of migrant workers, a special program in Austin, Texas, is designed to provide the essentials of a regular nine-month school term in a six-month period of concentration on basic skills. This year the program served 9,000 elementary school and junior high school pupils.

Some programs have made provision for a more extended relationship between pupil and teacher than is provided by the traditional curriculum organization. An ungraded program, for example, may be organized to permit pupils to remain with the same teacher for more than a year in order to encourage the development of more productive teacher-pupil relationships. In Detroit, student-teacher continuity in the primary grades has been extended to three years in some schools. In New York City, the Queens College project BRIDGE conducted an educational experiment in which three teachers spent about two-thirds of each school day with the same junior high school pupils over a period of three years. More often at the secondary school level, block-time programing is used to provide pupil-teacher continuity within the school day for pupils not ready for the multiple-class approach of the traditional junior high school. The University of Texas junior high school program in Austin uses block-time programing with an emphasis on reading and language skills in a project aimed at seventh-graders who are considered likely to be future dropouts. Cleveland has a similar special transition class for pupils entering the seventh grade who are not yet ready for junior high school. In addition to a special core curriculum they have remedial reading work and supervised study periods. A Centinela Valley (Calif.) pilot project applied the same approach to a special class of tenth-grade pupils.

In lieu of an ungraded structure, some programs have made use of transitional classes at the primary grade level, either to ease the pupil's entry into school for the first time or to ease his transition from one school situation to another. A junior first grade for the most immature of the kindergartners is used as a half-step between kindergarten and regular grade 1 in Boston's Operation Counterpoise. In small classes, teachers work to develop eye-hand coordination and auditory and visual perception discrimination. Whenever a child seems to be ready he is moved into a regular grade 1. Washington (D.C.) also has a junior primary grade level. A similar program for "late bloomers" is part of Philadelphia's language-arts program. It is designed for children who have spent at least one year in school and have not yet begun to read or write. A language-arts teacher gives them intensive work in listening and speaking, auditory and visual discrimination, reading readiness, and beginning reading and writing. As soon as the children develop competence they return to a regular reading group in their own classes. Boston's Operation Recap is a special class halfway between the third and fourth grade for normal learners who are reading at least one year below grade level. The program emphasizes spelling, handwriting and reading, and written and oral language work. Pittsburgh combines such a transition class with an ungraded early primary structure going through the third grade. Pupils not ready for the fourth grade move into a special class designed to bring them up to grade level. A pilot kindergarten program in Racine (Wis.) was designed to keep disadvantaged children from falling behind by providing a full five-hour school day to kindergartners to allow more time for readiness and enrichment activities. A kindergarten program in Nyack (N.Y.) also extends the kindergarten day, less formally, through a variety of enrichment activities for kindergartners who show evidence of information gaps upon entering school. Within the area of special classes, many schools serving disadvantaged pupils have programs for the chronically disruptive, the emotionally disturbed, and the mentally defective. Although such programs do, indeed, serve an area of disadvantage, they are not specifically directed toward the problems of social disadvantage with which this study is concerned. There are two additional kinds of special classes, however, which do have a particular relevance for the disadvantaged: classes for the non-English-speaking child, and classes for the academically talented child. Classes for the gifted, children who rank exceptionally high on standard IQ tests, have been in operation in a number of cities for some time, but such programs do not attend in any large degree to the needs of the disadvantaged. Among these children scores on standard IQ tests are usually both lower than the average and, it is suspected, much lower than they should be in terms of the existing potential for learning. In Oakland (Calif.), classes for academically talented children who are culturally disadvantaged have been set up in two elementary schools at the sixth-grade level. The children are recommended for the program on the basis of recognized potential as judged by teachers and other school staff members. Although their IQ scores are not high enough to merit their inclusion in a regular class for the gifted, they are provided with the same kind of enrichment program, the same services, and the same extra materials as are the classes for the gifted. In Chicago it is the practice of the school system to include children from the top 10 or 15 percent in low-achievement schools in programs for the gifted, although their IQ range may be no higher than 100 to 115. Chicago also has at least two partially state-financed demonstration centers in operation at Carver Elementary School and at Kelley High School, designed to provide special enriched programs for able and potentially gifted youngsters. Another program for students of above average potential is the one at Winston-Salem (N. C.), where the residential North Carolina Advancement School has been set up specifically to develop means of educating underachieving pupils through a combination of motivational techniques and training in basic skills.

The common aim of all these structural rearrangements and special classes is to suit the education to the child and to individualize instruction. This kind of individual program is, quantitatively, a very different problem in Los Nietos (Calif.), where 30 children are involved in a program of compensatory education than it is in Detroit, where more than 30,000 are included. It is also very different in a community like Mount Kisco (N.Y.), where the resources of a generally upper-class population can be brought to bear on small pockets of the underprivileged, than it is in Newburgh (N.Y.), where the limited resources of the schools are part of a generally depressed area. The underlying principle in individualizing instruction is the same however—that the likelihood of meaningful teacher-pupil contact is significantly related to the reduction of teacher-pupil ratio.

In recognition of this fact, many cities have set up formulas, based on measures of various economic, social, and educational achievement factors, by which extra personnel are assigned to schools serving predominantly disadvantaged populations. In addition, the introduction of a specific program of compensatory education into a given school or group of schools will usually result in the assignment of additional supplementary personnel. A program like Cincinnati's is typical. Five schools located in a depressed area and close to each other are grouped together to receive extra services. Five regular teachers and five remedial reading specialists serve the schools individually, and such additional staff as psychologists, visiting teachers, and other supportive personnel are assigned to the schools as a group. Although some programs have achieved success without extra personnel, most of the programs of any size have made provision for at least a part-time reduction of pupil-teacher ratio, and have seen to it that the classroom teacher had recourse to an extra head or an extra pair of hands when she needed them.

The assignment of extra classroom teachers to a project school to reduce class size is perhaps the most useful technique from a teacher's standpoint. A number of communities, among them Newburgh (N.Y.) and Hartford (Conn.), have reduced average class size to 25 in project schools. However, in addition to being expensive, formation of new classes is sometimes impossible because of space limitations. In response to this problem, the Chicago school system tried putting a teacher who was free of class duties into project schools where no room was available to form extra classes. Two new classes of personnel who could effectively reduce teacher-pupil ratio developed from the experiment: special service teachers to work with the children in small groups for reading or arithmetic coaching, assist the classroom teachers, prepare curriculum materials, and so forth; and master teachers to help new teachers understand the problems of disadvantaged children and to initiate them into teaching methods that have been proved effective in the classroom.

A number of projects have made use of mobile personnel, variously designated as coaching teachers, curriculum experts, project consultants, project teachers, and so on, to provide a variety of services for the classroom teacher. These skilled teachers may present demonstration lessons, provide special instructional materials, maintain resource rooms, help with room decoration, provide small group instruction in the areas of remedial reading or literature enrichment; and, where no special new-teacher help is available, they may spend a good deal of time during the early part of the year providing needed assistance to new members of the staff. In San Francisco's School-Community Improvement Program, resource teachers are employed to give demonstration and observation lessons and to work with small groups of children when needed. In the McAteer project in Berkeley a special resource kindergarten teacher in each school provides assistance to the regular teachers in classroom planning and selection of materials, and is also available for work with children and their parents. Pupil adjustment workers serve as roving trouble-shooters in Hartford and also take over the classroom when the teacher needs to leave. In Boston, the Operation Counterpoise program makes use of special master teachers who instruct their own homerooms in reading and arithmetic and are then relieved of the remainder of their regular teaching program in order to perform a variety of coordinated, supervisory guidance and counseling functions for a team of five or six elementary school teachers and their pupils.

The addition of almost any kind of personnel to a school staff will help a classroom teacher to some degree, either by reducing her classroom load or by relieving her of duties which would otherwise devolve upon her. The organization of remedial classes in reading or mathematics during the school day draws off pupils weaker in those subjects from their regular classrooms leaving the classroom teacher free to provide a richer program for her remaining pupils. In the Kings County (Calif.) compensatory project, the project pupils are drawn out of their regular classrooms not for remedial work, but for enrichment activities. Special teachers in art, music, speech, language arts, science, or library may help the teacher and the pupils by coming into the classroom to teach special lessons, demonstrate special materials or techniques, or provide enrichment activities to groups of talented children in various subjects.

Similarly, the addition of special personnel in guidance or psychology may provide for a more rapid handling of school adjustment problems and relieve the teacher of the necessity of coping single-handedly with immediate crises. In the McAteer programs in Los Nietos and San Diego (Calif.), specific provision has been made for substitute teachers to take over the classroom in order to allow the regular teacher time to meet with parents. In Cleveland, parent contacts are handled by visiting teachers who move between home and school, providing classroom teachers with special help in understanding home problems that are affecting the children in school. New York has paid school-aides, nonteaching personnel originally employed to relieve teachers in special service schools of lunchroom duty, who now perform a variety of functions from taking inventory and repairing library books to supervising handwashing and escorting ill children to their homes.

There is no rule which dictates that the personnel added to a classroom to reduce teacher-pupil ratio need be professional, or paid. In a number of projects the use of volunteer aides, particularly in the primary grades, has proved a most valuable way of increasing teacher effectiveness without at the same time collapsing the school budget. In San Francisco, volunteer parents serve as classroom aides, "admiring, buttoning aprons, tying shoes, cutting, pasting, admiring, and listening," and by so doing effectively reduce the classroom teacher's load. In the same project a group of volunteers were also trained as storytellers and assigned to project classrooms. An aide may be used to maintain order in the classroom during a free play period so that the teacher can provide special reading readiness or other "catch-up" work for a small group of slower learners. School resource volunteers in Berkeley are available upon request from the classroom teacher—and the demand outstrips the supply—to perform any and all needed functions from correcting papers to providing special enrichment activities for groups of students. Volunteer personnel in such special areas as music, art, dance, creative writing, or science may come into the classroom to provide special information and inspiration, regularly, or on a one-shot basis as visiting lecturers. Although most of the volunteer tutoring projects are conducted in after-school time, volunteers have also been used, as in Milwaukee's university tutorial program, to tutor pupils during the school day as well as to assist generally in the classroom. Although in some cases volunteers may provide simply another pair of hands, they are sometimes trained for specific jobs. The Urban Service Corps in Washington, D.C., has provided services and personnel of all sorts to the Capital's schools, ranging from volunteers to offer music and literature enrichment activities, to specially trained counselor aides and remedial reading aides, who provide assistance to professional personnel in those areas. The Junior Volunteers Project in New York City utilizes the abilities, talents, and time of six hundred 13- to 15-year-old junior high school students who are drawn from the neighborhood served and provided with extensive inservice training.

Volunteer classroom personnel can be parents or other adults, or they can be young people. The Kings County (Calif.) compensatory education program makes use of student teachers from a local state college to supplement the work of the classroom teacher. Two of the other McAteer programs in California provide notable examples of intraproject cooperation. In Indio, the Coachella Valley McAteer project uses bilingual future teachers as classroom aides in the elementary school grades and uses high school students from the project school neighborhood as interpreter aides in teaching and counseling. In Fresno, junior high school project pupils helped run a nursery school program, and fifth- and sixth-graders provided reading help for primary grade pupils. The latter practice is one that has been explored in several programs.

One of the more extensive and ambitious volunteer programs is that of the Council of the Southern Mountains in Berea (Ky.), the Appalachian Volunteers. These volunteers are providing a program of individual attention for pupils in eastern Kentucky's rural schools that includes both remedial work and enrichment. They are also working to establish libraries in about 400 rural schools, through the Books to Appalachia Drive conducted with the help of the national p.t.a. last spring.

With or without extra personnel, many compensatory programs have attempted to develop ways of making the maximum use of their experienced teachers to improve the competence and effectiveness of their less able or less experienced colleagues. In some cases, a regular time is set aside—in the morning before classes, for example, or at lunch—for teachers to meet and share ideas. In San Francisco, project teachers shared methods with regular classroom teachers through meetings, descriptive bulletins, and demonstration lessons. In a Syracuse project, released time during school hours is provided for team planning of the instructional program utilizing a team consisting of an instructional specialist, four or five teachers, and resource persons as needed. A Columbus (Ohio) program developed a similar kind of planning team consisting of five classroom teachers and one enrichment teacher. A number of less formal programs have been organized to provide for teacher cooperation in sharing insights and techniques in planning programs or preparing materials for the project.

But whatever the size of the class, no matter how it is planned and conducted, it is ultimately what gets taught that counts. Innovation in teaching the disadvantaged has affected not only who is in the classroom, but what is in the classroom as well. To describe a certain program as an innovation is to suggest that it has never been done before. The fact is, that in many schools serving disadvantaged neighborhoods, certain activities are considered innovations but may be commonplace in more privileged schools. The disparity in the amount of supplies and services provided to schools serving disparate economic groups is a documented fact. In many project schools the use of movable desks in the classroom, or the introduction into the curriculum of special art classes, student government activities, band practice, scientific experimentation, or field trips, represents genuine innovation for that particular school or school district.

Moreover, the emphasis in compensatory educational programs has been not merely on providing some kind of education to the disadvantaged, but on developing a curriculum which is pertinent to the real life situation of the children involved, and which takes advantage of the tendency noted particularly among the disadvantaged, but characteristic of many children, to do rather than to be told. The Project Able program in Hillburn (N.Y.) has put emphasis on "doing" activities throughout the curriculum, and in addition devotes a half-day a week to participation activities like dancing, dramatics, science experiments, and field trips. This general emphasis on approaches to learning that require the active physical participation of the children is part of many compensatory programs. Another emphasis is on multiple-level learning materials. Although the eventual goal of these programs is to raise the academic achievement of all the children, materials must be provided that are within the scope of their present ability. Consequently, one effort in this direction has been to provide multilevel materials which allow for extensive individual differences even within a given classroom. In order to accomplish this, many projects have had to devise a good deal of original teaching material to suit the needs of their particular disadvantaged population. The aim, and the end product of much of the curricular alteration, has been to see the curriculum as a continuous vertical learning sequence rather than as a series of grades, each with a separate and isolated content. This kind of overview has often been the function of curriculum coordinators who are added to many project staffs to help unify both the innovations and the familiar into a coherent whole.

Although much of the emphasis in compensatory programs has been placed on reading and language development, an expanded notion of what constitutes learning and learning materials has affected all the academic areas. In mathematics, whether new or old, manipulative materials provide for independent discovery of basic number concepts. Abacuses, geometric figures, fractional parts, peg boards, and other concrete objects have enlivened the more traditional and abstract approach to teaching mathematics. Scientific apparatus, on all levels of complexity for all grade levels, has been utilized to enable students to learn through experimentation the fundamental facts of science. In Pittsburg (Calif.) the science curriculum was revised into a gardening and practical botany curriculum with a reduced emphasis on reading and text and an increased emphasis on direct experiences in raising plants, soil testing, and other practical approaches to science. Much of the experimental work on which fundamental curriculum revision can be based is still being done. Stanford University is conducting two experimental programs—one a total program and one a partial program—concerned with revision of the mathematics curriculum in terms of the disadvantaged. Many schools have brought together local teachers and administrators for consultations aimed at developing curriculums suited to their particular local situation.

The efforts at making the curriculum concrete are part of an overall emphasis on a multisensory approach to learning. At all grade levels there has been an extensive use of audiovisual aids: film strips, overhead projectors, tape recorders, and the like. Closed and open circuit TV has been used extensively in two ways. First, to tune in on local educational situations; second, to televise special material to a number of classrooms in one or more schools. In a few projects programed workbooks have been used to individualize instruction in science, arithmetic, and social studies. In Pasadena, a library containing not only books, but filmstrips, pictures, tapes, and records has been set up for pupil and teacher use.

The use of specialists in art, music, and other special fields has served to upgrade instruction in those areas. Special art classes and individual or group music instruction are often supplemented in the classroom by art prints and phonograph records. Grade-level music performance groups are used to motivate interest in participating as well as listening. In the social studies, science, and English, investments have been made in new textbooks that provide a high interest level for pupils with a low reading skill. But in terms of content, little could be done until very recently about the inadequacies of content in the available social studies and history books. Faced with the traditional texts which dealt little if at all with the place of Negroes and other minority groups in American life; and faced, at the same time, with classrooms filled with minority group children, many compensatory programs have placed great emphasis on devising enrichment materials that will provide these children with a sense of having a significant place in the culture. In the primary grades there has been a concentrated effort to enlarge the pupil's self-awareness and improve his self-concept in a general sense. This is done through the frequent and public use of his written name, through the installation of full-length mirrors in classrooms, and through photographs of children in the school prominently displayed on bulletin boards and in school publications. At the higher grade levels, participation in Negro History Week is almost universal among project schools serving largely Negro populations. The children investigate the lives of important Negro citizens, make bulletin boards and display pictures of Negroes at work in the community, put on assembly programs celebrating the contribution of Negroes in America, and otherwise seek for sources of pride for themselves and their community. In addition, supplementary readings from the works of Negro authors and books on Africa and Latin America are made a regular part of high school curriculums. Where other minority groups are involved, the schools attempt similarly to encourage pride in self and community. In a Merced (Calif.) program to teach correct Spanish to Mexican-American pupils, the pupils' pride was reinforced by a study of Hispanic culture that included establishing a relationship with a school in Mercedes, Uruguay. In Akron (N.Y.), a program for Indians of the Seneca tribe brought in Indians who had achieved status as models for the pupils.

But perhaps no techniques for enlarging the self-awareness of the disadvantaged child and simultaneously enriching his educational experience have been so widely used as those of taking the child into the community and bringing the community to the child. This is done by field trips and visits from guest speakers. It is no figure of speech that disadvantaged children inhabit ghettos, particularly in big cities. Crowded into the oldest and most run-down sections of the cities, many of them have never been further than two blocks from home. For Negro children in Harlem, downtown New York with its theaters and restaurants might as well be Paris, 2,000 miles away across the ocean. Rural children, particularly in western areas, are, by contrast, confined by too much space. Geographically isolated, they know nothing but their own small towns, and perhaps one or two neighboring ones, in which the local movie, if there is one, is the principal source of what might be called cultural enrichment. For both these kinds of children a field trip can open windows on the world. A list of the kinds of places to which children from project schools have been taken would fill pages. Detroit maintains a bus and a driver solely for field trips. Chicago has a special budget allocation to provide a free bus program to children without funds of their own. The system is made more economically feasible by using, during school hours, the buses used to transport the physically handicapped before and after school.

San Francisco devotes an entire project to field trips and complementary pre- and post-trip activities. Research projects preceding trips, panel discussions, written compositions, and other activities after them are used to extract a full measure of educational benefit from the experiences. Albany also made wide use of field trips and the experiences which could be derived from them to supplement its Project Able program. On foot and by bus, classes were taken to restaurants, libraries, art exhibits, museums, famous buildings, flower gardens, airports, and industries. They took science field trips to local woodlands and game farms and social studies field trips to the capitol building. When they returned to class they might make a scrapbook, or a beaver diorama, or a map of the route they had used on their trip. They might write thank-you notes, or stories for the school newspaper. The trips were also used to motivate research, reading, and composition, and to provide the children with experiences in group deportment and in performing introductions.

Field trips may provide the city child with his first view of the whole city he lives in—as in the San Francisco project where first-graders were taken by bus to a high vantage point to look over the city. Or he may get his first view of a natural wonder—as in Pittsburgh where project children were taken to Niagara Falls. Or he may get his first view of a real cow. A field trip may explore the past in museums and historic sites; the present in newspaper offices, defense installations, and city construction sites; and the child's own future in visits to universities, hospitals, or other places where he can see, often for the first time, Negroes or other minority group members working as professionals. Field trips for rural children may be excursions to the city, dinner in a restaurant, a trip to a dairy, or to a university. Where programs are designed to instill a work orientation or to promote healthy attitudes toward jobs, field trips are often made to factories or offices to help make real the world of work. Many compensatory programs make a special effort to include a variety of adults on field trips—parents, if they can come, so that they can share and talk about the experience later with their children; other teachers, principals, or volunteer college students, to provide the children with the experience of being with a number of literate and interested adults.

When the child cannot, or does not, go to the community, the community can come to the child—in the form of visiting firemen, literally or otherwise. Guest speakers, particularly successful minority group members or graduates of project schools who are working in a field for which the children are training, are especially effective in raising the sights of disadvantaged children. Albany combined its field trips with an extensive program of guest speakers who demonstrated everything from puppet-making to grooming and jazz, who described such disparate occupations as nursing, refrigerator repairing, and the writing of children's books, and who talked knowledgeably about places in the world ranging from California to exotic Montevideo. In addition to themselves and their knowledge, guest speakers may bring pieces of the world, in the form of geological specimens, museum models of birds and insect life, printing plates, or tools of the trades. In Pittsburgh, a visiting pharmacy student demonstrated how a druggist compounds cough medicine and ointments. It is as much the contact with a community leader, or a professional person that is of benefit to the pupils, as it is the particular topic of discussion.

Visits to and from the community are a major emphasis in curricular enrichment for the disadvantaged, but much of the emphasis in curricular change has focused on the language arts. No area of the curriculum has received as much attention in compensatory programs as reading and language development. Indeed, the attention given to all other subjects combined in compensatory programs does not equal the attention that is given to reading, alone. The reason for this concentration of attention is obvious. Without an ability to read not only adequately, but well, a pupil stands little chance of achieving academic success. The effort devoted to the training of reading teachers, to new approaches, methods, and materials in teaching reading, and to the encouragement of reading as an enrichment technique is sufficient evidence of the vital importance of reading in the learning hierarchy of skills.

Reading and language development

Further evidence of this importance is the extraordinary attention paid to remedial reading in programs for the disadvantaged. Indeed, remedial reading ranks with guidance as the most widely used single approach to compensatory education. Remedial reading teachers are not new in educational circles, but in the past they often served several schools and devoted only a small portion of each week to any given group of students. Currently, in many programs, the extensive needs of disadvantaged children in the area of remedial reading have called for the employment of reading specialists of much more extensive availability, often one or more teachers per school. Although these teachers may serve other functions within a language program, remedial work usually takes top priority unless there is a special teacher assigned only to remedial work. In Kansas City (Mo.), a reading specialist who is also available for consultation by classroom teachers, conducts small remedial classes of 6 to 10 pupils during school hours, using materials related to the reading levels of each pupil. When the pupils return to their classrooms, however, they work with materials of their assigned grade level. In San Francisco, special project teachers in the elementary schools give special reading help twice each week to grade-level groups of about 12 children. At the secondary school level, remedial work is carried on in a reading laboratory to which pupils in need of help come from their regular classes. In some San Francisco high schools all project pupils are assigned to a nine-week developmental reading program after which they are transferred into courses that lend themselves to flexible scheduling. In Baltimore there are 23 reading centers throughout the city to which children are assigned for remedial reading instruction. The child is a member of his homeroom class at his own grade level, but is instructed in reading in a reading center for one hour a day. In addition, two to five extra periods a week are set aside for English instruction in schools in disadvantaged areas, and eighth-grade pupils who are behind in reading can elect three additional periods of English for remedial reading instruction. The area of remedial reading is one in which volunteers have made extensive contributions.

The assumed relationship between the quality of oral language development and success in reading has led to an increased emphasis on speech and conversation development, particularly in primary school programs for the disadvantaged. This is an extension of the preschool emphasis on oral language and is based on the same rationale. Indeed, one of the benefits often cited for putting more adults, or fewer children, in the classroom is that a reduced teacher-pupil ratio allows time for more individual conversation and small-group discussion. The Willow Manor Oral Language Project in Oakland (Calif.) was specifically devoted to the encouragement of language usage. Teachers were encouraged to examine the curriculum for situations that might require speech from the children, regardless of the specific subject matter involved. Storytelling, dramatics, and singing were extensively used. Special listening tapes were developed to give children more opportunity to hear speech used well. Use of audio equipment to enable children to hear correct speech as well as to make recordings of their own voices is a widely used technique for developing oral language skill. In Buffalo, a speech therapist was employed in a school improvement program, not only to help children with speech problems, but to introduce into the regular classrooms once-a-week, 30-minute lessons that included poetry readings as well as specific remedial speech practice.

Role playing has proved a useful tool for improving the ability of disadvantaged children to communicate orally and in other ways. Acting out a situation may often be the first step in getting what is apparently a non-verbal child to describe a situation in words. In San Francisco, the drama demonstration project is a special program for seventh- and eighth-graders that emphasizes the use of drama throughout the day. In addition to providing the pupils with a special curriculum, the project allows them to participate in selecting and helping to stage out-of-school dramatic productions with the help of community agencies.

In the area of language, the problem of the use of languages other than English is one with which a number of school systems have had to cope. In Chicago this problem has been met in some schools with "opportunity rooms." Here non-English-speaking pupils who are new to the school are taught subjects in which language is a major factor. In special classes limited to 25 pupils, activities like physical education, music, art, and assembly are given, along with a regular class at their own grade level. New York City, with its extensive Puerto Rican population, has implemented the recommendations of the well-known Ford Foundation-financed Puerto Rican Study (1953–57) with what is called the non-English-speaking program. At the elementary school level most non-English-speaking pupils are assigned to regular classes where there is more English language stimulation. But special non-English coordinators and special instructional materials are provided to schools in which they are registered, and pupils whose language ability is considered limited enough to handicap them are provided with special language attention daily. In conjunction with its non-English program, New York also conducts Operation Understanding, a program of teacher exchange between New York and Puerto Rico, designed to provide an enriched experience for the pupils and the teachers involved. Another extensive program is the one in Texas that provides English language instruction to more than 20,000 Mexican-American preschoolers. At a higher grade level the same population is the object of a special program in Tucson, devoted to teaching English as a second language. In Philadelphia, an exchange teacher from Puerto Rico was hired to work for part of the day with Puerto Rican children in classes utilizing both Spanish and English. In Oxnard (Calif.), a language resource teacher is employed to give English instruction to the non-English-speaking pupils and to assist the regular teacher in preparing special instructional materials. In Chicago, Cantonese-speaking children in one program have all school work with their peers, except in primary grade reading classes. Spanish-speaking pupils in a program in Merced (Calif.) are grouped in daily Spanish classes according to their ability to read, write, and speak Spanish. The Merced program is an attempt to instill in seventh- and eighth-grade Mexican pupils a sense of pride in their own cultural heritage by teaching them how to speak their own language well and by acquainting them with job opportunities open to bilingual applicants.

The programs of remedial language arts have not been limited to school hours. After-school study centers in a number of communities offer remedial instruction in reading through the services of teachers or tutors, and remedial reading summer schools are regularly scheduled in several cities. San Francisco even has a before-school reading improvement program three days a week.

The greater the success of the regular teaching program, of course, the less the need for remedial work. Therefore the improvement of the teaching of reading by sharpening teacher skills has assumed major importance in many compensatory programs. Often it is not a question of simply sharpening existing skills, but of teaching new ones, for there has been a rapid production of approaches and techniques for the teaching of reading, not the least controversial of which is the Initial Teaching Alphabet. The issue of just which of these approaches is the most effective in teaching the disadvantaged is yet to be resolved. Studies that may help resolve this problem are being conducted now in New York, Nashville, and University City, Missouri. A program at City College in New York also explored the significant factors in a given method which are related to teacher understanding and use of that method. But the various techniques for teaching reading and the principles of learning reading are the subject of inservice workshops in a number of programs.

New Haven's reading program, for example, that serves about 13,000 pupils, includes extensive inservice education for teachers through workshops, bulletins, attendance at professional meetings, and classroom demonstrations. New York has city-wide television courses on the teaching of

79

reading. Similar large-scale programs to improve the teaching of reading are part of many school improvement projects. These efforts, it should be noted, are not always, or even usually, directed specifically toward the disadvantaged, although undoubted benefits accrue to the least competent readers from any program of reading improvement. One program which *is* directed to the disadvantaged, however, is the extensive program of inservice education for Negro teachers of reading in the South. It is a project of the Education Improvement Project of the Southern Association of Colleges and Secondary Schools in Atlanta. But inservice workshops are not confined to the elementary school level where the teaching of reading has always been a major area of concern. Cleveland has a junior high school reading program which emphasizes the upgrading of the teaching of reading for all subject-matter classes. Six junior high schools have continuous inservice workshops for teachers in these schools and neighboring schools, directed at helping teachers to recognize reading-connected academic difficulties at the higher grade levels, as well as making them competent to help with reading problems regardless of the subject matter involved.

The training of skilled teachers of reading is not limited to workshop time. The initial step in upgrading a reading program is often the introduction of special personnel designated as reading consultants, reading specialists, language arts specialists, or consultants, who not only conduct the training workshops, but work in the classrooms as well. Sometimes the specialists themselves will teach. Reading improvement teachers in New York City actually teach a minimum of 18 classes a week while the regular teacher takes time out for a period of reading preparation. More often the function of these specialists, over and above the workshop sessions, is not to teach reading themselves, but to help the classroom teachers to do so.

In Boston, a reading program sponsored by the Action for Boston Community Development (ABCD) is specifically designed to improve teacher skills. Pupils in the upper primary school grades are grouped homogeneously according to reading ability and spend 40 minutes each morning and 30 minutes each afternoon in a developmental reading program. Lessons are conducted by the classroom teachers while a special reading teacher assigned to the project, acts as a consultant in the use of materials and techniques. At the junior high school level in the same program, reading work occupies an hour a day.

There are two major ways in which a number of compensatory programs have utilized special reading personnel: to demonstrate or conduct classes for regular teachers, and to function as resource people providing sources of information on new materials and new reading techniques. In addition, a reading specialist will often conduct the reading tests that determine how the children are assigned to reading groups. Testing and subsequent homogeneous grouping of children by reading levels is an almost universal practice. Through subgrouping within the classroom, even greater homogeneity is achieved. Equally universal is the effort, in reading as well as in other curricular areas, to use a multisensory approach to learning through providing an increased variety of touch, taste, smell, and sound experiences with which the child will need to deal verbally. Plants, animals, foods, pictures, and records are brought into the classroom — anything, no matter how commonplace they are among middle-class children, that can represent a new experience or evoke a new word from a deprived child who has never been exposed to these objects.

In Philadelphia, to use a fairly common example, one beginning class of readers built its lesson around a live puppy that had been brought to class. The children's reading was based on their experiences in playing with the dog. The use of experience charts, word cards, and child-invented stories are techniques that have been used to encourage self-selection of both subject and vocabulary.

The enrichment of prereading experiences and related individual reading materials at the primary grade level answers a fundamental need for disadvantaged children — that is, to make learning to read a personally important goal and a personally relevant function. The provision of appropriate reading materials for these children is one of the areas in which the schools have had to meet a substantial challenge. The typical middle-class family situations described in the typical readers for beginners, often seem to an urban slum child to be critical of himself and his family. The presence of the father as a major figure in the home — the depiction of as simple an act as the family sitting down to a meal together — may be so unfamiliar to the child from a fatherless urban slum home, or to the Indian child who forages for himself in the frequent absence of both parents, that he is instantly alienated from the material and often from all reading as well. One solution has been to let the children develop their own reading materials. In Racine's kindergarten project, children's pictures on ditto masters were often used to illustrate children's stories that they dictated to the teacher, and reproduced in a monthly "newsletter" sent home to their parents. Minneapolis has an elementary reading materials development program that involves a writer-coordinator, reading teachers, and classroom teachers in a project to explore new methods and materials. Dayton's Talent Development project has made use of child-created reading materials. Trenton has emphasized child-centered creative writing and reading programs. In Rochester (N.Y.), a new Project Able program, Project Beacon, has employed a writer and an illustrator-photographer in order to develop new, illustrated reading material based on the children's experiences. As far as published materials are concerned, the field is opening up, but the results have yet to find their way into a substantial number of classrooms. Various publishing houses and educational institutions are working on readers that are more representative of city and multi-ethnic group cultures and that will be more relevant to disadvantaged children than stories about Dick and Jane. Perhaps the most widely known of these contributions is the "Jimmy Series" of pre-primers, developed in the Detroit Public Schools, in which Negro characters appear, the first Negroes ever used in a basic first-grade American reader. Detroit's integrated urban environment series now covers grades 1 through 3 and provides primary grade children in Detroit and several other cities who have made use of it, with a series of primers featuring urban settings, so-called natural speech patterns, and a set of racially integrated characters.

In secondary schools there has been an effort to provide appropriately advanced and interesting information at a variety of simplified reading levels, in addition to making these materials relevant to the lives these children live. Hunter College in New York is developing the Gateway English series of reading materials for city junior high schools. In Jay (Maine), the director of a small project for slow-learning boys developed a dittoed reader that dealt with experiences, such as family arguments, with which these children could identify.

Within the framework of the existing published material, various projects have attempted to personalize and enrich the reading experiences of their pupils. In Buffalo, for example, a reading specialist analyzed the reading needs of each class in the school. Sets of basic readers were matched with the children's reading ability and, in addition, take-home books and supplementary readers were placed in classroom libraries. The children were thus exposed to hundreds of books from which they might select the books that interested them to take home, to read in class, or to just look at. In Flint (Mich.), mothers cut up and bound individual stories from old school readers to provide easy reading booklets for the children. Flint also made available a child's dictionary to the family of every project school child in grades 4 through 6. In many project school classrooms, current-event materials are provided to help overcome the absence of magazines and newspapers in the children's homes. In Kansas City, a morning and an afternoon newspaper are delivered to each classroom in project schools to be taken home by the children on a rotating basis. In Chicago, textbook funds are used in some schools to buy current-event materials for each child.

While almost any experience which enlarges the awareness of a child and encourages either oral discussion or reading can be classed as language enrichment activity, a number of project schools have instituted programs which directly encourage the use of language as a creative tool. Puppetry, creative dramatics, the use of teletrainers and tape recorders, creative writing courses, newspapers, home newsletters, special research projects—are all encouragements to exploit language imaginatively. The publication of the children's poetry and stories in school bulletins is a stimulus to an interest in reading and writing.

Philadelphia has an extensive program of language enrichment centered around the work of language-arts teachers. Among other activities these teachers conduct a special program in literature, reading, functional and creative writing, and other language skills for an ungraded group of potentially talented intermediate children who might otherwise get lost among

their classmates. In addition, the language-arts teacher conducts a literature program for all of the elementary school children while their classroom
teachers attend an inservice training workshop. This literature program
may include a movie, film-strips, or a read-aloud story; the classroom
teacher is provided with a summary of the movie or a copy of the storybook
for follow-up work.

In the ABCD-sponsored reading program in Boston, project school reading consultants devote one-fifth of their time to able pupils whom they
meet with in groups for one hour a week to discuss a book the children are
supposed to have read during the previous week. Tapes of the discussions
are made to be used in enriching the regular classroom program. In these
programs, as it is in others, the goal is to expose children to reading and language, to the written and spoken word, in as many guises as possible in
order to encourage the widest interest in reading. Reading encouragement
takes a variety of forms. An Oakland project has experimented with keeping the school library open during the lunch period. In many programs librarians have been added to the staff as a means of providing for longer
hours—before and after school, at lunch time, or in the evening—during
which children may use the library. In some of the older urban schools, special programs prompted the founding of school libraries where none had
existed at all. In Buffalo, books are given as prizes to pupils in weekly reading contests. In Detroit, second-hand paperback books are bought for 10
cents each and used to form lending libraries in English classrooms. Flint
has a Bookworm Club for grades 2 through 6, in which each book that is
read wins a sticker on one of 15 segments of a bookworm.

Several school projects have instituted programs aimed specifically at encouraging reading outside of the regular school program. In Detroit, reading clubs have been started in after-school time and on Saturday mornings
under the leadership of a paid or volunteer leader. In these clubs, children
may explore subject areas of interest to them in "nonschool" books, and
receive a certain amount of individualized reading instruction. Detroit also
has an elementary school lending library in a highly disadvantaged area of
the city. It is open two afternoons a week after school and even the young-
est children are encouraged to borrow books. This kind of a program re-

quires, as one observer put it, "a librarian who accepts the idea that a victory for books is their use by children," rather than a concern for the safety and integrity of the book. At one project school, a library caravan buses the children to the nearest branch of the public library one day a week under the supervision of one school representative and mothers or teen-age volunteers.

In Chualar (Calif.), the firehouse became the site of the first community library, established under school auspices. Book fairs at which used books or books purchased on consignment are sold to the children at cost, are another frequently used method of encouraging the ownership and reading of books. In Los Nietos (Calif.), children's books in English and Spanish are provided for Mexican-American mothers to read to their children. And in Flint, primary grade children were sent home carrying books and wearing tags that said, "Please read to me." Older children had bookmarks asking "May I read to you?". In addition, the Flint schools encouraged reading by asking parents not only to read to their children, but to read to themselves in their children's presence as a way of encouraging respect for and interest in reading.

The practices described in this chapter have ranged from teacher recruitment, placement, and training, through various modifications of curricular organization, to innovations in remedial work and enrichment programs. Although they are complex and varied in detail, it is worth repeating that the programs of which they are a part are usually a good deal more complex and varied. Yet it is clear from what has been described that within the confines of the school day, the schools of the United States, taken as a group, have marshaled their whole battery of approaches, techniques, and materials on the problem of educating the disadvantaged.

5. Extensions of school programs and community involvement

The innovations which have taken place within the schoolroom and in the school day are only a part of the constellation of approaches that have been utilized in compensatory programs. The conventional under-use of school plant and school personnel, that has long been a topic for discussion among school economists, becomes a concern of sociologists as well, when the school happens to serve a disadvantaged neighborhood in which other facilities for education, social life, recreation, and family services are limited or nonexistent. Many schools serving a disadvantaged population have found it useful, and often imperative, to leave open the school doors to after-school educational, cultural, or recreational activities. In fact, some educators have felt that the school must eventually provide a seven-day-a-week, 365-day-a-year program for its disadvantaged pupils and their parents in order to compensate for the limited opportunities in their homes and neighborhoods for the stimulation and encouragement of academic development.

Extending the school day and year

Actual extension of the school day, as for example, in the Willowbrook program[1] in Los Angeles where pupils are actually kept in school for an extra hour of intensive training in skills, is less common in compensatory programs than after-school or weekend activities that either supplement or complement the regular school program. Of all the out-of-school activities that have been invented, enlarged, or resuscitated for educating the disadvantaged, the most widespread is the institution of the after-school study center, tutoring center, counseling center, or all three. In the last few years, small and large tutoring and study hall programs have sprung up by the dozens in major cities, and in fewer numbers in smaller communities, all across the country. Given the chronic shortage of money and personnel which underlies so many of the school's problems, this is probably not surprising, for study-tutoring centers, like preschool programs are often staffed

---

1. See Willowbrook (Calif.), p. 218 in Directory.

by volunteers. And the study center will unquestionably continue to grow stronger than ever under the stimulus of funds provided for supplementary educational centers under the Elementary and Secondary Education Act of 1964.

It is not possible to make a clear-cut distinction between study centers and after-school tutoring and counseling programs, even though at the extremes they may differ markedly from each other. On the one hand, there is the volunteer program that aims only to provide a quiet place for homework with a minimum amount of supervision and free from the distractions of television and family activities; on the other hand, there are organized remedial classes with paid teachers conducting remedial work for small groups in reading, mathematics, or the social studies. But these two kinds of programs are the extreme ends of what is really a continuum in which, for the present at least, the simpler program seems always to be tending to move in the direction of the more complex program. Once you have the quiet place, in other words, and someone to supervise it, you might as well have a few reference books; and once you have a few reference books, you might as well have someone to help the pupils use them, and so on. Programs that begin with a simple aim, like the project in the community of Ken-Gar in Montgomery County (Md.), initiated as a volunteer tutoring project in private homes, often end up, as did that program, involved in much more ambitious and extensive programs of assistance. In many cases, once the initial effort has made clear the extent of the need and the availability of help to meet it, tutoring programs started by volunteers have been taken over by the school boards and incorporated, along with the volunteer tutors, into the school progam.

Where programs of this kind have been organized by, or adopted by the school system, study centers are often located in the school itself, either in classrooms or in libraries. Sometimes they are, like the volunteer programs, located throughout the community, in churches, homes, community centers, or other available facilities. In Syracuse, study and counseling centers are located in a school, in a community center, in two rented converted stores, and in the county jail – where a program of counseling and tutoring is provided for juvenile offenders. Staffs for the programs are equally varied. Volunteer college students who are preparing for teaching make up the staffs of study centers in San Francisco. In Oakland, many of the tutors are secondary school pupils, selected on the recommendation of their counselors and trained in a summer workshop for their assignments as tutors. They are paid $1 an hour for two to four hours of work a week. The Crusade for Opportunity in Syracuse trains and hires high school students from deprived areas as homework helpers in neighborhood study centers. They also use local high school students as readers for an after-school story hour for elementary school children. In Philadelphia, parents of project children supervise homework centers. In New York City, volunteer parents, not necessarily the parents of project children, give reading help and after-school conversational English practice to children for whom English is a second language. In other cities, women's clubs or other groups of volunteer adults have provided similar services.

Formally organized remedial programs are often staffed by paid teachers. New York City has before- and after-school study centers in school libraries, where high school students, under the guidance of members of the regular teaching staff meet in classes of no more than 15 students for remedial work in English. Programs of this kind are considered supplementary to the regular in-school programs of remedial work, and in the case of the New York programs, enrollment preference is given to pupils who do not receive remedial help during the school day. Many communities have such programs, directed especially at remedial work in reading, and that utilize the services of paid classroom teachers. Milwaukee, for example, has an after-school reading center program in which special teachers conduct remedial reading classes from 4 to 5 o'clock in the afternoon. Chicago has similar programs for pupils suffering from varying degrees of reading retardation. Most large cities have, in fact, a multiplicity of tutoring or study center programs. There are an estimated 100 programs operating in Los Angeles alone. The specifically remedial programs represent only a small part of the total activities that are going on. New York City and Milwaukee, for example, have volunteer after-school study center programs in addition to the programs described above. The New York centers, operating in about 176 elementary schools, provide small-group remedial instruction in reading and arithmetic, library services, and homework help, and have an average weekly attendance of 5,000 pupils.

In many study hall programs like this one, attendance is purely voluntary and pupils come on their own for assistance in homework, for "how to study" advice, for help with research or library projects, or just to study in the company of their peers. In Sacramento, a series of neighborhood study centers was developed to provide the place, the materials and, on demand, the individual help and encouragement for effective study. Pretty much the same combination of ingredients is characteristic of hundreds of programs, whether they are community or school based, in operation throughout the country. Many centers are open on Saturday mornings as well as during the school week. In Austin, a Saturday morning program provides tutoring and enrichment to 400 elementary school children.

This combination, tutoring help with enrichment, is a part of many programs that have used, for example, volunteer college students to help children on a one-to-one basis. Sharing almost any activity which might be used to top off an afternoon of study with an interested young adult, can represent a genuinely enriching experience. And all is not *meant* to be work in the out-of-school programs. Just as field trips have provided both fun and education during school hours, cultural events, hobby classes, sports programs, social events, and other recreational-educational activities have been used to enlarge the experience of disadvantaged children during afternoon, evening, and weekend hours.

One of the more venerable programs that offer this sort of enrichment is New York City's All-Day Neighborhood Schools. For many years they have provided after-school activities, usually cocurricular, for children in selected elementary schools. Coverage for the extended school day is provided by extra teachers who are available from 10:40 a.m. to 3 p.m. to help classroom teachers. From 3 p.m. to 5 p.m. they provide a program of storytelling, dramatics, singing, rhythms, painting, clay modeling, and other enrichment activities for children who are recommended to the program. In a somewhat similar program sponsored by ABCD in Boston, a corps of teachers was recruited and paid to plan after-school and Saturday activities with individuals and groups on the basis of special interests the pupils have revealed in class. Cultural activities and field trips, special classes in music, science, or art were organized according to pupil interest – with uninterested pupils encouraged to participate as well. Special activities ranging from woodworking to putting out a school newspaper are part of an extensive program of after-school enrichment in Newburgh. A program along the same lines is being initiated for able pupils in Cincinnati schools. Buffalo has developed a program that includes before-school as well as after-school enrichment activities. Special classes in science, music, art, and other areas of interest are offered to pupils in grades 7 through 12, along with remedial work when necessary. In Richmond's Human Development Project, teachers are paid for supervising an after-school program of reading, study, art, and music appreciation. In addition, pupils are welcome to come to the program 15 minutes early to participate in various cocurricular activities.

After-school special interest clubs have been organized in one Chicago project modeled after the Urban 4-H Clubs. Cooking, sewing, science, camera, and other clubs were set up to help grade-retarded 11- to 13-year-olds make better use of their after-school time. After-school band, orchestra, and glee club programs represent a familiar type of enrichment activity. Big-brother projects, in which adult or high school volunteers take elementary school children on excursions to stores, parks, museums, or other community points of interest, also make significant contributions to out-of-school education. Phoenix has a Careers for Youth club program in 13 schools that provides enrichment and career guidance for its members. Rochester conducted a special Saturday morning typing program for center-city fifth- and sixth-graders. The pupils, instructed in class by teachers from the business education department, are permitted to take the typewriters home for weekday practice. There is, in fact, no end to the special interests that a school, determined to do so, can accommodate. In New Haven, the Prince Street Community School offers among other after-school activities, arts and crafts, a knitting club, a newspaper club, a tumbling club, a drama club, and sports clubs. They also offer a game lounge, a teen-age lounge, groups for modern dance, model building, weight lifting, and basketball, as well as parent-teacher sports groups.

Afternoon and evening concert programs, dance groups, and choral and instrumental performances in the school auditorium have further extended the use of the school plant, bringing these cultural forms into communities where they have not previously been stressed. Project children are often provided with free tickets for school performances. But exposure to cultural activities is by no means limited to the activities that can be brought to the school building. Trips to ballets, concerts, art museums, plays, folk dances, music festivals, puppet shows, opera, and other cultural events are a common method of bringing to the disadvantaged child a broadened awareness of the world. In large cities the opportunities for such experiences are numerous and tickets are often available when the need is known. Chicago, in fact, appointed a cultural resources consultant in 1962 who coordinated the multitude of activities that were available in the city and the multitudes of children who would profit from participating in them. In many communities, funds to provide for admission and transportation to events like concerts, plays, circuses, ice shows, and the like have come from service or charitable organizations. In many cases, when the need has been publicized, sponsors of these events have made direct donations of tickets.

Just what cultural enrichment means to a particular child in a particular school in a particular community depends on a host of factors: What is available locally? What kinds of things that are not available locally can be gotten to? What kinds of experiences would be meaningful to these children? It is an area in which the general comment is less significant than the specific event and the child's reaction to it. For a country child, a Saturday program of enrichment can mean a trip to the city. And for many of the upstate communities of New York State the "city" is New York City. South New Berlin (Conn.), a town of about 450 residents, 200-miles north of "the city," was the site, in 1963–64, of a Rural Talent Search Program involving 8 tenth-grade pupils. At 5 a.m. one Saturday morning in early winter, these pupils got into two cars driven by their guidance counselor and remedial reading teacher, to begin the 200-mile trip to New York City. They arrived in the city at 9:15 a.m., parked the cars in the midtown area, and took a tour of the Radio City area. Taxis took them to the United Nations and a crosstown bus brought them back to the New York Public Library at Forty-second Street. Walking down Fifth Avenue they window-shopped their way to the Empire State Building where they went up to the top for a view of the city. By subway they traveled to Eighty-second Street and the Museum of Natural History where they toured the Hayden Planetarium and saw the show. Then back by subway to Times Square, to eat by candlelight at a restaurant the students thought was "plushy," so the guidance counselor didn't tell them it was really quite ordinary. They walked up from Times Square to Radio City Music Hall for the movie and stage show, and after a final walk around the Radio City area they went back to the cars to begin the 200-mile trip home. A heavy snowstorm made them two hours late. What may be particularly significant about the trip is that since no community funds were available to pay for it, the guidance counselor herself financed the trip out of funds provided for extra counselor time and felt "well paid by the pleasure and satisfaction received."

To benefit from such a trip a child need not live in the country. Although the physical distance from Harlem may be less than it is from South New Berlin, the psychological distance may well be greater. A trip to the heart of his city can be enriching for the urban slum child too. But for a city child, a Saturday outing can also be an all-day excursion to the country, or to a local park, or it may be a weekend camp-out. In Cleveland, the Hough Community Project used day-long camp excursions as a laboratory for science nature study. The trips often provided much needed triumphs for children who had recently arrived from the rural South who were able to identify plants and animals unknown to their city peers. In Detroit, sixth- and seventh-grade pupils were taken to the country for a week at a time and made a contribution to the cost of their outing by cutting, hauling, and selling Christmas trees, washing cars, mowing lawns, and selling cakes and cookies, all under the supervision of the school staff and parents. In Boston, ABCD has organized a regular weekend camp program stressing vigorous physical activity, and combining useful work around the campsite with a recreational program. The use of organized physical activity as an approach to improving self-discipline and attitudes toward school has also been used in a morning program in Washington, D. C. More than 100 boys from special classes in two schools participate in a program of organized physical exercise, showers, and breakfast from 7:30 a.m. to 9 a.m. The program is led by physical education majors from local universities, aided by a dietician and two home economics majors.

As effective as the after-school and weekend programs of enrichment and remedial work are, there is perhaps no single area of extracurricular activity that has so convincingly demonstrated its usefulness in compensatory education as the well-planned summer school program. The extension of the school year into the summer months has, in many urban communities, provided for an eye-opening exploration of possibilities in the teaching of the disadvantaged. In one sense, summer school is almost always compensatory, since it has traditionally provided a catching up time for pupils who have fallen behind during the regular school year. New York City, for example, has a special summer program that permits vocational high school students who would otherwise not graduate on time, to make up courses in which they have failed. And there has more recently been a trend toward using the summer as a time to get children ready for their first school experience, a trend that was established in Project Head Start.

But the degree to which summer school is actually compensatory for disadvantaged children depends on the degree to which it is deliberately organized to be so. Where attendance at summer school involves a tuition fee, for example, the disadvantaged pupil may be specifically excluded for financial reasons. Recognizing this, some cities have eliminated the charge for summer programs. Chicago made its regular summer school free in 1954, with a resultant upsurge in attendance. Subsequently the city developed a number of special summer schools for elementary school pupils in disadvantaged areas, specifically designed to explore new ways of educating these children. Full-time classroom teachers are supplied to these schools along with a variety of supplementary personnel, special equipment, and an allocation of funds for bus transportation for 11 field trips. The program provides for classes of no more than 25 pupils, and is so organized as to allow for flexible grouping and regrouping of the children, according to their ability for work in various subject areas. The teacher's day consists of an hour of inservice training, a 9 a.m. to 2 p.m. school program during which she eats lunch with the children, and then another period after school for planning, conferences, relaxation, or further inservice training.

The advantage of this kind of summer program is that it permits the setting up of school situations closer to the ideal, where the emphasis is on the individual. Students at New Haven's free summer school had an opportunity to explore such new and interesting subjects as "Play Production," "Mathematical Excursions," "Oceanography," and "Crystals," as well as to do remedial work in small relaxed classes conducted on a no-examinations, no-marks, no-credit basis. The teachers found that the more informal atmosphere was conducive to trying out new materials and new approaches to reaching and teaching the students with whom they had been less than successful during the school year.

Detroit views its summer school as a laboratory for curriculum change. An extensive planning session precedes the summer school which is usually divided into two parts—remedial and enrichment classes, or a recreational and club program—both of them supplemented by an extensive program of field trips. Afternoon and evening recreational and club activities involve adults—parents and school neighbors—as well as the children. Detroit also conducts summer welcome programs for students who move (in late spring or early summer) to the school district from such areas as Puerto Rico or the South where customs, language, and educational standards may be different.

Milwaukee has set up a center-city summer school using teaching interns from local universities as staff. Syracuse also used teaching interns, in this case from the local urban teacher preparation program, to supplement regular teaching staff in a summer school program. Portland's Sabin Summer School was conducted in conjunction with a program of teacher-training focused on educating the disadvantaged child.

A special summer reading program in Dade County (Fla.), started in 1962 and serving more than 14,000 pupils in the summer of 1964, provided daily hour-and-three-quarter classes devoted to reading, oral language work, and an extensive program of supervised recreation. Special training sessions for the teachers and an intensive effort to involve the parents are significant aspects of the program. In Baltimore, the p.t.a. has organized and financed summer programs that use school facilities, but not school funds, to provide summer activities and education for center-city children through the services of a staff composed largely of volunteers. Less extensive summer school programs, primarily for remedial work, are conducted in a number of communities. In Brentwood, Long Island, remedial tutoring in reading and mathematics is provided by former students who are now attending college. Two tutorial programs, staffed by volunteers, supplement regular summer school programs in Los Angeles.

Another kind of program is the one sponsored by the Urban Service Corps in Washington, D. C. The Widening Horizons program uses volunteer adults to take thousands of junior and senior high school students on summer tours of Washington attractions, from the halls of Congress to the Folger Shakespeare Library.

Summer day camps or sleep away camps have also been made part of the schools' activity. The ABCD program in Boston has developed several camp programs using a variety of approaches to remedial and enrichment programs. One camp, for example, will schedule formal remedial work in addition to regular camp activities. Another camp will work to develop academic skills through nonacademic activities that require reading and computation, such as weather forecasting, menu-planning, keeping of archery and rifle scores, exploring with compasses and charts, and so forth.

In Syracuse, the extended compensatory program being developed under the Mayor's Commission for Youth includes plans for a summer reading camp in which able but underachieving seventh- to ninth-graders participate in a program of reading, counseling, and recreation. High achieving but disadvantaged high school students serve as junior counselors.

There are, in addition to all these school based efforts, a number of college based summer programs that are specifically designed to encourage higher education. By providing concentrated academic work in a college setting, they attempt to elevate the achievement and the motivation of pupils for whom college attendance is considered a reasonable possibility. The majority of these programs, like those at Hofstra University, Yale University, Princeton University, Georgetown University, and Franklin and Marshall College, to name only a few, usually concern themselves with high school students. But there are also summer programs, such as those conducted by the University of Detroit and Brandeis University for eighth-

and ninth-grade students, that aim at instilling in able students an even earlier orientation toward college.

There is one sense in which these precollege programs, although they are not public school based, are representative of all programs of compensatory education. They do have a specific goal, to prepare the students involved in them for college attendance; but they also have a more general goal, to increase the desire of the students to seek such an education, and to raise their aspirations for themselves. And it is this more general aim that they share with all programs of educational compensation. For running through all the programs and practices is a common thread of intention—to reach the student and to motivate him to want to achieve. Whether this is done through teaching methods and materials that help him initially to succeed, in spite of himself, or through teacher training that improves his chances of having sympathetic and competent leadership, it is ultimately how the student feels about himself and the possibilities for his own achievement that will determine the effectiveness of the program. And because it is student attitude which is at the heart of successful learning, it is counseling and guidance which are at the heart of many programs of compensatory education.

Guidance and counseling services

To the extent that any relationship between a teacher or administrator and a student involves the component of instilling motive and direction, guidance has always been at the heart of school life. But what has been designated as guidance in the school system has often been a crisis-oriented activity, and what has been called counseling has traditionally been largely vocational. Personnel specifically trained in understanding the social, psychological, and intellectual development of children have been utilized primarily to help teachers deal with the failing, the underachieving, or the disruptive students. There has been little effort in the past to provide systematic guidance for all students. Instead, help has been directed to those students who have been referred to counselors by distraught or disenchanted teachers or administrators. With the increasing concern of educators for the fuller development of the disadvantaged, counseling and guidance activities have come to play an increasingly prominent role in school life. Together with programs for reading improvement, some form of guidance is the one almost universal component in projects for the disadvantaged. Guidance personnel do, unfortunately, continue to be involved in their traditional preoccupation, dealing with the misfit. But there is more emphasis on early detection of misfits through elementary school guidance. A St. Louis program focuses on early identification of, and assistance to, those children who exhibit behavior patterns likely to lead to later school problems. A number of cities have initiated guidance programs at the elementary school level.

Seattle initiated a pilot guidance project in some elementary schools using personnel designated as pupil service coordinators. Boston has an intensive adjustment counseling program for elementary and junior high school pupils who have been referred because of symptoms indicating emotional, behavioral, or environmental problems. A school adjustment counselor provides individual pupil diagnosis and counseling, and also visits the pupils' homes to help solve family problems. Often these problems are solved by arranging for social agency referral. The counselors work closely with teachers and administrators in order to keep them apprised of ways in which they might better deal with the child in the classroom. Junior Guidance Classes in New York City provide a special resource for disruptive disturbed children under 10 years of age who can benefit from this therapeutically oriented program. Another New York facility, the well-known Northside Center for Child Development, uses group psychotherapy for potentially disturbed youngsters as an approach to solving behavior problems severe enough to cause serious difficulties in school adjustment. Although programs such as these are not exclusively designed for the disadvantaged, these children are usually well represented in the areas served.

At the secondary school level, the disruptive student, unless he is severely emotionally disturbed, is usually dealt with as a potential dropout. Most of the transition and dropout prevention classes described so far contain a large complement of guidance, in addition to curricular modifications and opportunities for early work experience.

But a major emphasis in current programs for the disadvantaged is the provision of guidance not merely to the disruptive students, but to all students in a project school. A great many programs are specifically guidance oriented. Less emphasis is placed on actual changes in the school organization or curriculum than it is on individual and group counseling designed to increase the student's self-understanding, to enhance his self-concept, and to improve his motivation and attitudes toward school.

New York City's Project Able is specifically designed to measure the usefulness of providing full-time guidance services in a high school setting. In many large programs, universal individual counseling is often limited to an initial interview in the fall with each child (with or without his parents), to discover any special problems the child may have, and to establish a basis for continuing or sporadic contact. Coupled with group guidance and teacher-based guidance services, this kind of program involves more frequent and more regular contact between the counselor and his counselee than has been the usual practice. One of the first steps in putting a guidance oriented program into effect, therefore, has usually been the employment of extra guidance counselors and such supplementary personnel as psychologists, psychiatrists, and social workers on a full- or part-time basis to reduce case loads to a level where more extensive encounters are possible. Some cities have made use of nonprofessional personnel to complement or supplement the activities of the professional guidance counselor. In Riverside County (Calif.), for example, high school students were used as interpreter aides in a program serving Mexican-American students. The Urban Service Corps in Washington (D. C.) has trained adults as counselor aides to relieve the guidance counselor of a number of peripheral duties.

The emphasis in individual counseling sessions is on establishing personal contact with each pupil about whom much is usually already known through available school records, through tests, and through comments from his teachers and administrators. One of the activities of the Coachella Valley McAteer project was an attempt to measure the self-image of the population, many of whom were Mexican-American migrant children. This was done through interviews and a project-designed self-concept scale. The program also included interviews with "successful" pupils in order to attempt to determine the kinds of circumstances which fostered academic achievement among these children. Since the compiling of as complete a file of information as possible on each student is one of the first steps in providing intelligent counseling, guidance programs ideally work closely with the rest of the school staff including social workers, home visitors, or other personnel who can provide information about family situations. In Kings County (Calif.), the McAteer program used local college social welfare students to visit project students' homes and prepare social histories of the children.

Over and above simply making contact, the purpose of an individual counseling session is to help the pupil set personal goals, and to help him find ways of dealing with personal problems and attitudes that are interfering with his ability to achieve those goals. Most individual guidance is oriented toward improving the student's self-concept, morale, and personal organization; toward helping him with the selection of courses appropriate to his temperament and his abilities; and, at the higher levels, guiding him toward appropriate career goals. One of the efforts of a counseling program in Washington, D. C., was to convince qualified students, together with their parents, of the necessity of taking the more difficult academic subjects that would equip them to continue their education. Individual guidance may have a particular function in transition situations. Oakland has a special reception service to receive, counsel, study, and properly place incoming pupils. A similar reception room service is provided under the auspices of the Youth Opportunities Board of Los Angeles.

In most guidance programs much of the educational and vocational counseling takes place in group guidance sessions. While individual interviews establish rapport and enable the student to talk out his personal attitudes, goals, and problems, group sessions are useful for exploring common attitudes which may be supportive or antithetical to academic success. Furthermore, these sessions can play a significant role in developing mutual peer group emotional support or in redirecting peer group standards. In an early experimental guidance program in White Plains (N.Y.), a group of underachieving junior high school students took part in both individual and group counseling sessions. The group meetings evolved into "bull sessions" for discussing study habits and peer group expectations, as well as for planning such activities as weekend camping trips, visits to colleges and museums, and attending concerts. In this program, occupational and educational information was introduced in individual counseling sessions, but more often this informational function of guidance programs is served by group guidance sessions. Sessions of this kind may be utilized to help ease the transition of seventh- and eighth-graders into the more departmentalized secondary school program by providing them with information about just what the secondary school program will be like. Chicago provides pupils in disadvantaged areas with intensive educational guidance during the last half of the eighth grade in order to encourage high school attendance. Or guidance sessions may be used to help the pupils become aware of educational opportunities open to them in their present school.

Weekly or even daily group guidance sessions are often incorporated into the school day with the counselor acting as a teacher and introducing materials related to careers, career planning, and vocational opportunities. Brentwood, Long Island, has a 10-week course for ninth-graders called "Exploring Occupations." At the same time that guidance has expanded its personal counseling role, it has enlarged its informational role as well. It has become the function of guidance personnel not only to explore the student's vocational interests and aptitudes through tests, but to stimulate his latent interests, to inform him of vocational and higher educational opportunities in his community, to help him channel his in-school and out-of-school activities in order to prepare himself to accept these opportunities, and to consult with his parents and other resource people in order to gain their assistance in achieving his goals. In a program for Indian students of the Seneca tribe in Akron (N.Y.), guidance personnel conducted a survey of former Indian students in order to answer more effectively questions about suitable course selection, choice of academic subjects, college success, and so forth. In Merced (Calif.), one of the counselor functions was to provide Mexican-American students with information about job opportunities for the bilingual.

The use of models as a means of raising pupil aspirations is a common practice in vocational guidance programs. In Wilmington, Project Boys is a program of in-school therapy conducted by group workers from a neighborhood settlement house, supplemented by extensive personal contact between the pupils and educational models. Successful business men whose formal education ended with high school graduation come in to talk about job opportunities, graduates of the project school come back to tell about their lives and their work, and at Men's Day lunches the Project Boys share a meal with business and professional men from the local community.

Fundamental to the raising of student aspiration, however, is the raising of student confidence by providing him with opportunities for some immediate success; and because success in school is represented by academic achievement, remedial work, tutoring, and help in improving study habits loom large as adjuncts to many guidance-oriented programs. In the White Plains project previously described, one of the counselor functions was the organization of study groups. In Oakland, a group of teachers in a project school organized an "uplift committee" to plan activities designed to increase student self-esteem. In addition to providing help with grooming and manners, the program involved instruction in methods of study and help with oral language. This kind of an uplift approach characterized an entire district program in St. Louis where motivation of parents and children was obtained through involvement of the entire school staff, not merely through the solitary efforts of guidance counselors. "Mr. Achiever," a mythical character, broadcast weekly hints over the school radio on how to study and how to succeed in school. "Mr. Achiever's" advice and admonitions were also strategically placed on hallway bulletin boards and on the school grounds. Although such school-wide involvements in motivational guidance activities are not the rule, it is not uncommon to find that one effect of an enlarged guidance program in a school is the increased utilization of guidance counselors' help by the teachers and increased consultative exchange between all members of the school staff regarding both normal and abnormal student development.

One of the best known of the school-wide guidance oriented programs is the Higher Horizons Program in New York City. Initiated as the Demonstration Guidance Project in 1956, it originally served only a selected upper half of the classes in the schools in which it operated, but now revised and expanded, it serves all pupils from kindergarten to grade 12 in 50 elementary and 13 junior high schools. Because individual guidance is considered a significant aspect of the Higher Horizons Program, sufficient additional personnel have been added to provide for at least one individual interview with each child and his parents per year. In addition to an enlarged individual guidance program, the group guidance program involving counseling with parents and teachers, as well as pupils, has also been expanded. The Higher Horizons Program also provides, for the school served, an expanded and enriched educational program through the activities of program teachers assigned to each school. These special personnel assist classroom teachers, serve as resource persons for new teaching techniques and materials, and coordinate a program of remedial and cultural enrichment activities for the children. The Jacox Plan in Norfolk (Va.), designed specifically to replicate the transferable aspects of the New York program, provides a similar combination of guidance, remediation, enrichment, in-service education, and parental involvement to the pupils of one junior high school.

While the Higher Horizons Program involves the total population of the schools served, there are a number of programs, modeled in many cases after the original Demonstration Guidance Project, which have dealt with a selected portion of the school population. The students are chosen, not from the most disturbed, but from the most promising or from among those students ranked as seriously underachieving. One broad-scale effort of this type is the Project Opportunity portion of the Educational Improvement Project, sponsored by the Southern Association of Colleges and Secondary Schools in Atlanta. Through a cooperative effort among one or more colleges and their neighboring public schools, this program uses counseling, remedial work, and enrichment to attempt to elevate the aspirations and achievement of disadvantaged pupils chosen from the top 10 to 20 percent of their classes, in a number of communities in the South.

An earlier program of this kind was the McFarland Roosevelt Guidance Project in Washington, D. C. The program began in 1959 and concluded in the summer of 1965, when a group of about 150 pupils, who had originally been selected in the seventh grade, were graduated from high school. The program was designed to see whether an extensive concentration of guidance, remedial work, and enrichment could help disadvantaged children develop their talents more fully. The guidance program placed emphasis on helping individual students analyze their abilities and subsequently make appropriate course and career decisions based on their understandings. Another completed program, Project Mercury in Rochester (N. Y.), studied the effects of intensive individual counseling on the performance of 15 able but underachieving students. The students, who were graduated from school in June 1964, are being followed up for a five-year evaluation of the success of the program. The Rochester program was one of a number of New York State-sponsored Talent Search projects, which have used funds available under Title v-a of the National Defense Education Act to provide supplementary services to just such able but underachieving students. The Talent Search programs, most of which are still in operation, make use of various combinations of pupil and parent guidance, remedial work, and cultural enrichment through activities like field trips. Field trips that provide general enrichment are less common than vocationally or educationally oriented trips—to colleges and universities, to hospitals, offices, or factories—intended to make the students aware of the positive rewards of successful school achievement as a way of motivating them to greater effort. In Shirley (N. Y.), the counselor puts stress on providing information about financial help that is available for programs of higher education. In East Springfield (N. Y.), the guidance program emphasizes early provision of educational and vocational information in order to let the student know what he is working for. In Providence, the Cooperative Motivation program puts a similar emphasis on college orientation, combining visits to colleges with group counseling in which members of the college faculty participate. For the same reason, juniors are permitted to participate in College Day programs in disadvantaged areas of Chicago where interest in college attendance must be encouraged early. College motivation for the disadvantaged may well be one of the pleasantest tasks of the counselor.

One of the less rewarding but fundamental problems with which guidance personnel have had to concern themselves is that of nonattendance. Obviously no program of motivation or pupil reorientation can even begin to function until the pupil is physically accessible. High transiency rates (in one Philadelphia neighborhood the principal reported a pupil turnover of 85 percent in one year), particularly in urban communities have presented staggering problems to the schools in simply keeping track of pupils. In 1963 Chicago initiated a program called "Impact" designed specifically to cope with elementary school nonattendance. It enlisted the services of attendance officers and supplementary personnel in making home visits, which, if unsuccessful, were ultimately followed by placement of the pupils in special "Impact" rooms for intensive attention. In St. Louis, high school combat teams consisting of a guidance counselor, a social worker, and administrative assistants are utilized in combating persistent absence and tardiness. The fact is, the absence problem can no longer be handled in the old way by a truant officer. Problems of nonattendance are more apt to be dealt with now by guidance personnel, social workers, or home visitors who can direct concentrated attention at the root causes of the problem in the home. Truancy is one of the areas in which schools serving disadvantaged neighborhoods have been forced to recognize the significant role of parental attitude.

School-home-parent relationships

The truant child, particularly in the urban slum community, is no longer the overalls-clad barefoot boy of comic strip fame sneaking away from his parents on a particularly fine spring day with a fishing pole over his shoulder. The truant is more often a child, or a youth, who with the collusion of his parents, or at least without their active opposition, has simply stopped going to school. The parents of many of these children have understandably lost confidence in the ability, or even the willingness of the school to educate their children. In spite of the fact that low-income minority-group parents are often painfully aware of the value of education as representing one of the few available routes out of the slums for their children, they have often come to regard the instrument for imparting that education, the school, as an alien and possibly hostile force. Parental indifference as to whether or not a child attends school is by no means the only problem. In fact, as the Waxes and Dumont pointed out in their sensitive study of education in an American Indian community, Indian parents who live on reservations are often insistent that their children go to school because they are convinced that by simply "going to school" the child will get educated. The lack of involvement on the part of these parents arises from the fact that they have little interest in or knowledge of what the child does when he gets to school—little awareness of what "getting educated" means. For them the school is not necessarily hostile, it is only incomprehensible.

All too frequently, the school's middle-class bias has caused it to regard the parents of the disadvantaged as equally incomprehensible or, if comprehensible, antagonistic to the aims of the school. Indeed, the relationship between the school and the disadvantaged parent often deteriorates as the school career of the child progresses and the parent and the school begin to blame each other for the failure to achieve behavioral and academic competence. But an open breach between school and home benefits neither the antagonists themselves nor the child with whom they are both presumably concerned. In the long run, parental support and involvement have been proved to be crucial to the success of compensatory programs.

Among the school's primary efforts at improving home-school relationships are teacher reorientation programs, designed to help the teacher understand her pupils' families, from their food and sex habits to their predominantly practical attitudes toward knowledge. These programs *can* help to overcome antagonisms and misunderstandings that originate in the schools, but changed attitudes on the part of the school are not enough. It remains for the school to reach out to the parents as an expression of this change. Many parents, even those who have not become openly alienated from the school through contacts with unsympathetic personnel, are unwilling, or more often unable, to take an active role in supporting the educational process. Uneducated themselves, they are, like the Indian parents, simply unaware of what goes on in the school or of what they can do to help. The p.t.a., the traditional catalyst for home-school interaction, has not proved an effective instrument for involving a substantial number of disadvantaged parents. Most schools have taken a more aggressive approach to bringing the school to the parents and ultimately the parents to the school.

Initial contact with a family is frequently made through a notice sent home with a pupil inviting the parents to a meeting or some other school activity, or to request them to come to the school for a teacher conference, or simply to indicate that they are welcome at their child's school. In conjunction with making parents feel welcome, many center-city schools have publicized an "open door" policy and implemented it by attempting to make the entrance and reception areas of the school more attractive. Frequently, contact with parents is made through home visits instead of written notices, for a very simple reason. The kinds of hard-to-reach parents with whom project schools are usually dealing simply do not think of coming to school in response to any notice that does not threaten expulsion, failure, or some other dire possibility. A home visit may have one of several purposes. Because of the high mobility of many disadvantaged populations, there are often a number of new families to be welcomed into the neighborhood and the school. In Los Angeles, special school-community workers give priority to the task of welcoming and orienting these families as a means of combating perennial transiency.

Sometimes home visits have an immediate short-range goal. In Chicago, more than 1,000 parents were consulted on action to be taken as the result of a survey of their children's health. In a Houston antidropout campaign, teachers visited the home of each child and incoming seventh-grader with the immediate purpose of urging family planning for back-to-school needs. But more commonly an initial home-school contact has a long-range goal. It is meant to be the beginning of an extended parent-school relationship in which both will help in the education of the child. In Cleveland's home visit program, certified teachers are used to maintain a constant flow of information between school and home. These teachers inform parents about the child's adjustment to school and evaluate the child's home situation for the benefit of teachers and administrators.

Several school programs have employed this kind of special personnel. In many cases, trained social workers are designated as home visitors, visiting teachers, family workers, or home-school coordinators to provide just this kind of permanent liaison between home and school. Besides bringing and interpreting news of the school to the family and vice versa, family workers serve a significant counseling function. They may help parents to understand their own and their children's behavior. They may suggest ways in which the parents can assist the school program by lending support to productive behavior on the part of the student at home. They may counsel the child in the home or provide counseling for him outside of the home. Family workers have often found it necessary to help solve pressing family problems before the adults have time to worry about the child. Visiting teachers in Detroit do individual casework counseling when family problems are accessible to such an approach. When they are not accessible, the visiting teacher puts the family in touch with appropriate community agencies. Many schools have arranged for some of their personnel to play this intermediary role — bringing together local agencies equipped to handle social, physical, or emotional problems, and the families who need their help. In Philadelphia, school-community coordinators supply this service and a number of other services to parents, in addition to fulfilling a broader community function. The coordinators, who are local neighborhood people, even provide direct homemaking assistance in such areas as meal planning, budgeting, and housekeeping.

If no special personnel are hired to make home visits, regular school staff — guidance counselors, social workers, classroom teachers — or volunteer personnel like class mothers, are often used for home visits. When visits to the homes of parents are the responsibility of the teachers, special provision is often made for them to make these visits.

The pilot McAteer program in Palo Alto was devoted entirely to the improvement of home-school relationships. Teachers, given special inservice training in advance, were provided with released time to visit the homes of their students. The visits were followed by counselor-social worker sessions for evaluation of the success of the visit. In Oakland, visiting time for teachers was provided by early dismissal of classes — a practice that is followed in a number of school programs.

Just what transpires in a first home visit depends largely on the goals of the project. In Indianapolis, social workers visit homes to determine the school needs of the families in terms of such practical matters as clothing, school lunches, bus fares, and so forth. In Baltimore, the school staff visited parents in order to get their cooperation in promoting the kinds of habits, attitudes, and activities that would contribute to the children's school success. In Akron (N. Y.), the school social worker and guidance counselors visited the reservation home of each of their Indian students in order to provide a background for subsequent parent counseling, student counseling, or both.

Many times an initial home visit simply provides a chance for the visitor and the parent to get acquainted. If the visitor is a classroom teacher the opportunity to learn who is behind the child that comes to school may be invaluable. A visit is also an occasion to explain just what the school program is about and to enlist parent cooperation in fostering mutual school-parent goals for the child. Often that is all a home visit is meant to accomplish—to make a contact that, it is hoped, will be followed up by parents who now feel wanted and welcomed at their child's school. For this reason home visits are usually made early in the year and used as an occasion to extend an invitation to the parents to come to the school for a meeting, an open house, a parents' club, adult education activities, or some other school function. The Dade County (Fla.) summer reading program was initiated by a teacher-conducted house-to-house canvass explaining the program to parents and inviting them to come to school meetings to learn more.

Whether they are invited by written notice or by a personal visit, parents are often brought to school early in the year—or sometimes even before the semester begins—for meetings explaining the purpose and the goals of special compensatory programs. In Merced (Calif.), a project designed to teach correct Spanish to Mexican-American children was initiated by letters, written in Spanish, inviting parents to an explanatory meeting. A program in Flint, which put heavy emphasis on the parent as the motivator of the child, brought parents to school meetings at which they were given intensive counseling on ways in which they might promote the success of a reading-improvement project. In the St. Louis Banneker District program, parents were brought to an evening school meeting by their children. At this meeting charts were used to demonstrate to the parents the school's low academic standing and to ask for their help in improving the situation. The program put heavy emphasis on parental motivation—appealing to the personal pride of the parents and seeking to awaken their latent awareness that school was their hope for their children's future. Parents were presented with a pledge of cooperation to sign. This pledge promised that they would help their child by doing things like visiting his teacher, insisting that he do his homework, providing him with a library card, and seeing to it that he had a dictionary, a place to study, and suitable books to read.

Advice-giving of the most specific kind is a familiar feature of programs for disadvantaged parents. Many schools have special meetings and discussion groups for parents of preschoolers who will be entering kindergarten in the fall. At these meetings parents are helped to understand the ways in which they can prepare their child for the school experience and how, by talking to him and encouraging him to talk to them, they can promote his social and verbal development. This kind of meeting is organized not to explain a special school program, but to explain *school*; and although the substance of this kind of gathering is often didactic, the approach, at best, is not. Because they are designed to appeal to parents who are often socially insecure, ill-at-ease in the school setting, and educationally innocent, these school-parent meetings are a far cry from the p.t.a. meeting of the middle-class suburb. They may bring together the parents of one class, one grade, or several grade groups in one subject—numbering anywhere from 5 to more than 100—but preferably they are small, sociable, and informal. If the school has a family worker, social worker, or guidance counselor on its staff, these professionals will usually play a major role in parent meetings. If there have been home visits, the teacher, room mother, social worker, counselor, visiting teacher, or whoever did the visiting will either conduct the meeting or be actively present at a meeting of the parents he or she has visited.

Obviously there is a budgetary as well as a social value in attracting parents to a school meeting or to a series of meetings. More contact with parents can be provided with less personnel than in a one-to-one home visit; so special efforts are made to make the meetings interesting, productive, and responsive to the stated interests and desires of the parents. In a Quincy (Ill.) kindergarten project, parent meetings were built around discussion groups following the showing of films on the behavior of five- and six-year-olds. The parents then expressed an interest in what their children did at school so programs were developed around report cards, reading readiness, and arithmetic.

In Albany, parent meetings were conducted on such diverse subjects as how to help children in reading or arithmetic, child behavior, and local recreation facilities. In San Francisco, parents were shown photographic slides of their children in action to enable them to share an understanding of the techniques and materials used in the classroom. In Wilmington (Del.), "Family Life" program consultants on family life and children's literature provide guidance and information to parents by means of assemblies, individual and group conferences, and selected reading materials on special problems. In Springfield (Mass.), weekly parent-teacher discussion groups organized by grade or subject, promote parent-parent as well as teacher-parent relationships by sharing successful child-rearing practices and discussions of ways in which the home can reinforce the school learnings.

Programs may be developed to explain children to parents and explain parents to themselves. One school in Chicago organized parent discussion groups on the topic of sibling rivalry. Some programs have made special efforts to involve fathers in the school program, scheduling home visits or guidance sessions during evening hours. In Chicago, Father's Clubs have been organized under the supervision of male staff members. But one of the facts of disadvantaged life with which many schools have had to contend is that they are often dealing not with parents but with *a* parent. One Father's Club in Chicago was organized for children without fathers – and each child was asked to bring to school a male relative or other adult male who was interested in him.

In addition to providing for evening meetings or other activities involving parents as a group, some schools have adjusted the traditional parent-teacher conference to suit the special needs of the disadvantaged parent. At one school in Chicago supervised play is provided for infants and pre-school children whom mothers may have to bring with them to conferences. In other cases, conferences are scheduled for evening hours to suit the convenience of working parents. And conferences are not simply devoted to a critical analysis of the child's performance and exhortations to do better, but to discussions of what both parents and teacher can do to help the child succeed in school.

In the Los Nietos and San Diego McAteer programs, substitute teachers take over the classrooms so that teachers may have more time for work with parents. In a number of other programs the daily schedule is so arranged that teachers have two free periods a day, one for planning and one for parent conferences. Evening guidance sessions have also been made a part of many school programs. Not only does the child need to be helped to understand his own potential and the possibilities for fulfilling it, but parents need to be helped to develop realistic expectations of their children and realistic plans for their future. As a consequence a great number of guidance-oriented programs have scheduled evening counseling time in order to include parents in both individual and group counseling sessions.

The educational role of the school meeting and the parent-teacher conference is often supplemented by regular or intermittent parent newsletters. In the McAteer program in Monterey County (Calif.), a newsletter in Spanish and English is sent to the parents of project school children. These newsletters convey news about coming school events and help to keep the parents informed about what their children are doing in school. Frequently, they also contain more general information — lists of recommended books, telecasts, or movies — or suggestions to parents about helping and training their youngsters.

Open Doors, the newsletter of the White Plains (N. Y.) Project Able, devoted one issue to a list of books and toys suitable for Christmas giving, another issue to a list of places to go on family trips, and a third issue to tips for mothers on helping young children to learn to speak.

In Syracuse, parents were informed about the Madison Area Project by a Learning Caravan, amply supplied with photographs of the children in school, which moved about the project neighborhood. They also received a newsletter full of news, suggestions of trips to take, and things to do with their children.

Family outings have been encouraged by more than exhortation. In

Berkeley, Buffalo, Detroit, and many other communities, families have been included in school field trips. Family-school outings – nature walks, picnics, trips to college campuses, or community places of interest – are often initiated by the school as a way of encouraging families to undertake similar activities on their own.

In Baltimore, parents were taken to the local public library, shown how to use the library, and urged to come back with their children on their own. New Haven has free family concerts – evening concert programs at project schools are usually for parents as well as their children. Other kinds of evening programs at the school – family fun nights, game nights, parent sports programs—have been promoted as a way of encouraging family members to enjoy the school as well as to encourage their interest in the school.

Sometimes parents are brought to school to share in their children's accomplishments. In Albany, pupils wrote the invitations to a class program where parents were served refreshments prepared by the children. In a similar vein, one class in Pittsburg (Calif.) brought its bakery unit to a triumphant conclusion when the children made bread and butter for their parents. Parents have been proud observers at evening honor assemblies and, in Detroit, proud admirers of a display of their children's handicrafts. Parents have also been encouraged and helped to form clubs on their own— sports clubs, special interest clubs, sewing clubs, mothers' clubs, and similar organizations meet afternoons and evenings at many schools.

Although all these parent and child activities have their place in involving parents with the schools, it is probably true, as some educators have suggested, that one of the best ways to make parents aware of, concerned with, and favorably disposed toward education for their children is to provide them with education for themselves. Consequently a number of schools – urban, suburban, and rural – have begun to involve themselves in programs of adult education, ranging from basic literacy classes to courses in home management. Adult education, of the "Italian Gardens" and "Russian Made Easy" variety, has been around for a long time. The Mott Program in Flint, that provides courses on any subject requested by at least 12 people, represents the broadest kind of approach to adult education. But many projects have felt it was necessary to focus more specifically on the disadvantaged parents, most of whom would not think of themselves, without encouragement, as potential students. In Philadelphia, one of the functions of the school community coordinators is to encourage and to help parents sign up for courses that can make them not only more helpful parents, but more productive adults as well.

Basic education courses—sometimes with an approach as direct as "learn to read before your child does"—have been set up for parents in many communities. In White Plains, courses for parents were organized according to ability levels. Some adults learned to write their own names for the first time; in other and more advanced classes some work in mathematics and social studies was included. At one center in White Plains a nine-year-old boy came regularly to pick up his mother's homework when she got sick — a circumstance that suggests that adult education does have an effect on children.

One school in Sacramento set up an experimental program designed specifically to affect children through educating their parents. The Literacy Program for Culturally Deprived Dependent Parents offered instruction in language arts and mathematics and also dealt with problems of school and family management. In Detroit, adult after-school and evening classes are taught by teachers or lay people from the community. Classes range in subject from basic literacy to Yoga. In addition, classes in "helping your child" and in such skill areas as furniture repair, budgeting, sewing, and shorthand were set up in response to parent requests.

Many classes in large urban areas are set up to help recent in-migrants from rural areas to cope with the special problems of the city. Arriving from communities where living patterns are not only much different, but much less complex, these families find themselves in a drastically changed environment where everyday activities like planning meals, shopping, and managing their children can become major obstacles to family adjustment. Philadelphia's school-community coordinators, in addition to providing in-the-home help, have also arranged for classes in food preparation and other homemaking activities. In a Chicago school, mothers participate in cooking and nutrition programs, home sewing groups, and take field trips to supermarkets and department stores under the trained guidance of a home economist. Los Angeles holds home management classes in an apartment setting, training homemakers from low socioeconomic areas in homemaking skills. In Baltimore, a social worker organized shopping trips for parents so encapsulated that they had never been to the downtown stores.

As has been demonstrated in several projects, however, one of the more effective things a school can do to help the parents is to let the parents help the school, because many parents, like their children, are more interested in doing than in talking. In Quincy (Ill.), for example, two parent groups decided that they would like to improve the kindergarten room and spent as many as 10 Saturdays painting, decorating, and making toys. In the McAteer program in Willowbrook (Calif.), parents were involved in workshops to prepare materials for use in the classroom. In Pittsburgh, one American Indian mother who had been antagonistic to the school was brought around when she was asked to help make costumes for an Indian unit.

In many cities, surveys of parental backgrounds and abilities have enabled project schools to make use of parent talents in the classrooms, in assembly programs, or in supplementary school activities. One Philadelphia school has a parent talent night. In addition, school-community coordinators in that city have helped involve parents in such activities as supervising homework centers or teaching after-school classes for adults. Oakland has asked parents to assist as nurses' helpers, supply assistants, and library assistants. In Washington, parents have helped set up book fairs, establish libraries, and plan class field trips. In other programs mothers have been hired as paid assistants to supervise drill work, handle supplies, or act as aides in team-teaching programs.

There is another area in which the concept of mutual assistance has operated. Many urban schools have found that one obstacle to the formation of effective parent groups is the lack of indigenous leadership. In several cities leadership classes have been conducted as a way of developing an understanding among parents of the techniques of organization and of the effectiveness of organized activity. These parent leaders are looked upon as potential community leaders, the focus around which people from disorganized slum neighborhoods can group themselves to begin to move toward the solution of some of their own educational, economic, and social problems.

Community involvement

The interrelationship between the school, the children, and the parents develops against the background of a single entity of which they are all a part —the community. For better or for worse the school is firmly embedded in the community; and in the final analysis the existence of a viable community structure, of a healthy neighborhood in which children and their families can operate effectively and rewardingly, is the fundamental essential without which other strictly educational efforts will ultimately fail. As the prospectus from one of the project schools put it, what a child learns in school must ultimately have "use value" for him in meeting his family and community problems. If the child lives in a community where there is no reinforcement outside of school of the values the school strives to impart, and where there are no rewards for the successful attainment of the goals the school strives to establish, then the school's job will be made more difficult, if not impossible. In the selection of a school to be the beneficiary of a special program of compensatory education, it has mattered little whether the basis for selection was relatively low school achievement scores or relatively high neighborhood concentrations of social, economic, and cultural problems—the two go together. The problems of the schools are only symptomatic of the broader problems of population shift, economic change, and technological growth.

Among the earliest organized approaches to dealing with school problems are the Ford Foundation Great Cities Gray Areas Programs. In five cities, Oakland, New Haven, Boston, Philadelphia, and Washington, D. C., and one state, North Carolina, these programs were planned, with varying degrees of success, to encourage the mobilization of public and private community resources to deal with a whole gamut of interrelated problems: housing, employment, health, and schooling. In short, to deal with the problem of "human renewal." This approach has served as a model for the urban and rural Community Action Programs authorized under the new antipoverty legislation. One of the consequences of this broadened perspective on the interrelationship between school and community problems has been a reevaluation of the school's role in relation to these problems. And the most inclusive conception of the school's responsibility to emerge from this reevaluation is expressed in the idea of the community school. According to this view, the school, as the institution which occupies the central place in neighborhood life, should assume the responsibility for seeing to it that needed services in all areas are provided to the community the school serves.

For example, the community school concept in New Haven views the school not only as an educational center, but as a neighborhood community center. It should provide facilities for cultural, recreational, and club activities, serve as a center for community services, provide health, legal, counseling, employment, and other service activities, and be a center of neighborhood and community life. It should be available to help the community in the study and solution of local problems. Although no New Haven school is yet performing the full range of functions which the concept envisions, one of the activities of Community Progress, Inc. (the Gray Areas Program administrative entity in New Haven) was to initiate the implementation of the community school concept in six schools through the services of community-school coordinators. Each of these coordinators is assisted by a leisure-time-planning staff team. The team includes a neighborhood coordinator from Community Progress, Inc., a recreation supervisor from the Department of Parks and Recreation, and a group work supervisor chosen from an agency like the YMCA, YWCA, and so forth.

In Detroit, community schools are open from 8 a.m. until late at night. In addition to the regular school program, they offer afternoon enrichment and remedial activities to the children, after-school and evening recreational and educational activities for adults, and summer programs of education, enrichment, and recreation to adults and children alike. Furthermore, Detroit community schools have found that the availability of time and space within the schools has encouraged other groups to schedule meetings there. Disparate organizations such as the Department of Parks and Recreation and the Boy Scouts have utilized school facilities for holding meetings. Cooperation between various agencies and the school has also led to a sharing of facilities. The schools have used YMCA and YWCA buses and buildings; and in exchange for their use of the school swimming pools, the Department of Parks and Recreation permits the schools to use one of their large recreation centers.

In Detroit, family social service is provided by visiting teachers. Personnel designated as school-community agents and social workers trained in community organization, concentrate on developing local community leadership, on coordinating the work of community agencies, and on involving both parents and school neighbors in community and school sponsored programs. A number of programs have made use of these school community agents. Generally their role is to help coordinate the services of the school with those of other agencies working in the community and to seek to fill, or arrange to have filled, gaps in services as they discover them.

In Syracuse, one of the functions of the community-school coordinator is to help set up neighborhood study centers that offer a full schedule of activities for children and adults alike. The year-round morning program includes a story hour for preschoolers and an informal coffee hour counseling program for mothers. The afternoons are devoted to an after-school story hour for elementary school children that utilizes local teen-agers as readers. In the evening each facility is used as a study center, a neighborhood meeting place, the site of a guidance program for parents, and a reentry program for dropouts.

Philadelphia's school-community coordinators are doubly related to the community — they are selected from it and for it. They are lay people, residents of the neighborhood, chosen for their demonstrated effectiveness in working with members of the community. In addition to making calls on project parents, the coordinators help to foster the development of local community councils and, by putting parents in touch with the proper community assistance agencies, help to involve those agencies in the immediate school community.

Often it is in working to organize and focus the efforts of existing community service agencies on behalf of the neighborhood population that the school can play its most significant community role. The school cannot go it alone, cannot itself provide all the services the population needs. Indeed, the effectiveness of the school as an instrument for neighborhood improvement is always largely dependent on the degree to which it is successful in involving other contributors of time, money, and effort—social and civic organizations, religious and educational institutions, public and private social agencies, private groups and individuals—in the local problems.

One of the functions of the New Haven community school coordinator is to integrate the services of the existing public and private agencies that are operating or should operate in the school neighborhood. Ideally then, the school's role in community service is that of an intermediary—defining the specific population that has a need, finding an agency appropriate to meet that need, and bringing the two together. The McAteer program in Pasadena utilizes the services of an orientation teacher to introduce each new child to some community youth group. There are some areas, of course, where the school itself is the most appropriate agency to meet the need of the child. Where the emphasis is on education the school is often clearly the institution of choice. But where social services, recreational activities, or cultural activities are involved, many schools (urban schools in particular) are faced with a different situation. The community school is really a neighborhood school. It provides the encapsulated inhabitants of center-city neighborhoods with a single local facility that can centralize services for a number of their immediate needs while simultaneously teaching and encouraging them to take advantage of all that the larger community has to offer. The school, in other words, can act to encourage participation in a number of existing activities, the social, cultural, and recreational activities that most urban communities have available already. In many smaller communities, however, particularly in isolated rural areas, the opportunities for recreation and cultural enrichment that the school offers may be the only opportunities of this kind that are available in the community. Under these circumstances a concert, a dance recital, an art exhibit, or a program like the lecture series on the topic of prejudice held last winter and spring in Deposit and Windsor (N. Y.) can represent a significant contribution to the cultural life of the community.

In many communities the school's role has not been that of supplier or coordinator of community services. Sometimes the school has instigated action by other agencies or participated as an equal member in programs designed to benefit both the community and the school. In Minneapolis, for example, the Youth Development Demonstration Project, developed under the auspices of the Community Health and Welfare Council of Hennepin County, Inc., has involved the schools in a cooperative planning effort to focus the attention of existing agencies on a number of community problems. Personnel from various community agencies, volunteers, and school staff work together in the areas of youth employment, curriculum development, enrichment programs, and the provision of counseling services to families and school neighbors in disadvantaged areas of the city.

In Wilmington (Del.), one outgrowth of a school-conducted three-year experimental project on schools in changing neighborhoods was the establishment of an interagency council that involved 35 organizations. It fostered activities like the rehabilitation of buildings, the formation of neighborhood councils, the establishment of playgrounds, and other community improvement projects.

The encouragement of community involvement on the part of the school is based on the assumption that no one agency, for example the school, is equipped to provide the total range of services needed for the children or for their community. But where such help is not otherwise forthcoming many schools have, on occasion, taken it upon themselves to provide concrete social services like new shoes, used clothing, free lunches, shower and wash-up services, and sometimes free breakfasts for children who come to school hungry. In one urban school the principal made a practice of learning from the milkmen about children who had been locked out of their homes overnight and brought them in for a shower, breakfast, and a nap before they started school.

Project schools have also assumed the responsibility of providing for the special health needs of disadvantaged children. Through the services of a full-time school nurse and the availability at least part-time of a physician and a dental hygienist, many project schools have been able to provide more regular and more frequent checkups as well as more intensive follow-up services when there has been a referral for treatment.

But the auxiliary relationship between the school and the community is not a one-way street. Just as there are ways that the school can help to serve the broad range of community needs, there are ways in which the involved community can help the school to fulfill its primary educational role. Very often the school's first step in getting help from the community must be to disseminate information about just what the school is trying to do. In San Francisco, the School Community Improvement Program is one of a number of projects that mounted a public relations campaign in order to communicate the aims and procedures of its effort to the community. Where lower-class and middle-class neighborhoods meet, the school must often overcome the hostility of the latter in order to enlist community cooperation in its effort.

That funds invested in promoting a project can often provide a high rate of return in community interest and community assistance is clear. The degree to which an informed and involved community can foster the work of its schools has been amply demonstrated by the contributions of the Urban Service Corps in Washington, D. C., where volunteers have initiated projects ranging from tutoring for unwed mothers to arranging classes in custodial training for boys who are potential dropouts. Dropout programs are, in fact, one of the areas in which the assistance of the community — the business community — is essential. The cooperation of local merchants, manufacturers, and businessmen in providing useful and remunerative work for pupils in work-study programs is fundamental to the success of the programs. Once employers have been made aware of the need, the careful selection and subsequent supervision of students placed in jobs has proved to be the most effective way of breaking down employer resistance to the hiring of students from project schools.

Volunteer tutoring programs, volunteer school aide programs, volunteer programs of all kinds have been used to supplement the regular school staff in providing special services to disadvantaged children. In Boston, settlement houses, churches, and other community organizations provided tutorial services where none were provided within the school system. This is also true in many other communities. In New York City, a volunteer parent organization provides special English instruction to non-English-speaking children and tutors other children in reading, art, or music. Ten preschool programs in St. Louis are run by volunteer organizations. In Baltimore, a number of local service organizations are involved in selecting and screening personnel as volunteer workers in its HELP preschool program. Civic and fraternal organizations have been involved in helping with field trips and other school activities.

In Pasadena, a special program developed in conjunction with the Pasadena Art Museum, provides an after-school Junior Art Workshop for third-grade boys who are low achievers. In Chicago, the Urban Gateways and Fine Arts Program provides disadvantaged boys and girls with an opportunity to attend musical and other cultural events and provides them with background materials to help them get the most out of the experiences. In Hartford, Fox Scholars have donated money for records for the schools' music departments, the Hartt College of Opera gives performances at reduced rates, the Metropolitan Woman's Club donates the proceeds of bridge parties, and the high school commercial classes donate typing services for project school programs.

In Pittsburgh, various community agencies have provided luncheons, book review sessions, and other experiences to small groups of children. Through funds provided by outside groups, 16 children were enabled to attend a 10-week summer course in general science at the Buhl Space Academy. In Boston, one of the unique projects being undertaken under the Action for Boston Community Development program is a community school planning program in which a committee of lay and professional people are working, together with the principal designated, to develop curriculum and plant specifications for a new elementary school in a disadvantaged area of the city.

In almost every compensatory program, however small, the community has made some contribution — by providing leadership to start a girl scout troop, or by providing the money to pay for a field trip, or by contributions of time, money, and effort, or all three.

6. Compensatory practices in colleges and universities

The same social forces responsible for the recent development of compensatory education in the public schools—mainly the growing need for educated manpower in industry, increasing pressures of the civil rights movement, new conceptions of the educability of the "lower classes," and philanthropic stimulation and support—have given new impetus to the development of compensatory programs and practices on the college level. Current efforts to identify potentially able Negro and other socially disadvantaged youths and to help them go through college probably constitute one of the most dynamic trends in American higher education. And they involve a much larger proportion of the collegiate institutions than the proportion of public school systems involved in compensatory education on the elementary and secondary school levels.

Some colleges, of course, have long been active in giving special assistance to disadvantaged young people for whom higher education would otherwise be impractical. One thinks, for example, of Berea College in rural Kentucky, of Oberlin College in Ohio, and of one or two institutions in the East; and perhaps one should include also the vast majority of the Negro colleges in the South. But their activities in this regard were exceptional; the mainstream of higher education showed little or no concern for youths with educational handicaps born of poverty and discrimination. Indeed, prior to 1960, the literature was almost wholly barren even of discussions of higher education for the disadvantaged; only during the past three or four years has there developed a trend toward doing something about it.

Anticipating the now emerging trend by more than a decade, the National Scholarship Service and Fund for Negro Students (NSSFNS) sought early to direct the postsputnik national concern for identifying and developing "talent" toward the largely untapped reservoir among Negro students from depressed homes and inferior schools. The activities of NSSFNS in mobilizing philanthropic aid and institutional cooperation to bring hundreds of able southern Negro high school graduates with educational deficiencies to northern colleges and universities did much to stimulate current developments along this line. Strong ideological support for such developments came from emphasis in the 1961 Rockefeller Panel Reports on large groups "in which talent is wasted wholesale."[1] Further support came with growing recognition in college circles that conventional entrance examinations do not validly assess the academic potential of young people from disadvantaged environments. And the principle here involved was still further strengthened and expanded by the Educational Policies Commission's 1964 declaration that "The nation as a whole has never accepted the idea of universal opportunity as applying to education beyond the high school. It is time to do so."[2]

That idea, of course, is still far from being generally accepted, especially by institutions of higher education. The point of view of more than a few colleges and universities is reflected by responses to a questionnaire circulated in 1964 justifying their failure to develop compensatory programs and practices on such grounds as "the stigma of admitting poor students, most of whom do not succeed anyway"; and "we believe it is the task of schools to prepare students for college, not the responsibility of colleges to do the work of the schools." Although such explicit rejections of the compensatory principle are rare, implied rejections are reflected by such responses as "Since we do not have students who are handicapped by socially disadvantaged environments, this questionnaire does not apply to us"; and ". . . our constituency has not provided a sufficient number of cases for the university to justify setting up such a program as you describe." However, neither of these types of negative response is typical of replies by institutions currently inactive in the compensatory field. Much more frequent are such statements as "We do not have any compensatory programs at present, but are interested in possibly planning one"; and "We have not up to this time developed special programs and practices in the direction indicated by the questionnaire—we recognize the fact that we shall probably do so."

Although the vast majority of institutions of higher education have not

---

1. Rockefeller Panel Reports, *Prospect for America*. New York: Doubleday & Company, Inc., 1961.

2. Educational Policies Commission, *Universal Opportunity for Education Beyond the High School*. Washington, D.C.: National Education Association, 1964, p. 5.

yet undertaken any compensatory programs or practices, a very substantial number of them have. And it appears that many more of them have accepted, at least in principle, the need for and the validity of special approaches to help socially disadvantaged young people to enter and succeed in college. Their reports are evidence of the developing trend.

Extent and distribution of compensatory practices

In an effort to identify colleges and universities developing compensatory programs and practices, a six-page questionnaire was mailed during the spring of 1964 to the 2,093 institutions listed for the 50 states and District of Columbia in the United States Office of Education's *Education Directory, 1962-63: Higher Education*. The inquiry form noted that it is now "widely recognized that many potentially able college students are handicapped by socially disadvantaged environments, and/or inadequate precollegiate school experiences," and asked the institutions to report on their "special programs and practices to help overcome the socially-induced educational handicaps of such students," the nature and extent of such programs and practices, their objectives, effectiveness, and underlying rationale. Information gathered from their responses was supplemented by limited field trips, correspondence, and the collection of press reports during the following year.

Reports were received from 610 institutions of higher education, representing 28.6 percent of the 2,131 colleges and universities in the 50 states and District of Columbia during 1963-64. This 29 percent sample is roughly representative of all colleges and universities on several bases of comparison. It includes approximately one-fourth to one-third of the institutions in each of the nine geographical regions, in each of four type-of-control categories (religious, private, state, and city), and in three of five highest-level-of-offerings categories (from junior college to doctoral and professional). Only with regard to this latter criterion does the sample vary much from the pattern of all colleges and universities. Institutions offering the doctor's degree are substantially overrepresented; institutions on the junior college level are slightly underrepresented. In regard to the types of programs offered, the sample is highly representative of all colleges and universities. Nearly one-half (48 percent) of the reporting institutions are small, with fewer than 1,000 students enrolled during 1962–63; one-third (33 percent) had enrollments between 1,001 and 5,000; and about one-fifth (19 percent) had enrollments larger than 5,000. (See Tables 1 and 2.)

Of the 610 institutions, 224 (37 percent) reported that they were conducting a variety of compensatory practices – special recruiting and admissions procedures, financial aid, precollege preparatory courses, remedial courses in college, special curriculums, counseling, tutoring, and other practices; and 386 of the institutions (63 percent) reported that they were not conducting any compensatory practices. The geographical distribution of those reporting "Some" or "No" practices is summarized in Table 3.[3]

It may be noted that except for the small group of institutions in the Mountain Region, between 30 and 43 percent of the institutions in each region reported that they were conducting "Some" compensatory practices. These proportions of total institutions are substantially higher than was noted for the regional proportions of total institutions reporting either "Some" or "No" compensatory practices; the range is from 23 to 35 percent. Obviously, reports were received from a larger proportion of the institutions with "Some" compensatory practices than from institutions with "No" such practices.

Although institutions controlled by city or district governments constitute only 14 percent of the 610 colleges and universities reporting, they account for 22 percent of the institutions reporting "Some" compensatory practices. Of the city or district institutions replying to this inquiry, 57 percent reported "Some" practices, as compared with between 31 and 37 percent of those under religious, private, or state control. (See Table 2.)

There is a tendency for proportionately more of the larger institutions than of the smaller institutions to report "Some" compensatory practices. Whereas the proportions range from 41 to 55 percent for four enrollment

---

3. The division of the reporting institutions between these two categories involved judgments which may underestimate the size of the "Some" group. Many institutions that checked special recruiting, admissions, scholarship, and other practices on the questionnaire were nevertheless placed in the "No" category because, in the context of their responses to other questions, it appeared that these practices were not addressed specifically to socially disadvantaged students.

Table 1. Number, distribution, and selected characteristics of institutions reporting; percent of total of U.S. institutions, 1963-64

Selected characteristics	Number of institutions reporting	U.S. total, 1963-64[b]	percent reporting
Geographical region[a]:			
New England	69	196	35
Middle Atlantic	105	355	30
East North Central	116	355	33
West North Central	67	258	26
South Atlantic	74	326	23
East South Central	37	156	24
West South Central	40	174	23
Mountain	18	72	25
Pacific	84	239	35
Total	610	2,131	29
Type of control:			
Religious groups	199	868	23
Private (independent of church or state) . . .	159	505	31
State	157	405	39
City or district	86	353	24
Other	9	—	—
Total	610	2,131	29
Highest level of offerings:			
I. 2 years (less than 4) beyond 12th grade . .	125	640	19
II. Only bachelor's and/or 1st profl. degree . .	201	789	25
III. Master's and/or 2nd profl. degree	151	454	33
IV. Doctor of philosophy and equivalent . .	127	223	58
V. Other	6	25	24
Total	610	2,131	29

a. The regional classification is that of the U.S. Census. Included are the 50 states and District of Columbia.

b. Taken or derived from *Education Directory, 1963-64: Higher Education*. U.S. Office of Education, 1964, Table 4, p. 12. Data for Canal Zone, Guam, Puerto Rico, and Virgin Islands are excluded.

Table 2. Number and percent of institutions reporting "Some" or "No" compensatory practices, by type of control and size of enrollment

Item	Total	Number reporting "Some" practices	Number reporting "No" practices	Percent reporting "Some" practices	Percent reporting "No" practices
Type of control:					
Religious group	199	61	138	31	69
Private	159	54	105	34	66
State	157	59	98	37	63
City or district	86	49	37	57	43
Other	9	1	8	10	90
Total	610	224	386	37	63
Enrollment, 1962–63[a]:					
More than 10,000	59	27	32	46	54
5,001 to 10,000	58	24	34	41	59
3,001 to 5,000	44	24	20	55	45
2,001 to 3,000	47	22	25	47	53
1,001 to 2,000	111	39	72	35	65
501 to 1,000	102	37	65	36	64
301 to 500	74	23	51	31	69
300 or fewer	115	28	87	24	76
Total	610	224	386	37	63

a. *Education Directory, 1962–63: Higher Education, passim.*

categories above 2,000, they range from 24 to 36 percent for four categories of smaller enrollments.

The levels of academic programs offered by the 224 institutions reporting "Some" compensatory practices seem per se to bear no substantial relationship to the incidence of compensatory practices among them, as is shown by the following summary tabulations:

Two years, less than four. 29%
Bachelor's and/or first professional degree 26%
Master's and/or second professional degree 21%
Doctor's and equivalent 24%

Table 3. Number and percent of institutions reporting "Some" or "No" compensatory practices, by geographical regions

	Number reporting[a]			Percent reporting	
	"Some"	*"No"*		*"Some"*	*"No"*
Region	*practices*	*practices*	*Total*	*practices*	*practices*
New England	23	46	69	33	67
Middle Atlantic	42	63	105	40	60
East North Central	35	81	116	30	70
West North Central	25	42	67	37	63
South Atlantic	27	47	74	36	64
East South Central	16	21	37	43	57
West South Central	15	25	40	38	62
Mountain	10	8	18	56	44
Pacific	31	53	84	37	63
Total	224	386	610	37	63

a. See Appendix A for list of institutions.

Although proportionately more of these institutions are on the junior college level, the range among the four classifications is only 8 percentage points. (See Table 4.) The kinds of programs offered by these 224 institutions, however, are very definitely related to the presence or absence of compensatory practices. Although some institutions with compensatory practices are included in all 11 of the program categories shown, more than three-fourths of them are in only 4 categories:

c. Liberal arts and general, and terminal-occupational 43 (19%)
e. Both liberal arts and general, and teacher-preparatory . . 54 (24%)
f. Liberal arts and general, terminal-occupational,
    and teacher-preparatory. 31 (14%)
k. Liberal arts and general, with three or more professional
    schools 45 (20%)
    173 (77%)

When the 27 institutions in the other two "Liberal arts and . . ." categories ("b" and "j") are added to these, about 90 percent of the institutions reporting compensatory practices are accounted for. It is clear that compensatory programs are centered overwhelmingly in institutions whose programs are based on the liberal arts. Only minimally are they represented among institutions whose programs are mainly terminal-occupational, teacher-preparatory, or professional (that is, categories "a," "d," "g," "h," and "i" in Table 4).

Further evident from Table 4 is the concentration of institutions with compensatory practices in only 2 of the 44 highest-level and type-of-program cells: Ic (42) and IVk (41), which account for 37 percent of the 224 institutions. These are, respectively, junior colleges with liberal arts, general, and terminal-occupational programs; and universities offering the doctor's degree, with liberal arts, general programs, and three or more professional schools. Thus, given a liberal arts program as the base, there seems to be a tendency for compensatory practices to be carried on most frequently among institutions on the lowest and highest academic levels.

Information received by this inquiry concerning the numbers of disadvantaged students being helped by the 224 institutions reporting compensatory practices is incomplete, fragmentary, and in many cases ambiguous. Of 135 institutions with reasonably clear reports on this item, 31 (23 percent) reported assistance to between 1 and 10 students; 18 (13 percent) reported assistance to between 11 and 20 students; 14 (10 percent) reported assistance to between 21 and 30 students; and the numbers reported by the others range upward into the (highly-questionable) hundreds.

Thus it appears that in the spring of 1964, when these reports were received, almost half of the institutions with compensatory practices were assisting fewer than 30 disadvantaged students. These figures do not reflect enrollments in the special compensatory summer programs that a number of these institutions conducted subsequently, and in each of which from about 40 to more than 100 disadvantaged youths participated.

Information received about the ethnic identity of the disadvantaged students being helped by the compensatory practices here reported is also incomplete, fragmentary, and in many cases ambiguous. On the basis of meaningful reports from 131 colleges and universities, it appears that the disadvantaged students assisted were mainly white in 79 (60 percent) of the

Table 4. Number and percent of institutions reporting "Some" compensatory practices, by highest level of offerings and type of program; percent of U.S. total, 1963-64

Type of Program	Highest level of offerings						U.S. total, 1963-64	
	2 years less than 4 I	Bachelor's and/or 1st profl. degree II	Master's and/or 2nd profl. degree III	Doctor's and equivalent IV	Total	Percent	No.[a]	Percent
a. Terminal-occupational (below bachelor's)	2	—	—	—	2	1	52	2
b. Liberal arts and general	3	6	4	—	13	6	153	7
c. Liberal arts and general and terminal-occupational	42	1	—	—	43	19	378	18
d. Primarily teacher-preparatory	2	2	5	—	9	4	99	5
e. Both liberal arts and general and teacher-preparatory	7	30	14	3	54	24	560	26
f. Liberal arts and general, terminal-occupational and teacher-preparatory	9	14	8	—	31	14	240	11
g. Professional (not teacher-preparatory)	—	—	1	2	3	1	202	9
h. Professional and teacher-preparatory	—	2	1	5	8	4	74	4
i. Professional terminal-occupational	—	2	—	—	2	1	40	2

j. Liberal arts and general with one or two professional schools. . .	—	2	10	2	14	6	143	7
k. Liberal arts and general with three or more professional schools	—	—	4	41	45	20	190	9
Total	65	59	47	53	224		2,131	
Percent	29	26	21	24	100	100		100

a. Taken from *Education Directory, 1963–64: Higher Education*, Table 5, p. 13 (not including the institutions in outlying areas).

institutions; mainly Negro in 35 (27 percent) of the institutions; and mainly Asian, American Indian, or Mexican-American in 17 (13 percent) of the institutions. Whereas most of the Negro students came from urban communities, the white students came from urban and rural areas in approximately equal proportions.

This analysis of the extent and distribution of compensatory programs and practices among the nation's institutions of higher education, although accurately reflecting the answers to this questionnaire, tends nevertheless to be somewhat misleading. Several correctives should be borne in mind in assessing the data presented.

In the first place, 65 (29 percent) of the 224 institutions reporting compensatory practices are public junior colleges and community colleges, offering programs on the subbaccalaureate level. A few of them are known to have special compensatory programs that are expressly developed to aid underachieving students from depressed social environments, such as the "College Discovery Program" in two community colleges in New York City. It is probable, however, that most of the compensatory programs and practices reported by institutions on this level are not at all special, but are a part of their regular ongoing programs of public education beyond the high school. Of course, many socially disadvantaged young people are enrolled in these programs.

A letter from the Los Angeles Public Schools, which participates in the very extensive junior college program of California, illustrates this point. It enclosed a 1963 handbook, *Promising Practices For Expanding Educational Opportunities*, with the comment: "While there are no special college programs as such, this compilation of current effective techniques will indicate our efforts in this most important area." The point is further illustrated by this comment in a letter from Rockland Community College, located in a suburb of New York City: "A substantial proportion of our freshman students have always been from the bottom half of the high school graduating class . . . I suspect . . . that if we are enrolling the disadvantaged it is our basic admissions policy, our low tuition cost, and our accessibility that is doing the job, rather than the practices and programs which you list in your questionnaire."

In a very important sense, the regular programs of most junior and community colleges are inherently compensatory; but they are not special programs addressed specifically to what are here termed socially disadvantaged youth.

Second, 16 of the colleges and universities reporting compensatory practices are exclusively or predominantly Negro, 14 of them located in the South; and this latter group accounts for 24 percent of the 58 institutions reporting compensatory practices from the three southern regions. As has been noted, these and similar institutions do, indeed, serve large numbers of young people who have been handicapped by racial, social class, and academic influences, most of whom could not attend college elsewhere. Some of these institutions are known to have special compensatory programs in the sense that the term is used here—such as the Basic Skills Program for freshmen at Morgan State College (Md.). Most of them, however, might more appropriately be classified as "compensatory colleges," rather than as institutions with special compensatory programs.

Third, several of the northern institutions classified here among those with compensatory practices reported that their established general practices provide assistance for small numbers of disadvantaged youth as individuals. Swarthmore College (Pa.), for example, reported: "For many years we have had students from minority and culturally deprived groups as part of the Quaker tradition of the college, and we have always seen fit to handle these students in very much the same way that we deal with any other Swarthmore undergraduates. Being a small college, we are able to work with individual students prior to admission and after they arrive." Radcliffe College (Mass.) reported that the institution "has no special undergraduate program, but we are sufficiently flexible with respect to admission, financial aid, and tutoring to be able to assist a few socially disadvantaged students on an individual basis." Somewhat similar responses were received from a few other institutions. Their practices along these lines may properly be characterized as compensatory, but they are not special.

Thus far in this analysis, the terms "compensatory programs" and "compensatory practices" have been used more or less interchangeably, with meanings largely implied; but it is important at this point to define them explicitly. A continuing activity by an institution of higher education that helps disadvantaged students who could not otherwise do so to enroll and progress in college is here termed a compensatory practice. Examples are the giving of financial aid, modifications of admission requirements, and the provision of tutoring services. An organized group of related activities to the same end is here termed a compensatory program: concerted efforts to attract and help disadvantaged students through a series of practices such as those enumerated, and special precollegiate and college-level instructional programs.

It is probable that the number of institutions with some compensatory practices is much larger than the 224 reported to this inquiry. The number of reporting institutions with compensatory programs, however, is much smaller. On the basis of less than adequate data, it is estimated that fewer than 50 colleges and universities for which information is at hand are developing compensatory programs as here defined;[4] and they probably include the bulk of such institutions in the nation.

Types of programs and practices

Colleges and universities reporting compensatory programs and practices indicated the nature of such activities in their responses to a checklist in the questionnaire distributed during the spring of 1964, and also by means of descriptive statements and documents. The information thus obtained was supplemented from various sources during the following year.

It may be seen from Table 5 that practices designed to help disadvantaged students after entering college predominated among the institutions reporting in the spring of 1964. Almost two-thirds of the frequencies (62 percent) are accounted for by counseling, credit and noncredit remedial courses, instruction in study skills, tutoring, special curriculums, and lengthened time for completing degree requirements. Practices addressed to helping disadvantaged students enter college – financial aid, modified admissions criteria, preparatory courses, and recruiting procedures – were

---

4. The institutions so adjudged are designated by asterisks in Appendix A.

Table 5. Number of institutions reporting various types of compensatory practices: Spring 1964

Type of practice	Number of institutions
Special counseling and other guidance services	142
Special remedial courses in college, yielding no academic credit	128
Special instruction in study skills, test-taking, and so forth	89
Special remedial courses in college, yielding academic credit	63
Special tutoring in college	61
Special curriculum or sequence of courses	50
Lengthened time for completing degree course	43
Special financial aid	121
Modified admission criteria	90
Precollege preparatory courses (for example, during summer, and so forth)	72
Special recruiting procedures	68
Special postgraduate program	8

represented by a little over one-third (38 percent) of the frequencies noted.

It should be noted that the questionnaires returned by a number of colleges and universities provided responses to the checklist of compensatory practices but little or no further information. It is probable that some of the reporting institutions checked practices which they followed with students generally, but which were not directed especially toward aid to socially disadvantaged students. Thus the frequencies reported in Table 5 should be interpreted with caution. Information at hand is inadequate for differentiating clearly between those which reflect incidental help to disadvantaged individuals and those which represent compensatory practices addressed specifically to this end.

Unlike the compensatory educational programs on the elementary and secondary school levels reported to this inquiry (nearly nine-tenths were begun since 1960) most of the compensatory practices reported by institutions of higher education are said to have been in existence much longer. Information from the institutions reporting the academic years in which their compensatory practices were used (accounting for 699 of the 935 frequencies shown in Table 5) suggests that nearly two-thirds (64 percent) of these practices date back to the 1950s or earlier. In the light of general knowledge concerning the recency of widespread special efforts to help disadvantaged students enter and succeed in college, this finding underscores the caution noted above.

Developments since the spring of 1964, when the questionnaire survey was made, probably have resulted in relatively more emphasis on helping disadvantaged students enter college (as compared with helping them to succeed after admission) than is suggested by Table 5. Especially notable during that period was the burgeoning development of precollege preparatory programs in the summers of 1964 and 1965, as well as increased emphasis on compensatory recruiting, admissions practices, and scholarship aid.

General descriptions and a few illustrations should suffice to interpret the nature of these helping-to-enter and helping-to-succeed kinds of compensatory practices, together with some of the issues they involve. The analysis is based mainly upon reports by colleges and universities to this inquiry, but it also includes information obtained from the press.

Special efforts to recruit socially disadvantaged students have become a major emphasis in many colleges during the past few years. Particularly worthy of note is the quest for Negro students, both the disadvantaged and the affluent, by prestige institutions in the East. For a complex of motivations, this has become "the thing" to do. Long-practiced and continuing referrals by the National Scholarship Service and Fund for Negro Students (NSSFNS) are now supplemented by direct recruiting activities undertaken by the colleges themselves, including field trips to segregated or predominantly Negro high schools. College students take part in these recruiting activities at some institutions. An example is the student-inspired and operated "Project 65" at Bowdoin College (Maine), which undertook "to bring at least 65 Negro students to Bowdoin College by the fall of 1965."

Reflecting such special recruiting efforts, it was reported that the eight Ivy League and the Seven Sisters colleges admitted 468 Negro men and women to their freshman classes in the fall of 1965, more than double the number admitted in the previous fall and about 3 percent of total admissions.

At least two cooperative programs for recruiting Negro students have recently been developed by colleges and universities in various parts of the country. The Cooperative Program for Educational Opportunity, which involves 15 institutions in the East, undertakes joint efforts to recruit talented "students qualified for one of the colleges but who would not apply without encouragement." This agency is said to be largely responsible for the 1965–66 increase in Negro students admitted to the Ivy League and Seven Sisters colleges. Similarly, the College Assistance Program (Hoy Plan), sponsored jointly by NSSFNS and 110 institutions, undertakes to help disadvantaged youth find their way to college. It consists of regional groups of admissions and scholarship officials who visit Negro institutions "usually overlooked," seeking "to uncover talent and refer it to the right college."

The recent trend along this line is also reflected by the Minority Group Project of the American Association of Law Schools, which seeks "to counteract the factors which permit only a few Negroes and Puerto Ricans to enter the legal profession."

The socially disadvantaged youths attracted by these recruiting efforts, whether talented or not, usually require financial assistance to enter college; and institutions of higher education are increasingly making such help available.

Scholarship aid and other forms of financial assistance for individual students with demonstrated academic talent have, of course, been provided by many institutions over a long period of time; and it is probable that a large proportion – if not most – of the "special financial aid" practices reported here are of this type. They appear to represent extensions of the recently developed "talent search" to the disadvantaged, and are directed mainly toward attracting bright students who happen also to be poor.

Typical of this approach is the program of financial aid – together with special recruiting and admissions practices – recently begun by Duke University (N. C.) with support from the Ford Foundation. It seeks "to open access to higher education for this socially disadvantaged type of student who is academically talented and yet might not normally think of this type of private institution." Similarly, the special fund of $100,000 which the Regents of the University of California recently made available on a matching basis to the several campuses to be used for financial and other forms of aid to "students from disadvantaged cultures," undertakes "to bring into higher education talented people who because of environmental handicaps do not persist beyond the secondary grades." These are fairly representative of the prevailing approaches to financial aid for socially disadvantaged students.

A few institutions have established compensatory programs of financial assistance that seem to be available not only to the talented, but also to academic risks. Examples are the University of Michigan's Opportunity Award Program, begun in 1964, and the new Cornell University (N. Y.) financial aid program for underprivileged students. Another example is the Kansas City Special Scholarship Program, in which a number of colleges in and around Missouri participate on a matching basis. Initiated by the Kansas City Public Schools with philanthropic support, it seeks "to increase college attendance among students from economically, culturally, and educationally marginal segments of the population . . . especially Negroes." Of the 137 freshmen and sophomores attending college in the fall of 1963 with four-year scholarships under this program, 22 percent ranked below the sixtieth percentile on the School and College Ability Test (scat), and 45 percent ranked below the eightieth percentile.

Financial aid programs for disadvantaged students who might be judged as academic risks are almost always associated with other compensatory practices that are designed to help such students overcome their educational deficiencies.

One of the most impressive compensatory developments in higher education during the past few years is the increasing availability of funds for financial and related forms of aid directed specifically to socially disadvantaged students. Much of the money comes from the resources of individual institutions, like the scholarship programs at the University of California and the University of Michigan. Local philanthropy supplies the funds in some areas, as in the Kansas City program. Especially notable are the contributions of several great foundations.

A case in point is the 1964 Ford Foundation grant of $7 million to the National Merit Scholarship Corporation for the purpose of administering the National Achievement Scholarship program for Negro students. Beginning with 1965–66, this new program will grant at least 200 scholarships annually through 1969. Another case is the 1965 Sloan Foundation grant of $500,000 to support a program of scholarships (along with other forms of help) in 10 southern Negro colleges. The Rockefeller Foundation, the Carnegie Corporation, and others are similarly involved in compensatory programs.

Most of these new financial aid programs are directed mainly toward helping disadvantaged Negro students. However, a number of institutions, largely from their own resources, offer financial assistance to other disadvantaged minorities. Special scholarship aid for American Indians, for example, is provided by the University of Minnesota, the University of South Dakota, the University of Arizona, Fort Lewis Agricultural and Mechanical College (Colo.), and the University of Alaska. Grossmont College (Calif.) provides special scholarships for Mexican-Americans, American Indians, and Asians.

Obviously talented disadvantaged students can compete – not only for scholarships but also for college admission – on the basis of standards which apply to other students. But disadvantaged youths in the academic risks category generally require some modification of admissions criteria in order to enter college and demonstrate their potential. Increasing numbers of institutions are effecting such modifications. Thus, many disadvantaged students whose high school grades and performance on College Board tests, scat, or other entrance examinations would normally bar them from college are nevertheless being admitted on the basis of recommendations from their high schools or nssfns, often supplemented with personal interviews.

Such modifications of admissions criteria are commonly associated with other compensatory practices that are designed to help disadvantaged students succeed after entering college, but some related practices seem to be largely independent of other approaches. For example, Williams College (Mass.), on the basis of a 1962 Ford Foundation grant of $125,000, is conducting a 10-year study of students admitted "with less than outstanding grades and test scores but with promising qualities that defy scientific measurement." Up to 10 percent of each freshman class will be selected from "individuals with a flair, a forte, a strength of character" – presumably including the socially disadvantaged – who would not be eligible on the basis of their high school grades and performance on scholastic aptitude tests. Somewhat similarly, for the expressed purpose of making higher education accessible to more disadvantaged young people, the several colleges which constitute the City University of New York began in 1965–66 to admit students with a high school grade-average of 82 rather than 84, which was the previous year's cutoff point. This change was expected to bring an additional 3,000 students into the city colleges.

Probably the most dramatic compensatory development in higher education during recent years is the variety of preparatory summer programs conducted for high school students by a wide range of institutions. Although somewhat similar precollege preparatory programs – mainly with high school graduates – have previously been conducted by a few institutions, the big impetus for this type of program came during the summer of 1964, when hundreds of disadvantaged undergraduate high school students spent several weeks studying at some of the major institutions of higher education. Most of the programs, together with others, were also conducted during the following summer.

Typically, in these preparatory summer schools, high school students below the senior year are brought to the colleges with all expenses paid, and given instruction for from six to eight weeks in English, mathematics, study skills, and other fields. Skilled high school teachers generally give the instruction, and college students supplement it with individual tutoring. Enriching social and cultural experiences are usually provided. Some of the programs call for the learners to return in successive years. The general purpose is to identify disadvantaged students with college potential before the end of high school, and to strengthen their academic achievement and motivation so as to facilitate and encourage entrance into college. Most of the programs are directed toward talented youth, but some of them seek to involve academic risks.

Representative of this development was the Yale University (Conn.) summer high school of 1964, supported by the Ford Foundation, the National Science Foundation, the Cummings Engineering Foundation, and the Whitney Foundation. It was a six-week program for 103 tenth-grade, socially disadvantaged boys from all over the eastern part of the country — half of them Negroes, some of them southern whites. Somewhat comparable were the eight-week "A Better Chance" (ABC) summer programs during 1964 at Dartmouth College (N. H.), Mount Holyoke College (Mass.), Princeton University (N. J.), Oberlin College (Ohio), and perhaps other institutions, supported by the Rockefeller Foundation. Participating in each ABC program were between 40 and 60 disadvantaged high school students, many of them risk candidates for future college entrance. A unique purpose of one of these programs, Dartmouth's, was to prepare boys for admission to a cooperating group of 40 top-ranking preparatory schools — Choate, Phillips Andover, Groton, St. Paul's, Hotchkiss, and others — where many of them actually enrolled during 1964–65.

Also during the summer of 1965, Columbia University (N. Y.) conducted an eight-week program (Double Discovery Project) for 160 disadvantaged boys and girls about to enter the sophomore year in New York City high schools. About 40 percent were Negroes and 30 percent were Puerto Ricans.

At least one of the continuing precollege summer preparatory programs is for pupils below the high school level. During the summer of 1964, Rutgers—The State University (N. J.) began a program for an interracial group of 50 disadvantaged seventh-grade children. They were selected from nearby schools, and are to return each summer until they are ready for college. The number of students will be augmented each year until 200 are enrolled.

Although special summer programs for high school students, such as those cited, are perhaps the most dramatic among recent precollege preparatory programs for disadvantaged young people, they by no means constitute all of the college and university practices along this line. There are many others, with varying features, in all parts of the country.

Somewhat of a precursor to this whole recent development was the experimental "Operation Second Chance" which was conducted from February 1960 to June 1961 by the Bronx Community College (N. Y.), with support from the Ford Foundation's Fund for the Advancement of Education. It was "a program of special guidance and instruction in English language and mathematics . . . for New York City high school graduates who had sought and been denied admission to college." During successive semesters, student groups of 20, 40, and 12 – mostly socially disadvantaged young people – were given remedial instruction and guidance to help them qualify for college admission. The results were outstandingly positive, and this demonstration project led directly to the expanded compensatory programs now being developed by component colleges of the City University of New York.

The City University "Program to Discover College Potential Among the Young Men and Women of New York City" is a two-phased program, directed toward disadvantaged high school graduates and toward disadvantaged high school students. The first phase, the five-year College Discovery Program, began in the summer of 1964 at the Bronx Community College and the Queensboro Community College, supported by an appropriation of $500,000 from the New York State Legislature and an equal amount from New York City. Initially, 254 high school graduates were selected from nominees suggested by high school principals, all of them recommended as students with "native ability and drive which was not revealed in their academic grades." Approximately 234 of these students attended summer sessions at the two community colleges as special matriculants, taking remedial work in reading, speech, mathematics, languages (French, Spanish, or German), and sciences – in preparation for entry into regular college courses in the fall. It is planned to enroll 500 of these special matriculants in the program over the five-year period.

The second phase of the program, with funds provided by appropriations of $1 million from New York State and $500,000 from New York City, began in the fall of 1965, in cooperation with the New York City Board of Education. Its purpose is to identify high school boys and girls with undiscovered college potential and to improve their academic achievement and motivation for going to college. To this end, five Discovery and Development Centers will be established in high schools in the five boroughs of New York City. Each of these centers (a school within a school) will be organized as a two-year program, involving the eleventh and twelfth grades. Instruction will stress the development of reading skills, writing skills, study skills, and effective speech. Teachers of English and speech will be assigned reduced loads; class periods will be lengthened; guidance counselors will be provided; and summer classes will be conducted for students who need more than two years to attain college freshman achievement levels. Each student who successfully completes the center's program will be admitted to a unit of the City University of New York. A Social Dynamics Research Institute was established at the university in 1964 for the purpose of evaluating both phases of this program.

In cooperation with the local public school system in Pittsburgh (Pa.), the Carnegie Institute of Technology recently began a precollege preparatory program for disadvantaged high school students, with funds provided by a two-year grant of $106,800 from the Carnegie Corporation of New York. Known as the School-College Orientation Program of Pittsburgh (SCOPP), it seeks to strengthen the academic competence of underprivileged tenth-grade students "who, because of poor motivation, low level of aspiration, or poor preparation, would not normally think of college or prepare properly for it." Beginning with 43 participants in a summer school in 1964 and continuing on Saturdays throughout the year, the students were brought to the campus for instruction – expressly *not* remedial or tutorial – in biology, mathematics, and English. Program activities also include a series of cultural experiences for the students and counseling for both students and parents.

Several other institutions in Pennsylvania have also begun compensatory programs along this line. Examples are the precollege preparatory courses initiated during 1963–64 at the University of Pittsburgh; the Trial Admission Program begun during 1961–62 at Gannon College; and the Precollege Workshop Program (for rejected applicants) begun in the summer of 1963 at Point Park Junior College. The fact that this latter program involves a trimester fee of $315 plus books raises doubt concerning its accessibility to many socially disadvantaged students.

During the summer of 1965, Franklin and Marshall College (Pa.), supported by a personal gift from David Rockefeller, conducted an eight-week precollege enrichment program for 55 disadvantaged high school graduates. They were selected mainly from the 1965–66 entering freshman classes of five cooperating Negro colleges and universities – Cheyney State College (Pa.), Lincoln University (Pa.), Morgan State College (Md.), Delaware State College, and Florida Agricultural and Mechanical University.

These and related types of precollege programs are being developed at many other institutions across the country. To cite a few more examples: summer preparatory programs for disadvantaged high school students were conducted during 1964 and 1965 at Georgetown University (D. C.), Brown University (R. I.), Tuskegee Institute (Ala.), the University of North Carolina, Antioch College (Ohio), Jackson State College (Miss.), the University of California, Knoxville College (Tenn.), Northeastern University (Mass.), Luther College (Iowa), the University of Detroit, the University of Toledo, and others.

Thus, through special recruiting efforts, modification of admissions criteria, financial assistance, and a wide range of new preparatory programs for high school students and graduates, many institutions are helping a large number of socially disadvantaged young people, mainly Negroes, to begin college careers. These practices, although here described separately, are commonly associated in programs involving most of them. Despite the contrary impression suggested by the somewhat ambiguous frequencies of Table 5, there is no doubt that efforts along these lines constitute the most significant compensatory programs and practices currently being developed in the field of higher education.

These approaches to helping disadvantaged students enter college are paralleled by the practices and programs that are designed to help them succeed following admission. As has been noted, most common among them are special counseling and guidance services and noncredit remedial courses. Others include college-level remedial courses yielding credit, instruction in study skills, tutoring, special curriculums, lengthened time, and certain postgraduate arrangements. Most of these practices are generally well-known, and only a few of them warrant special comment here.

Although the practice of offering noncredit remedial courses – mainly in English, but also in mathematics – is still widespread, it appears to be losing ground. A substantial number of institutions reported that they recently discontinued this practice for a variety of reasons. The most common explanations were poor motivation on the part of students and lack of evidence that these courses improved subsequent academic performance. Several institutions reported that more stringent admissions requirements obviated the need for remedial courses. This suggests that their practices along this line may not have been truly compensatory.

The lengthened-time approach is illustrated by the special five-year undergraduate program that began at New York University in the fall of 1965, supported by a grant of $314,031 from the United States Office of Economic Opportunity. Involved are 60 disadvantaged boys selected from the June graduating classes of two depressed-area high schools in New York City: "Negroes, Puerto Ricans, and very poor whites with no expectation of going to college and few formal qualifications for higher education." They will study as a group at the university's School of Education, devoting the first three years to special remedial courses designed to qualify them for academic work on the junior and senior levels. The aim of this program is to prepare these students to teach in slum schools. Although relatively few institutions reported lengthened-time approaches, several noted that, obviously, extended time is "always available" to undergraduates who need it.

The Columbia-Woodrow Wilson Program at Columbia University (N. Y.) gives presumably disadvantaged college graduates an extra year of study in preparation for work on the graduate level. It undertakes "to select high ranking students from southern Negro colleges and give them what we refer to as a 'qualifying year.' This fifth year of study, while basically at the undergraduate level, also offers two or three graduate courses to the student so that when he reaches graduate school he does not find himself out of phase with the graduate school requirements."[5] Somewhat similarly, the so-called "buddy-schools" arrangement between Brown University (R. I.) and Tougaloo College (Miss.) includes a fifth-year program at Brown for

---

5. The report from Columbia University added: "Whether these students fall within your terminology of socially disadvantaged youth is for you to judge. . ."

Tougaloo graduates who need added preparation for graduate or professional studies.[6]

It appears that very few institutions are developing new compensatory curricular programs on the college level; most of those reported to this inquiry consist of the usual remedial courses and study-skills workshops. Notable, even so, are two comprehensive remedial curriculums developed during the past six or eight years.

In 1957, Morgan State College (Md.) began to require entering freshmen "who score in the lower half of both the English Placement Examination and the Psychological Examination to take the Basic Skills program." It is a one-year, noncredit program requiring from 19 to 21 clock-hours a week in a group of special courses in English, reading, science survey, social studies, physical education, health education, and military science. A student's performance in this remedial program determines whether he is dropped permanently or transferred to the regular college program.

In 1959, the Woodrow Wilson Branch of the Chicago City Junior College began to place all entering full-time freshmen who scored in the lowest tenth on a battery of intelligence, English, and reading tests in a special one year, noncredit remedial program, known as the Basic Curriculum. Approximately one-third of the entering freshmen are assigned to this program. They are required to take a three-hour rhetoric course, a two-hour remedial reading course, and a year's sequence in social science and natural science; and they may elect one course from a group of nonacademic courses, such as speech, music, art, typing, and remedial mathematics. Approximately three-fourths of these Basic Curriculum students complete the first year; about one-third of them enter regular college courses; and of this one-third only about 4 percent go on to finish junior college. Because so few of the students graduate, the college began in 1964 to reorient the pro-

---

6. The recent mutual-assistance pacts between paired institutions—one predominantly white and the other southern Negro—although outside the scope of this inquiry, are tangentially relevant. In addition to Brown and Tougaloo, they include cooperative agreements between Indiana University and Stillman College (Ala.), the University of Michigan and Tuskegee Institute (Ala.), Florida State University and Florida Agricultural and Mechanical University, the University of Tennessee and Knoxville College (Tenn.), University of North Carolina and North Carolina College at Durham, University of Wisconsin and Texas Southern University, and Cornell University (N. Y.) and Hampton Institute (Va.).

gram toward terminal ends, with emphasis upon consumer economics, speech, and job orientation.

Both of these special curricular programs appear largely to perform a screening function for public institutions which find it difficult to reject applicants with high school credentials. It is probable, however, that their emphasis upon remedial instruction makes some compensatory contribution to socially disadvantaged students.

One curricular innovation among college-level remedial programs involves the use of programed instruction. During 1962–63, for example, Knoxville College (Tenn.) conducted an experimental project with freshmen "to test an hypothesis that basic educational skills in remedial mathematics and English can be learned from automated programs as well as from familiar classroom practices." Programed learning machines were also used in the Gradual Learning Program which Whitworth College (Wash.) tried out for two years and then adopted as a regular program in 1964–65.

Special curricular modifications were involved in the Experimental Freshman Year program which the University of Southern Illinois conducted during 1962–63 for "educationally disadvantaged students."[7] Unlike three equated freshman groups with which they were compared, the students in the experimental group "had a completely new curriculum with emphasis on integrated studies, based on the concept that one learns to know himself and the nature of man through a sequential examination of universal systems – from the whole to the particular."

Although Northeastern University's Program to Increase Economic Opportunity for Negro Youth Through Higher Education on the Co-Operative Plan appears to involve no special modification of the academic curriculum, its work-study feature is unusual among compensatory programs addressed specifically to disadvantaged students. Begun in 1964 with support from the Fund for the Advancement of Education, the program enrolls 25 freshmen each year – "young Negro men and women who are qualified to profit from a college education, but who could not afford to at-

---

7. The respondent expressly rejected the term "socially disadvantaged students," but indicated that his preferred euphemism includes the "socially handicapped."

tend college without liberal financial assistance." In addition to their academic courses, these students are given related cooperative work assignments in a variety of career and professional fields with companies in the Greater Boston area.

This analysis of two big groups of compensatory programs and practices —those designed to help disadvantaged students enter college and others directed toward helping them succeed following admission — is based upon incomplete and otherwise inadequate data. Nevertheless, there emerges a reliable picture of widespread and varied efforts among many of the nation's colleges and universities to enhance the availability of higher education to socially disadvantaged young people. Moreover, the tempo of this development has accelerated markedly.

Objectives, rationales, and evaluations

The general purposes of these compensatory educational developments are apparent from the practices involved. Some further insight into the thinking behind them is afforded by a brief analysis of the objectives and rationales of the institutions reporting to this inquiry.

Practically all of the institutions reporting compensatory practices included statements about their specific objectives, most of which are really statements of general aims. They tend to cluster around several themes.

Most prevalent, of course, is the humanitarian aim of helping young people from disadvantaged social environments—especially those with talent — to develop their potential through higher education. Stated almost as frequently is the related aim of assisting these students to overcome academic deficiencies presumably resulting from poverty, discrimination, and inferior schooling. These two themes encompass the bulk of the objectives reported by the colleges and universities.

A few institutions stated broad social objectives relating to conservation of the nation's human resources, for example, "to enrich and upgrade the educational foundations of disprivileged strata." Perhaps noteworthy in this regard is the fact that several Roman Catholic colleges emphasized specifically the objective of relieving the pressing shortage of teachers by developing human potential otherwise likely to be wasted.

A number of institutions stated research objectives. For the most part, they reflect surveys or experimental investigations of the effectiveness of compensatory educational programs.

Rare but especially notable among the objectives stated by institutions of higher education is that of achieving a diversified student body. For example: "To benefit the institution by having on the campus students representing greatly diverse cultural and subcultural experiences, values, and so forth." "We endeavor to recruit qualified Negroes so as to have Negro youth in our student body." "To broaden the experiences of students by arranging for young people from other cultural backgrounds to attend the university." "To provide beneficial diversity in the student body."

What is especially significant about these objectives is their departure from the social uplift theme. They imply that a student body diverse in racial and social-class composition is beneficial for all students.

Only 40 percent of the 224 institutions reporting compensatory practices responded to the question: "What is the rationale behind the 1963-64 practices checked above?" Perhaps some of those not responding considered the answer too obvious to warrant a reply. Perhaps also, some of them had not yet formulated statements of rationale. For the most part, the statements submitted echo the general themes around which the asserted objectives tend to cluster.

Most of the responding institutions expressed the rationale behind their compensatory practices in terms of the social responsibility of colleges and universities: "Educators must not be passive in just passing through what comes to them; they must correct the situation of waste of able people – must help in hunting and placing them. . . ." "It is the social obligation of the institution to locate and provide for the education of highly promising but socially disadvantaged students." "A state college must serve the needs of all the children of all the people, provided they demonstrate some capacity to benefit from higher education." "The community college is committed to assisting in every way possible the citizens of the community."

Closely related to this social-responsibility rationale is the asserted obligation to further equality of educational opportunity: "The college has the obligation to equalize as nearly as possible the imbalance of opportunities experienced by students who apply. . . ." "Every person should be educated to his fullest capacity." "All people capable of profiting from a college education should be given the opportunity." "Most adults and virtually all high school graduates should have a chance at education beyond the high school."

A premise implicit in all efforts to remedy academic deficiencies among disadvantaged students – that conventional measures do not validly assess their college potential – was stated explicitly as the rationale behind the compensatory practices of many institutions. For example:

"We are not completely convinced that high school grades and particularly the College Entrance Examination Board give us the proper knowledge we seek."

"Current trends have raised the entrance requirements of degree programs . . . Students who would have been qualified for regular admission a few years ago are now admitted on probation or denied admission . . . Many of the students are deficient in basic communication skills, and often lack confidence in their academic abilities. Such students could benefit from a program aimed at these weaknesses. . . ."

"Reliance upon higher and higher admission standards does not attempt to take into account motivational factors which are admittedly important in attaining success in college."

"The underlying philosophy of Basic Curriculum is that the student's deficiency is more the lack of skills in reading, writing, and study techniques than it is a deficiency of innate intelligence."

"Many students from local schools . . . have not had curricular offerings given in larger schools. This applies to mathematics and languages particularly. Consequently, these applicants make lower scores in College Boards. They should be given some consideration, since they often prove their competence if they are given a chance to do college work."

Involved here, of course, is an issue concerning selective admissions that relates to students generally, not merely the socially disadvantaged, and around which there is currently much debate among college admissions officials. Apparently many institutions reporting compensatory practices have taken a clear position on the question. They seem to agree with

Kendrick's assertion that "we must suspect that children who are cultural-ly and socially disadvantaged are probably underestimated fairly often" on the basis of their college-entrance test scores. Perhaps they agree also with his admonition that even though "we have no warrant to assume that the score is biased . . . it is extremely important that an unusually thorough in-vestigation be made to determine whether or not the total environment of the candidate over the years justifies a suspicion that the test does not fit the student."[8]

Several institutions interpreted their compensatory practices in terms of their educational value to the advantaged as well as the disadvantaged stu-dents. Relevant are these unabridged statements of rationale by two insti-tutions which asserted the diversity-of-student-body objective.

From Rockford College (Ill.): "We believe that one of the advantages of the small liberal college is that students are thrown into close proximity physically, intellectually, and emotionally. If the college has a diverse stu-dent body then the experience gained in student to student interaction is broadly educational in and of itself and supports the more formal academic, intellectual, and creative activities sponsored by the college. This not only would meet the needs of advantaged students for growth and development through close experience with 'different' ideas, behaviors, and so forth, but also calls upon them to make a contribution of a personal nature to the growth and development of the less advantaged. Thus it sets in motion or elicits a spontaneous program which, because of its spontaneity, is difficult to formalize (especially on paper) and which we believe makes a greatly productive contribution to the development of the disadvantaged student and to his incorporation into the larger culture."

From Brandeis University (Mass.): "The practices checked indicate Bran-deis' rather low key efforts to assist socially disadvantaged youth in obtain-ing the fruits which college training and degrees will bring them in terms of social and occupational choice and mobility, and personal fulfillment. The practices are deemed twice blessed. First, in terms of benefits to the

---

8. S. A. Kendrick, "College Board Scores and Cultural Bias." *College Board Review* No. 55, Winter 1964–65, pp. 7–9.

student; second, in terms of benefits to the college. The first aspect is often the one emphasized but the second is of equal importance for without it the first cannot be realized.

"Students from socially disadvantaged areas bring to their more advantaged peers a way of looking and labeling which is a positive contribution to the latter's education. Socially disadvantaged students who are made to feel that they are making a real contribution are free of nagging guilt feelings about being marginal, unimportant, and so on. It is from this point of view that we make no major academic considerations for these students. They must not be made to feel as a group apart, but rather as full members of the community with unique, individual, and important contributions to make.

"We should make every effort (counseling, finances, and so forth), therefore, to bring them to the educational threshold – that point from which they can fully participate in Brandeis. We have not realized this ideal, as will be evidenced from some of the other answers."

The philosophical and theoretical premises which underlie any educational practice decisively influence its nature and the quality of its outcomes. It may be assumed, therefore, that the differing emphases revealed by this summary of the stated rationales behind institutions' compensatory programs and practices reflect real differences in their content and effects.

The institutions surveyed in the spring of 1964 were asked to note and send reports of evaluations of their compensatory programs and practices, mainly for the purpose of defining the nature and extent of such evaluation procedures. Many of those with compensatory practices reported informal evaluations, but very few of them reported and provided evidence of systematic appraisals.

The informal judgments expressed with regard to the several types of compensatory practices are not very revealing. Typical responses are: "very effective," "satisfactory results," "worked well," "moderately effective," "seems to be effective but too early to decide," "significantly improved academic performance," "ineffective," "much remains to be done," "not sure whether it's effective or not," "questionable," "little value," and "ineffective." A majority of responses were definitely positive.

Systematic evaluations ranging from simple before-and-after tests to carefully designed experiments were reported by eight institutions. They relate to the previously mentioned remedial English and mathematics program at Tuskegee Institute; the remedial first-year curriculums at Morgan State College and Woodrow Wilson Junior College; the programed learning experiment at Knoxville College; the Trial Admission Program at Gannon College; the Operation Second Chance project and College Discovery Program at Bronx Community College; and the School-College Orientation Program of Pittsburgh at Carnegie Institute of Technology.

A number of compensatory programs with evaluation research designs have been developed since this questionnaire survey was made. This is especially true of many of the precollege preparatory programs for disadvantaged high school students during the summers of 1964 and 1965. It is clear, however, that systematic evaluation of compensatory programs and practices in higher education is quite rare.[9]

Some general observations

This analysis of the extent and nature of compensatory programs and practices among the nation's colleges and universities reveals several developments and issues that invite emphasis and brief comment.

The major generalization warranted by the data is that a substantial number of institutions of higher education are attempting through a variety of approaches to help socially disadvantaged young people who could not otherwise do so to enter and succeed in college. Further, such efforts have grown markedly in extent and intensity during the past two or three years. It is important to note, however, that proportionately very few of the nation's colleges and universities have thus far begun to develop compensatory programs and practices; and most of those that have are serving very small numbers of disadvantaged students.

---

9. In this connection, it appears that extremely few research evaluations of such programs have thus far appeared in professional literature. The only ones known to this inquiry are: Morris Meister, Abraham Tauber, and Sidney Silverman, "Operation Second Chance." *Junior College Journal* No. 33, October 1962, pp. 78–88; and tangentially related, Kenneth B. Clark and Lawrence Plotkin, *The Negro Student at Integrated Colleges*. New York: National Scholarship Service and Fund for Negro Students, 1963.

The recently predominating emphasis upon assisting disadvantaged Negro youth to get a college education undoubtedly reflects the increasingly important role of the Negro people in the life of the nation. It is fully warranted. Nevertheless, there appears to be undue neglect in providing compensatory services on the college level for disadvantaged young people of other minority groups in different parts of the country, especially American Indians, Mexican-Americans, and Puerto Ricans. Moreover, except for the work of a few institutions, the vast population of socially disadvantaged white youths in rural areas, particularly in the South, seems hardly to have been touched by recent compensatory developments in higher education.

The large contributions of several great foundations to the support of many new financial aid programs, precollege preparatory programs, and other compensatory programs addressed mainly to disadvantaged Negro students are impressive. Although on a higher educational level, this development reminds one of an earlier period, just before and after World War I, when the massive intervention of another group of foundations[10] was decisive in stimulating the revival of Negro education following its virtual destruction during the last quarter of the nineteenth century.

Current and increasing efforts to attract socially disadvantaged college students tend to collide with recent trends toward higher and higher admissions standards, and most institutions resolve the conflict by restricting their recruiting efforts to disadvantaged students with already demonstrated talent. It would seem, however, that full commitment to the compensatory principle calls for increased efforts to enroll and help risk candidates among disadvantaged high school graduates.

The development of precollege preparatory programs for disadvantaged high school students – especially the new summer schools on college campuses – constitutes an alternate and very important approach to the problem of maintaining high admissions standards *and* recruiting larger numbers of disadvantaged students. It warrants further extension.

This recent burgeoning of precollege preparatory programs indicates

---

10. Including the Peabody Fund, Slater Fund, Southern Education Foundation, Anna T. Jeanes Foundation, Phelps-Stokes Fund, Julius Rosenwald Fund, General Education Board, and others.

that a number of colleges are beginning to move directly into the field traditionally preempted by the secondary school. That there is need for them to do so reflects widespread incompetence among public school systems in educating socially disadvantaged young people.

Whereas many of the precollege preparatory programs include imaginative and apparently valid curricular innovations designed to overcome academic deficiencies born of social disadvantage, this is seldom true of the special college-level curricular programs and practices serving compensatory ends. Most of the latter seem to fit the somewhat dreary pattern of remedial courses which have plagued many generations of low-achieving students with but little benefit to most of them. There is need for fresh approaches in special curricular programs for disadvantaged students on the college level.

Although the careful assessment of students' performance is frequent and practically universal on all levels of American education, the careful appraisal of educational programs is rare. It is not surprising, therefore, that very few of the compensatory programs in higher education have been systematically evaluated. That more of them be so evaluated is essential if the profession is to have reliable guidelines for further developments.

One cannot but be impressed with the humanitarian and more broadly social motivations which seem to underlie most institutions' efforts to attract disadvantaged young people and help them get a college education. One wonders, however, to what if any extent the prevailing "social-uplift" rationale operates to limit the effectiveness of such efforts. It would seem that a more fruitful guiding principle is that the interaction of students from different racial and social-class groups is beneficial to them all. Compensatory programs and practices which reflect this conviction, as is the case in a few institutions, are likely to be permeated by a spirit that makes a maximum contribution to educational development.

The conscious and impersonal social forces which gave impetus to recent compensatory developments in higher education are likely to continue their influence with increasing intensity, and current efforts along this line are far from adequate to cope with the growing need. Their further extension is both desirable and probable.

7. A critique of compensatory education

If the success of our efforts at facilitating the educational development of disadvantaged youngsters could be evaluated simply on the basis of the amount of enthusiasm and activity generated by those efforts, we would at once declare the majority of the programs studied successful. As was the case with the much heralded Project Head Start, the wide acceptance of the idea, the involvement of many segments of the community, and the political momentum building up behind such efforts, combine to give the impression of success. In communities large and small, in schools public and private, in preschool, elementary school, high school, and college, and in graduate and professional institutions all across the nation, we find growing concern reflected in special projects directed at the disadvantaged.

It appears at first glance that the efforts directed at desegregating our schools and improving educational opportunities for children from low income families have resulted in important and impressive modifications in the work of our schools. A wide variety of ideas for improving the effectiveness of the school has been advanced, hardly any one of which has not received at least a degree of consideration and trial in some school system during the past few years. In fact, there are some school systems in which practically every serious proposal has been tried with some group of its pupils.

Problems in program evaluation

The appropriateness of a practice or the success of a program cannot be adequately judged from the enthusiasm with which it is embraced or the speed with which the practice spreads. Educational innovation, unfortunately, has too long a history of approaching evaluation and decision making on such an inadequate basis. At the very least, evaluation of compensatory education would seem to require a precise description of the newly introduced educational practices, of the specific conditions under which they are initiated, and of the populations to whom they are applied; the careful identification of target population and of appropriate control groups for whom specified criterion measures are established; and the collection and analysis of data appropriate to the measures identified. Despite the almost landslide acceptance of the compensatory education commitment, we find nowhere an effort at evaluating these innovations that approaches the criteria suggested. Where evaluative studies have been conducted, the reports typically show ambiguous outcomes affecting unknown or amorphous educational and social variables.

This unhappy circumstance is likely to encourage premature and contradictory educational planning and decision making. On the one hand, apparent but meager gains by pupils in pilot projects may give rise to unduly optimistic interpretations, thus encouraging extensive long-term commitment to compensatory programs whose validity has not yet been established. On the other hand, lack of clear evidence that certain programs or practices are improving pupils' development to any significant degree may strengthen tendencies toward their abandonment, and even toward repudiation of the entire compensatory education effort. Neither of these reactions is warranted. It is clear beyond doubt that special problems exist in relation to the education of many children from disadvantaged backgrounds. It is also clear that some of these children are helped immensely by the special efforts of our schools. It is not yet clear exactly what helps which youngsters under what conditions. We do not know why certain practices that seem logically correct do not work. We have yet to determine which aspects of some of our more elaborate programs actually account for the reported changes. There remain unanswered critical questions related to motivation and to the reversibility of learning disabilities which arise from deprivations in experience. Some of these questions may be approached theoretically. For others, which must be examined empirically, answers may be sought from a critical review of our current experiences in compensatory education.

Assessing the major developments and trends

Viewed as a group, current compensatory programs are surprisingly recent. Of 76 programs for which starting dates were available, 93 percent were begun since 1960, and 43 percent just since 1963. Relatively few of them have been set up on a controlled experimental basis to determine whether specific innovations result in improved school performance; however, a number of them are concerned with the total effect of a multiphase program on the target population. For all their variety of means, the programs have generally suffered from one fundamental difficulty—they are based on sentiment rather than on fact. Or, at best, those facts on which they are based are the obvious ones: that a population exists which is not able to benefit from the education being served up by the schools, that that population has certain common characteristics (the programs are less likely to be sensitive to the differences) among which are low reading ability, low general school achievement, low interest and motivation level, poor health status, and so forth. The great majority of the programs are simply an attempt to "do something" about these problems. Their stated aims are usually couched in unarguable generalities, "to raise achievement level," "to raise the sights of the students," "to enlarge the students' horizons," "to awaken parents to the value of an education." The urge to do something has been so compelling that many of the programs have been designed without grounding in any systematic study of ends and means.

It is not inappropriate that the programs of special education for the disadvantaged have been described as compensatory. They are attempts to compensate for, or to overcome, the effects of hostile, different, or indifferent backgrounds. Their aim is to bring children from these backgrounds up to a level where they can be reached by *existing* educational practices. And it is in terms of this aim that we tend to judge their success or lack of it. A compensatory program in the seventh grade would be held successful if it enabled its participants to move into a "regular" eighth-grade program. Or, to cite another example, if preschool programs in general might measure their success by how well their graduates adjusted to traditional kindergarten and first-grade activities. In other words, the unexpressed purpose of most compensatory programs is to make disadvantaged children as much as possible like the kinds of children with whom the school has been successful, and our standard of educational success is how well they approximate middle-class children in school performance. It is not at all clear that the concept of compensatory education is the one which will most appropriately meet the problems of the disadvantaged. These children are *not* middle-class children, many of them never *will* be, and they can never be anything but second-rate as long as they are thought of as potentially middle-class children. (They may become middle-class adults, however, and some certainly have middle-class aspirations.) At best they are different, and an approach which views this difference merely as something to be overcome is probably doomed to failure. What is needed is not so much an attempt to fill in the gaps as an approach which asks the question: What kind of educational experience is most appropriate to what these children are and to what our society is becoming?

Once this question has been posed, it brings into focus the really crucial issue, that is, the matter of whom we are trying to change. We have tended until now to concentrate our efforts on the children. Unwilling to abandon what we think we have learned about teaching through our years of educating, with some success, the children of the middle- and upper-classes, we have tried adding and multiplying our existing techniques to arrive at a formula for success with less privileged children. We have tried to help them by giving them more of what we already know how to do—more guidance, more remedial reading, more vocational information, more enrichment activities. We have said to these children, "We will prepare you for our school system, we will help you to catch up when you fall behind, we will show you the kinds of lives other kinds of children already know about, and if you get discouraged and drop out we will try our best to get you back." But what we have not said is, "We will take you as you are, and ourselves assume the burden of finding educational techniques appropriate to your needs." We have asked of them a degree of change far greater than any that we as educators have been willing to make in our own institutions.

It seems significant, for example, that so much of the current work in the education of the disadvantaged has been directed either at preschool children or at youngsters who have dropped out of high school, while so little attention has been given to investigating the overall appropriateness of contemporary educational processes. If school people were not such a decent lot, one would think that these two emphases have been so widely accepted simply because they require the least change in the school itself. It is often easier to add extensions than to change the basic structure of institutions.

There are, of course, logical arguments to support the preschool emphasis. There is no question that children who grow up under different life conditions are likely to show different developmental patterns. Unless experiential input has been designed to produce the same learning readiness end, such readiness will vary. Consequently, it is not inappropriate to assume that children coming from privileged homes enter school with skills and competences different from those of children from less privileged homes. And since all these children, despite the differences present upon entry, must meet common academic standards, the disadvantaged child, it is argued, needs special remedial or enrichment experiences in order to better cope with the traditional school requirements.

Following the logic of this position, educational programs for nursery school-age children from disadvantaged backgrounds have gained wide acceptance, this despite the fact of early evidence suggesting that there is little value in the nursery or preschool educational experience in the absence of continuity and consistent high quality for the nursery, kindergarten, and primary grades experience. Special program gains seem to wash out in the absence of subsequent school experiences that build upon the head start.

The preschool movement, strengthened by massive federal support since the initiation of Project Head Start in the summer of 1965, has become one of the major forces in the nation's war against poverty and in the school's effort at meeting the educational problems of disadvantaged youngsters. The quickly organized national push, however, is not likely to do as well as its experimental precursors, for many of these programs do not consistently meet the needs of the children they enroll. While they rarely fail to provide an atmosphere that is warm and accepting, they are not always as successful in providing an atmosphere that offers psychological support to each child — some of whose needs may run more to order, firmness, and discipline than to a free, unstructured atmosphere and uncritical warmth. Preschool classes, more than any other compensatory programs, have often been started and staffed by ardent, well-meaning but untrained amateurs — a shortage of well-trained, professional teachers at the preschool level being only one facet of a personnel shortage that haunts all phases of compensatory educational programs. These amateurs bring to their work many virtues and some skills, but not among them frequently are the specific techniques for providing the kind of directed pre-academic experiences that will really equip these disadvantaged youngsters to start and move ahead in school. Although relatively little is known about the specific kinds of experiences that are most effective in encouraging language development and language acquisition, certainly more is known than is being widely utilized. Experimental programs that test the efficacy of new approaches to concept formation, to the acquisition of learning set, to the wider utilization of symbols, and so forth, are vital to provide us with continuing insights into the types of activities that should be included in a truly effective preschool program.

Certainly, as advocates of public education, we should welcome this downward extension of public education to include the three- to five-year-olds. However, we should be unprepared to accept this downward extension as a substitute for new, different, and greater effort in those school grades that are now traditional. It is also somewhat arbitrary, in the light of some of the work of Piaget and Hunt, to settle for intervention at the third year of life and not at the eighteenth month or during the first year of life. If we are serious about the importance of early encounters with the environment, it may be that we must take greater collective responsibility for influencing life experience from birth and even for controlling the quality of the physical environment before birth. It is unlikely however that our society will be ready for the revolutionary social changes involved in this kind of commitment for a good many years to come.

If preschool programs represent the earliest intervention we have yet become involved with, dropout programs represent the last intervention of the school into the lives of these youth. Unfortunately, their very lateness mitigates against their success. Where dropout programs operate on the junior high school level – and are really special educational programs modified to suit particular children rather than antidropout programs – they are more likely to be effective. Because the sad fact is that a high school dropout, or a young person who is simply waiting impatiently in school to reach the age when he can drop out, tends to be a youth for whom school has represented perennial failure. If when he drops out of school he does not find a job – which is most likely – his failure has been compounded. It seems highly unlikely that such a youth, lured back to school by the understanding advice of a guidance counselor, has any greater basis for success, whatever the concessions made by the school, than he had when he left. Nothing significant has happened to change his estimate of school, of education, of life, or of himself. Furthermore, in the case of minority group youngsters, the opportunity structure of the job market is, as they often know, such as to make their education almost irrelevant. Negro and Puerto Rican youngsters who graduated from high school were shown in one study to be earning, on the average, only about $5 a week more, seven years after graduation, than those who had dropped out. In addition, the lifetime earnings of Negro college graduates are about equal to those of white high school graduates. This is, of course, if they are employed at all. As one researcher commented, "We are almost in the position of counseling them to stay in school so that they can become unemployed high school graduates." Obviously the answer to the dropout problem lies far back along the educational track—back in grammar school and kindergarten where the failures begin. But for those who have passed through the system and come, frustrated, embittered, demoralized, and uneducated, out the other end, the answer would seem to lie in somehow providing them with experiences in formal education and work from which they can gain both a sense of personal responsibility and a sense of personal success. From such experiences, eventually, they may also gain the courage and motivation to face their previous areas of failure and so resume their commitment to learning. The weakness of so many of the dropout programs that have tried to do just this is that they have been unable, through no particular fault of their own, to provide meaningful work for meaningful pay to the youths they are trying to help. Of even greater significance, however, is the failure of the school to identify those approaches to curriculum content and organization that take into account the special learning problems of persons who are essentially adult but developmentally handicapped. Simple or complex changes in schedule, changes in sequence of material presentation, and changes in the quality or quantity of material presented are inadequate. If we succeed in holding these young people in school or in attracting them back to formal learning situations, and they learn only that we have not yet developed the capability to insure that they achieve literacy, concept mastery, and ability to utilize new knowledge, we cannot claim success for antidropout programs.

Even if the school succeeds in combining remunerative work and more appropriate formal learning experiences, it will, unfortunately, not have totally met the problems of potential school dropouts and ex-dropouts. Substantial modifications must indeed be made in curriculum material, content, and methods, but significant innovations will also be required in the job market. Work and formal learning have yet to be integrated in the development of new jobs—including those at the preprofessional or sub-professional level—which provide for upward mobility by making auto-matic provision for continued training. To settle, as so many programs do, for jobs—any jobs—is not only inadequate but uneconomical and basically dishonest. What do we gain when we invest training and placement re-sources in solutions which only postpone for a few months or a year the long-term problems of career development? To lure a youngster back into school and to train him for a vanishing job, to place him in that job and to claim that we have been successful, may contribute to the statistical suc-cess of a project, but makes no real contribution to the solution of the prob-lems of young adults who drop out or do poorly in school. Programs that follow such practices, and many dropout programs do, are simply practic-ing rank deception.

It is entirely possible that a successful attack upon the problems of school dropouts and unemployable youth will require not so much a greater effort directed at these young people, but a greater effort at identifying for them and facilitating their assumption of roles in the fiber of our society that have meaning. We know from the rehabilitative influence of military ex-perience on some of these youths that there is a tremendous potential for development and productivity latent in this population. The individual behavior traditionally associated with stability and upward mobility are likely to be most easily achieved as a by-product of involvement in activi-ties on which society places importance and for which it offers tangible rewards. One possible answer might be a Peace Corps or a National Service Corps less oriented than the present Peace Corps toward the altruistic concerns of middle-class young adults—an organization in which the pay is good, in which the work is challenging, and in which membership commands respect. Such a corps would come closer to answering the needs of these young people whose conditions of life leave them with little interest in volunteer community service. And, finally, it may not even be sufficient to the problems presented by this segment of the population to provide good pay for respected work. Because these young people tend to be alienated from the values and goals professed by the society at large, it may also be necessary that their work and their opportunities for education and self-advancement be directly related to influencing the political-social power structure. One of the characteristics of earlier periods in our nation's history when uneducated and alienated people succeeded in the system was the fact that opportunities then existed for these newcomers to move into and influence the power structure of the communities in which they settled. The work they did paid off not only in terms of money, but also in terms of homes, communities, institutions, businesses, and industries in which they had gained or could aspire to varying degrees of control. In other words, the work and the rewards were not artificial, and although they were also not guaranteed, they at least had meaning in a relatively open opportunity structure. It may be that what is critically missing from our programs for unemployable youth is any realistic opportunity for their participation in the decision-making processes that control their lives. To provide this opportunity, society may have to reexamine some of its basic economic and political tenets which have thus far precluded consideration of more radical approaches to the creation of new—and the rehabilitation of old—institutions, industries, and communities.

In the last few years it has become an acknowledged fact that teaching the disadvantaged is a specialized task. It cannot be left only to the newest teachers, who may have no choice in their assignments, nor to the older teachers, "left over" in the center-city schools after the pupils whom they knew how to teach have gone elsewhere. The growing recognition of this fact is evidenced by the degree to which teacher training and retraining projects figure in programs of compensatory education. Unfortunately, it is doubtful that any short-range orientation or inservice teacher training courses will move us far toward the long-range goal of providing satisfactory levels of instruction in disadvantaged schools. This is so because the problem of staffing "unpopular" schools is merely the most difficult aspect of an already difficult problem—an overall shortage of qualified personnel. Much of what has been written about teaching the disadvantaged has been written as if such a shortage did not exist. It is all very well to talk about screening teachers for their attitudinal suitability to teach in depressed area schools, but the fact is that in many communities there is almost no one to screen. It may be theoretically sound to propose the effective reduction of classroom size by assigning highly trained and specialized personnel to problem schools, but the fact is that before we can begin to multiply classrooms by reducing their size, we will have to get teachers into the classrooms we now have. This personnel problem is one that time will only intensify. By the early 1970s, one-third of the population will probably be in our educational system somewhere between kindergarten and graduate school. We are going to need teachers to manage all these classrooms and, without some concerted effort on the part of educators and of society in general, it is highly unlikely that we will have them.

Even if we had an unlimited pool of willing candidates from which to choose, we would still have no assurance that we could put into depressed area classrooms teachers qualified to provide the kinds of educational experiences these children need. Training programs have invested time and money in improving teacher competence and teacher behavior but neither research nor practice has yet provided definite guidelines as to what should be emphasized in such training. When Koenigsberg studied teachers who were thought by their administrators to be successful with disadvantaged children, she found no objective evidence of their superiority in this area. Some programs stress the human relations approach, but in our own investigations of this area, we have observed allegedly good teachers who, judged by colloquial standards, seemed to be lacking in the traditional human relation traits like warmth, support, and sympathy. Other programs stress understanding the culture and values of the poor. Yet we know that a good bit of this "awareness of the child's background" gets distorted into gossip about the number of men with whom their mothers sleep, and is seldom reflected in significantly changed teacher attitudes.

There is more than adequate justification for concern with the problems of teacher attitude. Unfortunately, much of this concern is expressed in suggestions that teachers be warm, accepting, supportive, nonpunitive, and so forth, while insufficient attention has been given to the value of an attitude of positive expectation – the expectation that these children *can* learn, and that teacher activity and curricular design *can* be effective in the teaching-learning process. There is increasing evidence that the teacher's awareness of the potential of her pupils not only influences her attitude as to what she may expect of them, but influences their performance as well. Clarke and Clarke (1954), in a follow-up study of a group of children who until they were three had been classed as mental retardates, found these children at age 10 to be of normal intelligence. At the age of three these children had been placed with foster parents who were told they were normal. A matched group of children who remained institutionalized were judged at the age of 10 to be essentially mentally subnormal. Rosenthal (1959), among others, has demonstrated that when psychology students are told that the children they are about to test are superior, those children perform significantly better than do other children who have been described as poor learners, although both groups of children are, in fact, equal in ability. In the light of such findings, approaches to teacher retraining focused on improving teacher attitude as a means of improving pupil performance might assume primary importance in compensatory programs.

As far as the problem of staffing depressed-area schools is concerned, the school systems might, as a first step, concern themselves with the functional ability rather than the paper qualifications of potential teaching personnel. If, as former Assistant Secretary for Education Keppel has observed, there are school systems in which teachers with two years of relevant experience in the Peace Corps are technically unqualified to teach, one would doubt the rationality of those systems. The use of volunteer or paid subprofessionals to perform nonteaching functions, and what would seem to be a general overcoming of the antipathy of school systems toward enthusiastic laymen in the classroom, suggests that in some school systems human needs are beginning to outweigh bureaucratic needs. This approach, of course, must be tempered with an awareness that good will is not for long an adequate substitute for technical competence.

It is not only movement from the bottom which has met with hostility in school situations. Many times the introduction at top levels of "specialist" or "resource" personnel has met with a kind of stony resistance on the part of the classroom teachers with a resultant underutilization of the services these auxiliary personnel are offering. It is rarely profitable to introduce into an existing school hierarchy a curriculum expert who is not at the same time a human relations expert, because it takes a particularly sensitive person to provide assistance to experienced personnel without at the same time causing resentment. One suggested approach to this problem is the retraining of the status people already in the school, although one would have to evaluate the degree to which the older, more established teachers are actually susceptible to retraining.

Aside from any hostility derived from a concern for status, some teachers are honestly convinced that, given the overcrowding of the classrooms in many of these schools, any additional personnel should be given classroom assignments in order to reduce overall classroom size. In evaluating the Higher Horizons Program, the 10 percent of the teachers who recommended canceling the program felt that the special Higher Horizon's personnel could much better be used in the classroom. And the fact is, that until programs are designed with more effective built-in evaluative procedures, there is no one who can tell them they are wrong.

Probably the most productive approach to changed teacher behavior and attitudes is that which emphasizes providing teachers with new and improved tools. It is instructive in this respect to recall the experimental work of K. S. Lashley. In the middle twenties it was a widely held view that laboratory rats were unable to discriminate among geometric forms. They could make brightness discriminations, but experimenters consistently found that rats could not discriminate between, say, a triangle and a circle. Lashley hypothesized that the problem lay not in the rats' inability to discriminate, but in the experimenters' failure to devise an adequate learning situation. So Lashley modified the demands of the learning situation by reducing sources of extraneous stimuli, limiting the range of alternative responses, and increasing the drive state of the experimental animals. Under the changed conditions for learning, he was able to teach rats to make discriminations among a variety of geometric forms.

If appropriate learning situations can be designed to enable rats to learn discriminations they are supposedly unable to make, is it not possible that appropriate classroom situations and procedures can be devised to enable all children to learn those things many children are already learning? We cannot expect the teachers in their individual classrooms to find for themselves all of the necessary teaching techniques and learning situations appropriate to these children. Taking a cue from the experience with the new mathematics curriculum, the Zacharias Commission has stressed the importance of new instruments and methods that work in achieving behavioral change in teachers. It is easy for teachers to slip into attitudes of defeat and indifference when they see little return for their efforts – and it is hard for them to remain indifferent and unchallenged when their efforts begin to meet with success.

A weakness of teacher training programs and of our overall programs of education for the disadvantaged is our failure to match the revolutions taking place in society with a revolution in the teaching-learning process. We have not yet removed the burden of proof from the shoulders of the learner and placed the responsibility for the success of the academic venture on the shoulders of the school system, where it belongs.

In no area is this misplaced responsibility more obvious than in the area of curriculum innovation. Remedial education programs have been developed, teacher-pupil ratio has been reduced, new materials have been produced, classroom grouping has been modified – all sensible and appropriate changes, but they represent no basic alteration in the teaching-learning process. They are likely to result in increasing the number of children who succeed, but they are unlikely to meet our era's real challenge to the schools, that of insuring that all children, save those with significant neurological defects, achieve competence in the development and use of ideas as well as mastery of the basic academic skills.

Most of what is being done in the area of curriculum change is being done in line with a tradition of unscientific innovation in the school system. Many of the innovations consume considerable time and money. Few of them are based on identifiable theoretical premises or verifiable hypotheses. Very often these innovations appear to have resulted from isolated, poorly controlled trial and error discoveries, and all too often the new practice is supported only by the exhortation of its enthusiasts. For example, there is little empirical evidence or theoretical basis for judging either homogeneous or heterogeneous groupings as providing the more effective learning situation. Homogeneous grouping may, indeed, provide an *easier* teaching situation, but in practice it often serves simply to segregate the minority-group children from their more privileged peers. Given the evidence suggesting that segregation is, per se, a handicap to the achievement of educational equality, and given, in addition, the social problems of the time, it might be well for school systems to examine the premise on which they have overwhelmingly adopted homogeneous groupings. It is quite possible that the more difficult teaching situation provided by heterogeneous grouping is also the more productive in the total development of the child.

Team teaching is another structural modification for which the justifications are largely those relating to more effective use of personnel, rather than to any presumption that it is an effective method of handling disadvantaged children. Where block-time programing has been introduced at the junior high school level, its introduction has been justified on the basis that these children are not ready to move out of the single-teacher, single-classroom situation. If these children at a secondary school level need identification with one teacher, it might be appropriate to assume that the greater flexibility which team teaching allows to the administration in the use of personnel does not necessarily result in psychological benefit to the children themselves. On the other hand, perhaps the need for personal identification with the teacher may be better met under team teaching conditions where the higher teacher-pupil ratio allows for more meaningful, if not more consistent, teacher-pupil interaction.

These structural rearrangements, like a number of other innovations which have been called compensatory, are really attempts to bring the schools up to date. Such additions as audiovisual aids, science equipment in the elementary schools, and programed learning, are simply modernizations that may or may not have relevance to providing appropriate education for the disadvantaged.

One of the most interesting things about these efforts at modification and improvement is the absence of anything really new or radically innovative in pedagogy. Most of these programs utilize common sense, or traditional procedures, or both, which are or should be a part of any good educational program. In fact, it is something of an indictment that these practices have not been introduced earlier into the education of the less privileged.

But if curriculum development is to be significantly innovative, we might well give greater attention to the effect of intragroup interaction on the teaching-learning process. Professionals concerned with such fields as decision processes and psychotherapy have developed elaborate systems of theory and practice based upon concepts of group dynamics. This sophistication has not yet been appropriately applied to education. Other advances in curriculum development and modification might well be achieved through exploring different ways of organizing learning experiences to meet individual differences in readiness. This readiness may vary with respect to the functional capacity to discriminate between things seen, heard, tasted, or felt. It may vary with respect to habit patterns that have been established around these sensory functions. Readiness may vary, based upon the dominance of one aspect of sensory function over another. The plea here is for curriculum development that takes into account available knowledge concerning significant variations in the organization and operation of the senses. Work with neurologically impaired subjects has provided insight into the significance of variations in sensory and perceptual function for efficiency in learning. This work has also made us aware of the possibility that normal individuals vary widely with respect to behaviors dependent upon such functions. But of greatest significance is the contribution that work with these neurologically damaged subjects has made to the design of modified procedures for teaching and training. Because man's function is not alone determined by his biological characteristics but also by his encounters with the environment, it may well be that children whose life experiences vary, have significant variations in function. If this is in fact the case, the leads provided by the special education model should be rich with possibilities for curriculum design for socially disadvantaged children. Furthermore, if individuals, independently of experience or station in life, differ with respect to the degree to which they are inclined to respond with one or another of the senses, it may be that one of the significant variables in learning ability and disability may be the quality of support provided for the learning experience when the pattern of the learning task presented does not complement the sensory organization of the learner. Understanding the interaction between these two phenomena in the learning process will provide a new dimension along which curriculum materials may be designed and content organized.

Our concern with learner-environment interaction provides a new life space for the curriculum. From developments in programed instruction we have learned something of the usefulness of modifying the rate and sequence in which learning experiences and materials are presented. We have yet to explore the significance of larger scale modifications in sequence, where instead of breaking down and reordering the structure of a single concept, broad categories of curriculum material and content are subjected to such sequential modifications. However, the formal curriculum elements are not the only elements in the environment which impinge on the learner. Of equal importance are the social, psychological, and physical environments in which learning occurs. This is not to say that educators have heretofore been indifferent to these environments. The importance of the climate for learning is "old hat" in education. But innovation will grow from our awareness of a far broader set of dimensions along which these environments may be manipulated. In recognition of variations in response patterns, *within* as well as *between* learners, dependent upon the circumstances and nature of the learning task, the various aspects of these environments may be manipulated to achieve certain learning outcomes.

These examples by no means exhaust the possibilities for new or greatly modified approaches to curriculum design. However, concepts such as these are rarely found in the programs that have been studied. It may be that behavioral scientists will need to assume a greater responsibility for the application of their competencies to theoretical and applied problems in education. In any case, it is probably unreasonable for us to expect that the present generation of professional educators will be able to take the giant strides required for curriculum innovation that will answer the challenge.

Growing interest in improving opportunities in higher education for the disadvantaged has led many of our colleges and universities to draw their newest student bodies from an increasingly wide variety of social, ethnic, economic, and cultural groups. Some of these new college students are the first members of their cultural or ethnic groups to attend these institutions, and large numbers of them are succeeding in college, defying pessimistic predictions of their chances for success. Sometimes these achievements are simply the result of discovery programs which provide an opportunity for college study to young people of ability. In other cases, success follows special remedial and enrichment programs in which youngsters who were functioning at modest levels were helped to correct their weaknesses in preparation and to move ahead. Still other members of this new collegiate population are counted among those who have taken advantage of the opportunity provided by the growing number of junior or community colleges. Increasingly, the new college group will include young people who have spent their summers and much of their free time during their last few undergraduate school years in special college preparatory programs. In short, it can be said today that any young person of above-average ability can find an opportunity for collegiate study, particularly if he is Negro. Unfortunately, these talent search programs and changed admissions policies have not routinely received a broad enough interpretation to enable them to assist other disadvantaged groups, including poor white youth. Furthermore, they have only skimmed the cream. They have not yet moved far enough from dependence on traditional indices of talent or potential to draw from the mass of youngsters who are academically handicapped because of their socially or economically disadvantaged status.

In facing the many problems involved in weak prior academic preparation the colleges face a substantial challenge. Where the issue has been engaged, emphasis has been placed on remedial work and enrichment experiences, special counseling, guidance and tutorial work, extended time to complete requirements, or the selection of students who show promise of rising above their limitations to succeed. None of the existing programs have begun serious work on such problems as the modification of the mental postures and learning patterns in inefficient young adult learners; the devising of alternate input systems for the acquisition of knowledge banks for the student who suffers from major deficits in information as well as impaired skills for acquiring it; the relationship of the availability of social or cultural reference groups to persistence and attrition rates among minority group college students; and the differential interaction between aspiration, motivation, opportunity, resource mobilization, and achievement. These are problems which seem to lie at the heart of the college adjustment problem for students from disadvantaged backgrounds. While we have delayed in using the remedies – financial assistance, modified admissions policies, talent searching, and remedial course work – that are now improving opportunities for these students, solution of problems on this level has never demanded more than an application of existing resources. The second-level problems whose solutions are likely to make the real difference in providing educational opportunities for the disadvantaged will require more systematic investigation and concerted effort.

Even as we direct our attention to the next steps, let us not be unmindful of the fact that woefully little is being done at the level at which we *do* know what to do.

The greatest part of the effort in compensatory higher education is being conducted in the Negro colleges. These are the colleges that have struggled longest with the problem and remain least able to mount the required effort. Moreover, as our great institutions of higher learning begin to offer help to students from disadvantaged backgrounds, they select those who are most likely to succeed, thus tending to rob the less prestigious Negro colleges of those very students who might raise institutional standards. Given society's increasing need for the kind of liberating education peculiar to the traditional college, it may now be time for the strongest institutions to assume a greater share of the burden of educating those young adults whose adequate development and achievement of academic excellence present the greatest challenge, giving the weaker institutions a chance to share in the education of the best prepared. For it may be that great teaching is not best measured by how much the excellent student learns at his teacher's feet but by the extent to which a teacher can help the less prepared student to approach excellence.

Given the rapidly proliferating efforts directed at helping the disadvantaged, and the almost universal emphasis on compensatory education to the neglect of education appropriate to developmental need, and given the virtual absence in these programs of any rationale based on a systematic conceptual framework for understanding the learning styles and the needs of disadvantaged children, what new directions or emphases are indicated?

In the search for improved approaches to educating the disadvantaged, one of the most fundamental needs is for some clarification of the relationship between conditions of life, characteristics of the learner, and success in the teaching-learning process. The attention so far given to characteristics of disadvantaged children has resulted in overgenerous generalizations. Several investigators and too many observers have been content to identify conditions and characteristics frequently encountered in some of the disadvantaged and then assumed these factors to be typical. Further, the fact of concurrence between certain conditions of life, certain characteristics, and poor school adjustment has been interpreted as indicative of a causal relationship, although the evidence supports only a conclusion that these phenomena are correlated. The primary need, then, in improving educational opportunity for disadvantaged children is to understand the nature and cause of their poor school adjustment.

Although it is probably true that adverse conditions of life do not facilitate academic achievement in most children, we have no firm evidence that such conditions preclude academic success. In fact, there are enough cases of success despite adverse conditions to make untenable the conclusion that difficult life circumstances preclude success in school. There are many good reasons for improving the living conditions of the disadvantaged and there is certainly no good excuse for an affluent society to fail to do so. However, if the school continues to point to these conditions as the excuse for its failures, it is not likely to mount an appropriate attack upon the pedagogical problems involved.

This is not to argue that the school and school people should not be concerned with these conditions. It is only to argue that the school's concern with conditions of life must not be a substitute for its primary concern with the teaching-learning process.

The characteristics earlier referred to, upon which much of compensatory education is based, also occur in more privileged populations. Inefficient utilization of formal learning situations and other learning disabilities are not confined to the disadvantaged. Our focus on these characteristics, most of which we presume to have negative implications for school learning, is not unlike our focus on behaviors and circumstances thought of as pathologic in neurotic and psychotic persons. Inadequate attention has been given to the fact that many "normal" and functioning individuals also have these characteristics and circumstances in their lives. So the "pathologic" signs are neither true indicators of pathology nor are they "typical" of the subject population. In fact, the subject population does not exist as a unitary group, but as a multivariant group. To think of this population as a single group, to identify its problems as common, and to prescribe a single program for all, is a seriously fallacious approach to the educational problems of the disadvantaged. These educational problems are the products of varying combinations of factors, and within a given subgroup the circumstances and contributing factors may vary even more than they do between subgroups. So, important as identification of characteristics may be, the qualification and specification of these characteristics and conditions in relation to the developmental tasks to be mastered are the essential prerequisites to educational prescription. The programs of compensatory education studied have not followed this sequence.

Guided by a concern with compensating for certain conditions and modifying certain characteristics (whether they are relevant to the learning task or not), the schools have utilized a variety of pedagogical procedures and materials. But since the nature of the relationship between the conditions, the characteristics, and learning taskmastery has not been fully understood, use of these procedures and materials can only be justified by tradition and pragmatic experience. Consequently, children who are judged to be deficient in language development are exposed to experiences that give them more about which they may speak; they are exposed to a variety of labeling procedures which are designed to insure that they have word symbols for the things and events in their environment; and they are provided with examples or models of adults using correct and fluent verbalizations in the hope that through the process of identification they will develop good language usage. What will be the likely result of these measures if the critical variable is sensitivity to the social necessity or survival-need represented by language facility? If there is validity to the Strodtbeck finding that differences in language usage in middle-class and lower-class families are due to differences in patterns of parental decision making in these families – making sensitivity to elaborated language forms essential in the former and sensitivity to signs and direction-giving adequate in the latter – this emphasis on directed cognitive experience may be inappropriate. The need may be for greater emphasis on directed and manipulated affective experience designed to develop sensitivity to elaborated language forms as an essential tool of survival.

Probably because we are conscience-stricken by our prejudices toward, and our neglect of, the disadvantaged, much of our school personnel training effort has been directed at better understanding the culture and values of the lower status groups. The assumption seems to be that in order to teach well we must understand the life of the learner, in order to motivate we must be able to identify parallels in the life of the motivated, and in order to empathize we must know the meaning of experiences to the recipient of our compassion. We have no evidence that this is so. It is quite likely that knowledge of the pupil's life may make the teacher somewhat more at ease or at least somewhat less vulnerable to shock, but few of us are really able to straddle cultures and to utilize knowledge of other cultures creatively. Even fewer of us have the capacity to adapt experiences from our own value systems to alien value systems without being patronizing. Of greater importance, however, is the question of whether good teaching and effective learning can transcend one's identification with a particular set of values or a particular culture. The history of education indicates that they can. The upper class has always received the best education and few upper-class members are educators. Education has been the vehicle of upward mobility for the lower class and certainly by the time they function as teachers, educators are not members of the lower class. Understanding of differences in culture and values may be helpful in teaching, but such understanding seems to be a noncritical variable and preoccupation with it may be diversionary in the education of the disadvantaged.

The importance of the interview and psychotherapeutic counseling as instruments for change in attitude and behavior has been greatly exaggerated. Although few programs have been developed with an intensive psychotherapeutic emphasis, almost none of the programs studied are without a significant guidance counseling emphasis. These counseling components which vary from information-dispensing and motivational exhortation to reflection of feeling and the provision of advice and support tend to be based on the same assumptions as psychotherapy. The heavy dependence on counseling reflects the views that greater insight into factors which seem to be related to the behavior results in a modification of the behavior, that atypical behavior reflects lack of correct information or correct interpretation, that habitual behavior patterns are subject to change under the impact of interaction with a person of higher status. These and a host of other assumptions have some validity. However, the counseling emphasis does not provide for the role of experience – direct confrontation with life – upon the development and change of attitudes and behavior.

Where one's life experience, or at least one's perception of the opportunity, corresponds to the values, goals, and behaviors stressed in the counseling situation, one may expect somewhat more positive results. When the major events of one's life and one's awareness of the opportunity structure contradict the hypothetical world of the interview, it is folly to expect positive results.

Too many of the guidance components of compensatory education programs are based upon superficial and infrequent pupil-counselor contact. Most of the encounters with guidance counselors are far removed from meaningful involvement with the real problems in the real world. Too often the guidance counselor represents a degree of sophistication with regard to the priority problems of the pupil that borders on naivete. Usually the guidance focus is on talking about the problem when the need is to do something about it. Too often, unfortunately, the support that the status person could provide is not given because life circumstances often rob these young people of trust in that segment of the population represented by the counselor.

Guidance programs in which the counselor performs an active helping role seem to be more effective. Often the counselor's value is established more readily on the basis of his having taken an action in the pupil's behalf. Arranging for a change of teacher, help in finding a job, mediating a parent-child conflict, coming to the pupil's defense in the face of the police, or taking a correct stand in the civil rights struggle are actions that may do more to establish a relationship than months of counseling. For the disadvantaged youngster who daily meets and often copes with many concrete difficulties in living, a focus on help with these problems may be the most productive approach to guidance.

It is not suggested here that information, support, reflection of feeling, advice-giving, and verbal reinforcement are to no avail. The importance of relationship therapy and models in guidance are not to be demeaned. The point to be made is that, particularly with this group, guidance efforts directed at control and modification of the environment, efforts directed at positive intervention to change the negative and destructive elements in the lives of these children, are likely to be more productive than efforts directed at change of attitude and behavior through verbal and other vicarious experiences.

Some promising guidelines

Ten years ago when one could make a contribution to the situation simply by calling attention to the fact that education for the disadvantaged was a problem, a critical approach to the review of the few real efforts then in existence would have been inappropriate. However, today when work in this field has almost become a fad, it is essential that we do not let our enthusiasm blind us to the limitations of our efforts. The predominantly critical view taken of these programs is born of the fear that quantity of effort may be mistaken for quality of achievement. Weaknesses and limitations in these programs have been stressed in order to call attention to the fact that we have not yet found answers to many of the pressing educational problems of the disadvantaged. To assume that we have the answer is to subject multitudes of children to less than optimal development. More seriously, to settle for the beginning effort now mounted is to lay the basis for the conclusion that children of low economic, ethnic, or social status cannot be educated to the same levels as other children in the society. This conclusion could be drawn because despite all of our current efforts tremendous gains are not yet being achieved in upgrading educational achievement in socially disadvantaged children. We are probably failing because we have not yet found the right answers to the problem. To act as if the answers were in is to insure against further progress.

Even though we do not know how best to educate socially disadvantaged children, we cannot afford to wait for better answers. The presence of these children in our schools, the demands of increasingly impatient communities, and the requirements of an increasingly complex society demand that we apply the best that is currently available even as we seek to improve. Our current experiences by no means leave us without leads. There are several ideas and practices which show promise.

1. *Effective teaching* – None of the programs studied have come up with a substitute for effective teaching. They have also failed to develop *the* effective approach to teaching. The teachers who are judged to be successful are those who have developed sensitivity to the special needs, the variety of learning patterns, and the learning strengths and weaknesses of their pupils. These teachers have also developed a wide variety of instructional techniques and methodologies by which they communicate knowledge with which they are very familiar, and attitudes of respect and expectation which they strongly hold.

2. *Child-parent-teacher motivation* – In the absence of revolutions in educational technology, one of the most promising areas for emphasis is that of motivation. Few programs have generated more enthusiasm for learning or better pupil gains than those which involved teachers, parents, and children in active and creative motivational campaigns. Utilizing a wide variety of motivational schemes, these programs have raised the level of expectation on the part of teachers, have greatly increased parent participation in the

school as well as home-based learning experiences, and have helped young-sters to find pleasure and reward in learning.

3. *New materials and technology* — One of the significant developments of the current period is the emergence of instructional materials more widely representative of the variety of ethnic groups which exist in this country. The better material in this category not only includes more appropriate graphic art but the prose is more pertinent to the realities of the pupil's life. The development of improved literacy techniques is worthy of note. Among these are the Initial Teaching Alphabet, Color Coded Words, the Progressive Accelerated Reading Technique, and the Talking Typewriter. Many of the better programs make good use of some of the excellent pro-gramed instructional materials as well as of inexpensive-to-costly teaching machines.

4. *Peer teaching and learning* — Drawing upon a long-ignored technique employed by Maria Montessori, some programs have caused children to make significant gains in academic achievement as a result of helping other children learn. Most often the pattern is that of older children serving as tutors for younger children with both showing gains from the experience. The practice not only has many tangential social benefits, it also has the advantage of replicating the naturalistic out-of-school experiences of chil-dren, where they generally tend to learn from each other.

5. *Psycho-educational diagnosis and remediation* — It is well established that disadvantaged children are a high-risk population with respect to de-velopmental abnormalities. The higher incidence of developmental defects and learning disabilities makes careful psycho-educational diagnosis of cru-cial significance in programs serving these children. Obviously it is not enough to diagnose; prescription and remedy must follow. Excellent pro-grams will include or at least have access to such staff and facilities.

6. *Learning task specific grouping* — Considerable controversy has devel-oped around homogeneous versus heterogeneous grouping. Such a dichot-omy clouds the issue. Clearly there are some learning tasks which are easier for some children to master and for some teachers to teach if they are pre-sented to a group all of whom are at much the same level. Mastery of other tasks may proceed faster in heterogeneous groups. There are some tasks

that require small group instruction, and others for which small groups are wasteful if not inefficient. Grouping of youngsters for instruction should flow from the nature of the learning task and not from the bias of the teacher or the school system. In work with disadvantaged children the social gains which may also be derived from flexible grouping should not be ignored.

7. *Extensions of the school* — Although school learning is focused in the school, its quality is significantly influenced by factors outside of school. Where competing forces operate outside of school, it is often necessary to extend the school day, week, or year so as to increase the period during which the school's influence may be felt. The All-Day Neighborhood School, weekend activities, and summer programs are among the variations used. In a few instances boarding-type schools are being tried, combining certain status and quality elements to the extended exposure to the school environment.

8. *Staffing* — There are few solid guidelines to staffing programs for the disadvantaged. However, the more promising trends give emphasis to:

a. the selection of teachers who have good basic backgrounds in academic disciplines, combined with particularly good instructional skills. Most programs stress some appreciation for the cultures from which pupils come, but instructional techniques that work seem to provide the best payoff.

b. the use of indigenous nonprofessionals as teacher aides is increasingly stressed although some critics of this development call attention to the possible influence of "negative models," particularly in language usage.

c. in addition to strength of staff, quantity of staff is also stressed. Combined with team teaching, where a master teacher supervises several less skilled teachers, the use of junior-level personnel can be used to advantage.

d. considerable emphasis in some programs is being given to the use of male models. Visitors and part-time people are used when men are not in ample supply on the regular staff.

e. a wide variety of supporting staff are being used. These include social workers, psychologists, physicians, nurses, community organizers, remedial specialists, guidance specialists, and home-school liaison officers drawn from the surrounding environment.

9. *Social or peer-group support* – Particularly in work with adolescents and college-bound youth the peer group or appropriate social or ethnic reference groups are used to provide morale support, an island for temporary retreat, or reference-group identification. This is particularly important in young people whose upward mobility may appear to be taking them away from the groups with which they identify.

10. *Financial assistance* – Many of the administrators of college programs have recognized the necessity for providing some financial assistance for youth from disadvantaged backgrounds. This need is not so readily recognized at the high school and elementary school level. However, many of these children's families simply cannot provide the pocket money which makes school attendance and social participation possible. The need for stipends is urgent for many of these children. Another unusual pattern of financial assistance consists of modest aid beginning as early as the seventh grade and continuing through college. In one of these programs, college is guaranteed while the student is still in junior high, as long as the pupil continues to demonstrate that he can qualify for this assistance.

11. *Improved opportunity* – Improved opportunities in college as well as in other post high school endeavors is viewed by some programs as a major factor. The view held is that perception of opportunity is in itself enough to move many of these youth from a position of lethargy and alienation to active involvement in their own development.

These several trends have made for considerable improvement in education for the disadvantaged. They flow logically from what is known about these children and from the best traditions in education. Their further development may be expected not only to enhance the quality of the educational experiences which our schools and colleges provide for children and youth handicapped by poverty and discrimination, but also to strengthen the profession's competence in serving the needs of learners of all social classes and races.

New directions

These approaches to improvement in the education of disadvantaged young people, although promising, will not alone suffice to cope with the new demands which rapid social change now poses for our schools and colleges. More fundamental than the task of providing compensatory education for the disadvantaged is that of defining educational goals which are appropriate for the emerging world of tomorrow. New directions must be charted for the education of all of our people.

The educational tasks faced by the United States in the next three or four decades have been enlarged and complicated by three revolutionary developments. The first of these is an explosion in the quantity of knowledge available to man. It has been traditional to consider that the body of knowledge doubles every 15 years — that today's information is, at worst, outdated tomorrow. However, in the light of the pace with which new discoveries are emerging, and in the light of the advances in technology which permit rapid processing and integrating of both new and old information at higher levels, this morning's information may well be outdated before noon. It is no longer possible for any individual to be master of the knowledge available in any basic discipline. Moreover, as knowledge expands, the distinctions between disciplines break down, thus extending the breadth of knowledge required to solve problems in any one of them. Meanwhile there is every indication that the information pool will continue to grow — not by arithmetic, but by geometric, progression.

The second aspect of the triple revolution involves the massive increments in technological competence. The industrial revolution combined the power of the machine with the skill of man. But today we are embarked upon a new era — the cybernetic era — in which the skill of the machine is added to the power of the machine. Its principles of organization and its implications are as different from those of the industrial era as those of the industrial era were from those of the agricultural era. The union between the computer and the automated self-regulating machine can result in a system of almost unlimited productive capacity which, in contrast to the mechanical systems which preceded it, requires progressively less, not more, human labor. Cybernation will force the reorganization of our economic and social structures to meet its own needs.

The third aspect of this triple revolution consists of the significant changes in the realm of political, social, and economic relations which have taken place over the last two decades – the civil rights-human rights revolution at home, the rise of underdeveloped nations abroad, and the new forms of military weaponry that have limited war as a method of resolving international conflicts.

These revolutionary developments have serious implications for education. To enable our educational efforts to match the demands of this changed and rapidly changing situation, we must focus attention on remodeling the concepts and structure of education so that the schools of the future will not only be more appropriately aligned with the needs of that future society, but will also be a positive force in facilitating transition in that society.

Probably the most significant change – or at least the one with the most serious implications for education – will be the change that requires the schools to shift away from an emphasis on simply rewarding the successful student. The emphasis will have to fall instead on the schools' responsibility for insuring success in academic, emotional, and social learning for all students save a very few who are truly mentally defective. The future will also demand of us that we abandon our focus on more and more content mastery and substitute for it a primary focus on learning to learn as a continuous process throughout life. The vast amount of knowledge available to man, together with the demands of the advanced technology by which our society moves, will require of our student-future-citizens skill in the management of knowledge. Similarly, changes in the politico-social sphere will make more necessary than ever before competence and skill in intrapersonal and interpersonal management.

A society which approaches education with these concerns might appropriately give attention to five specific educational goals. The first of these is a renewed commitment to effective teaching – sufficiently effective to provide for all students the mastery of *basic communication skills*. A real commitment to the goal of developing universal competence in speech, in reading and writing, and in arithmetic computation has crucial implications for education and for society. For education, it will mean the development of the kind of materials, methods, and conditions for learning that are appropriate to the different background experiences and learning styles of children other than those for whom most of our educational practices have been designed. These practices have not even succeeded with all the pupils for whom they were designed, and they have failed completely to meet the needs of most of the children who have been designated "socially disadvantaged." Consequently, a genuine determination on the part of the schools to assure universal mastery of basic communication skills would constitute a self-imposed challenge of some magnitude. The school has no choice about taking on such a challenge. In the agricultural and industrial eras, physical strength and manual skill were sufficient tools for man's survival, but it is increasingly clear that the survival tools of the cybernetic era are communication skills. If the schools cannot universally provide these tools, they will be institutionally dysfunctional in modern society.

Let me remind those who lack the courage to meet the challenge that our concepts of educability have consistently followed society's demand for educated persons. At one time it was only the religious and political nobility from which educable persons were thought to come. When the Reformation and the emerging industrial revolution required that more people be educated, we learned that educability existed in broader categories of humankind. Gradually in the West, there came a general acceptance of the notion that all white people were at least potentially educable, and in this country it was only the Negro who could not be taught. When, at last, out of humanitarian concern and society's need we began to discover that Negroes could learn, we came to accept a tacit responsibility for the education of all people. But though we have accepted the theory of universal educability, we have not attained universal education — at best we have learned how to teach that majority who meet certain rather stereotyped criteria. However, educability is a function of societal definition and societal need, and I submit that in the latter part of the twentieth century educability will be defined in the broadest and most inclusive terms. It is in those terms that the school will be challenged to produce.

A second goal of education, only somewhat less crucial than the mastery of basic skills, involves providing students with an attitude of readiness toward, and an increasing capacity for, continued learning. We must teach people to think of the acquisition of knowledge as a lifetime undertaking, not as a pastime for youth, because accelerating technological innovations are effecting profound changes in our job structure. Occupations are rapidly altering. We are seeing a developing stratification of people on the basis of intellectual function and technological skills. Over the last 10 years the proportion of white- to blue-collar workers has altered radically. Now for the first time white-collar workers outnumber the blue-collar workers, and the trend is not likely to reverse itself. We already have the capacity to install a productive system based primarily on machine power and machine skills. The coming replacement of man by the machine will destroy many more existing jobs and render useless the work contributions of vast numbers now employed. When that time comes, and it is coming rapidly, obtaining employment in one of the new fields will depend largely upon the level of adaptive skill and the quality of education of the applicant. Unemployment rates compiled in 1959 for those with seven years of schooling or less, reached 10 percent, compared with just over 3 percent for those with 13 to 15 years of schooling, and just over 1 percent for those with 16 years of schooling or more. A willingness to learn, and continued practice in learning, will stand in good stead those who would be employed in such a marketplace.

But motivation for learning is not, of itself, enough. In any given field, or group of related fields, available and necessary knowledge has already outstripped any single individual's capacity to master content. Only the student who by practice, by utilization of techniques of selection, discrimination, and evaluation has honed techniques which will allow him to sort out the worthwhile from the worthless and the significant from the insignificant can escape being inundated in a sea of paper. Those who would succeed tomorrow, must learn not only how to acquire, but how to manage knowledge.

And this is the third of the tools with which educators should consider themselves obligated to equip tomorrow's students — the techniques of managing knowledge. Successful functioning on an intellectual level consists not in having a headful of facts, but in problem-solving, in knowing how to conceptualize problems, and how to pursue the information which will provide solutions. The intellectual leaders today are those who have mastered the techniques of conceptual analysis and synthesis. And, increasingly, those who would succeed must gain competence in these skills – in the identification and analysis of principles and in their subsequent reassembling around new data to produce newer or more advanced concepts. These are the skills necessary to the successful functioning of today's intellectual elite. Tomorrow, in a highly technical society, they may be necessary for most of us, not only to enable us to do productive work, but also to provide us with armor against the ravages of idle leisure.

For leisure may well be the most important industrial by-product of our coming generation. As an outgrowth of a computerized age in which 2 percent of the population will be able to produce all the goods and food that the other 98 percent can possibly consume, leisure will replace work as man's most time-consuming activity. At a meeting in 1964 of leading political and social scientists, the president of the American Academy of Political and Social Science recommended such revolutionary measures as the establishment of departments of leisure in the 50 states, and the compulsory teaching of leisure skills in the public schools. He was immediately challenged from the floor as being hopelessly conservative in his approach. An economist at the meeting claimed that we face such an explosive increase in leisure that within a mere 10 years we may have to keep the unemployed portion of our population under sedation unless we can quickly figure out something better for them to do. Unemployment will be concentrated among the older workers and the youngsters entering the labor force and, according to Theobald (1963), "no conceivable rate of economic growth will avoid this result." Of the 26 million people who will enter the job market during this decade, 9.8 million will have less than a complete high school education. Many, if not all of these people, will face a lifetime without market-supported work.

How these people are to be kept solvent is a problem which we educators are not immediately asked to deal with. How they are to occupy themselves is at the heart of our concern. Even now America is a land of golfers, travelers, bowlers, amateur painters. After finding free time for all the marginal chores of living – mowing the lawn, taking a fishing trip, driving the kids to the library – what will a man do to fill his extra leisure hours?

Americans are ill-equipped to absorb leisure in any but the smallest doses. Our education, our informal training, our mores, our Horatio Alger kind of tradition, our puritanical mythology honoring the no-play-hard-work-equals-success tradition, have made us a people who feel guilty about "wasting time."

It must, then, become the fourth goal of our new educational system to teach our students just how creative and how elevating the wise use of leisure can be. Such a change may well be among the most difficult asked of us. Our public school system has always been a training ground for its students to "get ahead." It has consistently expounded the principle that only hard work and study will prevent failure after graduation. But it has rarely equated hard work with pleasure or self-satisfaction. It has more enthusiastically taught English as the language of business letters than as the language of Shakespeare, Thoreau, and DuBois. Our schools will have to start teaching a drastically new philosophy, one appropriate to our new age of abundance. The new educational standards will have to reflect, as well as encourage, a basic alteration in our cultural standards. The pursuit of pleasure will have to be accepted as a virtue. But at the same time, pleasure will have to cease being equated with nondoing and idleness and come to be associated with self-management, with self-imposed and self-chosen activity. To a people freed from the need to work we shall have to teach the skills of leisure as if our lives depended on it — and indeed they may.

For now, in the latter half of the twentieth century, we have reached a point where the abundance of knowledge and technology available to this country would allow us to create a society based on humanist rather than survival values. In earlier generations, when the hard realities of life seemed on every hand to run counter to copybook maxims about justice, equality, and humanity, the school necessarily based its teaching of these values on exhortation and fabricated example. Now, the school could well take as its fifth goal the education of citizens whose competencies in self-management and human relations render them capable of an appropriate creative response to the fact that we now possess the material potential to create a society truly respectful of human rights, a society where respect for one's fellow man no longer conflicts with his need to provide for his family and himself. The challenge of the new condition is to match the formal learning experience to this new reality and to meet the new opportunity of a freer social system with a new approach to educational methods and to a new organization of society. The great danger is to pretend that there has been no fundamental change and to go on using methods that were not completely useful even in the old days, thus missing an opportunity to advance learning and behavior when such an advance is not only possible but desperately needed. The failure of man to create a humane social order under the new conditions will carry with it the threat of society's suicide, because the same conditions of scientific advance and material plenty that make it possible for man to now be truly human, also make it possible for him to be definitively and conclusively antihuman.

Appendix A

Colleges and universities reported to be conducting compensatory programs and practices, by regions and states

Note: Asterisks designate institutions with programs here adjudged to be substantial. (See page 134. See also footnote 3 on page 125.)

New England

Connecticut:

Central Connecticut State
  College
Post Junior College
Yale University*

Maine:

Aroostock State Teachers
  College
Bowdoin College*
Nasson College
St. Francis College

Massachusetts:

Amherst College
Anna Maria College
Brandeis University
College of the Holy Cross
Gordon College
Mount Holyoke College*
Northeastern University*
Queen of the Apostles
  College
Radcliffe College
Springfield College
Williams College*
Worcester Junior College

New Hampshire:

Dartmouth College*

Rhode Island:

Brown University*
Roger Williams Junior
  College

Vermont:

St. Michael's College

Middle Atlantic

New Jersey:

Bloomfield College
Newark State College
Princeton University*
Rutgers—The State
  University*

New York:

Barnard College
Bronx Community College*
Brooklyn College of The
  City University of New
  York*
Broome Technical
  Community College
Catherine McAuley College
City College of The City
  University of New York*
Columbia College,
  Columbia University*
Columbia University,
  School of General Studies*
Cornell University*

Epiphany Apostolic College
Hofstra University
Manhattan School of Music
Manhattanville College of
  the Sacred Heart
Mater Dei College
New York University*
Polytechnic Institute of
  Brooklyn
Queensboro Community
  College
Rockland Community
  College
Staten Island Community
  College
Union College
Westchester Community
  College

Pennsylvania:

Albright College
Carnegie Institute of
  Technology*
College Misericordia
Drexel Institute of
  Technology
Franklin and Marshall
  College*
Gannon College*
Hahnemann Medical College
Harcum Junior College
Immaculata College
Indiana University of
  Pennsylvania

Lincoln University
Moravian College
Point Park Junior College*
Saint Francis College
Swarthmore College
University of Pittsburgh
West Chester State College

East North Central

Illinois:

Central YMCA Junior
  College
College of Jewish Studies
Concordia Teachers College
Kendall College*
Rockford College
Southern Illinois University*
Thornton Junior College
University of Chicago*
Western Illinois University
Wilson Junior College*

Indiana:

Anderson College
Ball State University
Indiana University
Purdue University

Michigan:

Andrews University
Community College and
  Technical Institute (now
  Lake Michigan)
Lansing Community
  College
Lawrence Institute of
  Technology
Madonna College
Michigan State University*
Northwestern Michigan
  College
Siena Heights College

South Macomb County
  Community College
Spring Arbor College
University of Detroit*
University of Michigan
Wayne State University

Ohio:

Borromeo Seminary of Ohio
Central State College
John Carroll University
Mary Manse College
Ohio State University
Rio Grande College*
University of Toledo*

Wisconsin:

Marinette County Teachers
  College

West North Central

Iowa:

Cornell College
Grinnell College
Luther College*
Marshalltown Community
  College
Morningside College

Kansas:

Baker University
Mount St. Scholastica
  College
St. Mary of the Plains
  College
University of Wichita (now
  Wichita State University)

Minnesota:

Hibbing Junior College
Moorhead State College
Rochester Junior College

University of Minnesota-
  Duluth
University of Minnesota-
  Minneapolis*

Missouri:

Avila College
Calvary Bible College
Cardinal Glennon College
Evangel College
Northwest Missouri State
  College
Southwest Missouri State
  College
Tarkio College
Westminster College

North Dakota:

North Dakota State
  University
University of North Dakota

South Dakota:

University of South Dakota

South Atlantic

Delaware:

Wesley College

District of Columbia:

District of Columbia
  Teachers College
Georgetown University*
Immaculata Junior College

Florida:

Daytona Beach Junior
  College
Hampton Junior College
Junior College of Broward
  County
Pensacola Junior College

Georgia:

Andrew College
Brenau College
Columbus College
Fort Valley State College
Oglethorpe College

Maryland:

Anne Arundel Community
College
Essex Community College
Morgan State College*

North Carolina:

Agricultural and Technical
College of North
Carolina
Duke University*
Guilford College
North Carolina College*
North Carolina State
University at Raleigh*
Sacred Heart Junior College
University of North
Carolina at Chapel Hill

Virginia:

Clinch Valley College of
The University of Virginia

West Virginia:

Morris Harvey College
West Virginia State College
West Virginia University

East South Central

Alabama:

Miles College*
Talladega College
Tuskegee Institute*

Kentucky:

Bellarmine College
Campbellsville College
Centre College of Kentucky

Mississippi:

Jackson State College*
Mississippi State University
Southeastern Baptist
College
William Carey College
Wood Junior College

Tennessee:

East Tennessee State
University
Knoxville College*
Le Moyne College
Tennessee Agricultural and
Industrial State
University
University of Tennessee

West South Central

Arkansas:

Agricultural, Mechanical
and Normal College
Henderson State Teachers
College
Little Rock University
Southern State College

Louisiana:

Southern University
Tulane University

Oklahoma:

Connors State College
Sayre Junior College

Texas:

Baylor University
Odessa College
Paris Junior College
Ranger Junior College
Southwestern Assemblies of
God College
Texas Southern University
Texas Western College

Mountain

Arizona:

Eastern Arizona Junior
College
Grand Canyon College
University of Arizona*

Colorado:

Adams State College*
Fort Lewis College

Idaho:

College of Idaho
University of Idaho

Montana:

Dawson County Junior
College
Western Montana College
of Education

New Mexico:

Eastern New Mexico
University*

Pacific

Alaska:

University of Alaska

California:

American River Junior
  College
Cerritos College
Contra Costa College*
Foothill College
Glendale College
Grossmont College
Long Beach City College
Long Beach State College
Los Angeles City College
Oakland City College
San Jose City College

Stanford University
Stanislaus State College
University of California-
  Berkeley*
University of Santa Clara
University of the Pacific
Ventura College
Whittier College
Yuba College

Hawaii:

Maunaolu College
University of Hawaii

Oregon:

Mount Angel College
Southern Oregon College
University of Oregon

Washington:

Columbia Basin College
Olympic College
St. Martin's College
Wenatchee Valley College
Whitman College
Whitworth College

Bibliography

American Council on Education, "Higher Education as a National Resource." *School and Society*, Vol. 91, May 4, 1963, pp. 218–221.

Anastasi, Anne, and D'Angelo, Rita Y., "A Comparison of Negro and White Preschool Children in Language Development and Goodenough Draw-A-Man IQ." *Pedagogical Seminary and Journal of Genetic Psychology* [*Journal of Genetic Psychology*], Vol. 81, December 1952, pp. 147–165.

Ausubel, David P., "How Reversible Are the Cognitive and Motivational Effects of Cultural Deprivation? Implications for Teaching the Culturally Deprived Child." *Urban Education*, Vol. 1, No. 1, Autumn 1964, pp. 16–38.

Beckey, Ruth Elizabeth, "A Study of Certain Factors Related to Retardation of Speech." *Journal of Speech Disorders*, Vol. 7, September 1942, pp. 223–249.

Bellamy, Edward, *Looking Backward*. Cleveland, Ohio: The World Publishing Company, 1945, 311 pp. (out of print). Available through Modern Library, Inc.

Bernstein, Basil, "Language and Social Class." *British Journal of Sociology*, Vol. 11, September 1960, pp. 271–276.

Bernstein, Basil, "Social Class and Linguistic Development: A Theory of Social Learning," Chap. 24, pp. 288–314 in Halsey, A. H.; Floud, J.; and Anderson, C. A.; eds., *Education, Economy and Society*. New York: Free Press of Glencoe, Inc., 1961, 640 pp.

Bernstein, Basil, "Social Class, Linguistic Codes and Grammatical Elements." *Language and Speech*, Vol. 5, 1962, pp. 221–240.

Birch, Herbert G., *Brain Damage in Children: Biological and Social Aspects*. Baltimore, Md.: Williams and Wilkins Co., 1964, 199 pp.

Birch, Herbert G., and others, "Reactions to New Situations—An Index of Individuality in Childhood." *American Journal of Orthopsychiatry*, Vol. XXXII, No. 2, March 1962, pp. 341–342.

Board of Education of the City of New York, Bureau of Educational Research and Bureau of Educational and Vocational Guidance, *Demonstration Guidance Project: Fourth Annual Report, 1959–60*. New York: Board of Education, 68 pp.

Brazziel, William F., and Terrell, Mary, "An Experiment in the Development of Readiness in a Culturally Disadvantaged Group of First Grade Children." *Journal of Negro Education*, Vol. 31, Winter 1962, pp. 4–7.

Carroll, Rebecca Evans, "Relation of Social Environment to the Moral Ideology and the Personal Aspirations of Negro Boys and Girls." *School Review*, Vol. 53, January 1945, pp. 30–38.

Carson, Arnold S., and Rabin, A. I., "Verbal Comprehension and Communication in Negro and White Children." *Journal of Educational Psychology*, Vol. 51, April 1960, pp. 47–51.

Clark, Kenneth B., "Segregated Schools in New York City." Paper read at conference, "Child Apart," North Side Center for Child Development, New Lincoln School, New York, April 1954.

Clark, Kenneth B., and Plotkin, Lawrence, *The Negro Student at Integrated Colleges*. New York: National Scholarship Service and Fund for Negro Students, 1963, 59 pp.

Clarke, A. D. B., and Clarke, A. M., "Cognitive Changes in the Feebleminded." *British Journal of Psychology*, Vol. 45, 1954, pp. 173–179.

Coles, Robert, *The Desegregation of Southern Schools: A Psychiatric Study*. New York: Anti-Defamation League, July 1963, 25 pp.

Davidson, Kenneth S., and others, "A Preliminary Study of Negro and White Differences on Form I of the Wechsler Bellevue Scale." *Journal of Consulting Psychology*, Vol. 14, October 1950, pp. 489–492.

Davis, Allison, "The Future Education of

Children from Low Socio-Economic Groups," pp. 27–54, in Elam, Stanley, ed., *New Dimensions for Educational Progress*. Bloomington, Ind.: Phi Delta Kappa, 1963, 190 pp.

Davis, Paul H., "Changes Are Coming in the Colleges." *Journal of Higher Education*, Vol. 33, March 1962, pp. 141–147.

Day, R. E., *Civil Rights U.S.A.; Public Schools, Southern States, 1963: North Carolina*. Staff report submitted to the United States Commission on Civil Rights. Washington, D. C.: Government Printing Office, 60 pp.

Deutsch, Cynthia, "Auditory Discrimination and Learning: Social Factors." Merrill-Palmer Quarterly, Vol. 10, July 1964, pp. 277–296.

Deutsch, Martin, *Minority Group and Class Status as Related to Social and Personality Factors in Scholastic Achievement*. Society for Applied Anthropology, Monograph No. 2. Ithaca, N. Y.: Cornell University, 1960, 32 pp.

Deutsch, Martin, "The Disadvantaged Child and the Learning Process," pp. 163–179 in Passow, A. Harry, ed., *Education in Depressed Areas*. New York: Bureau of Publications, Teachers College, Columbia University, 1963, 359 pp.

Deutsch, Martin, "The Role of Social Class in Language Development and Cognition." *American Journal of Orthopsychiatry*, Vol. XXXV, January 1965, pp. 78–88.

Dreger, Ralph Mason, and Miller, Kent S., "Comparative Psychological Studies of Negroes and Whites in the United States." *Psychological Bulletin*, Vol. 57, September 1960, pp. 361–402.

Educational Policies Commission, *Universal Opportunity for Education Beyond the High School*. Washington, D. C.: National Education Association, 1964, 36 pp.

Ferry, N. H., "College Responsibilities and Social Expectations." *Teachers College Record*, Vol. 65, November 1963, pp. 99–111.

Gallagher, J. J., "Social Status of Children Related to Intelligence, Propinquity and Social Perception." *Elementary School Journal*, Vol. 58, January 1958, pp. 225–231.

Goff, Regina M., "Some Educational Implications of the Influence of Rejection on Aspiration Levels of Minority Group Children." *Journal of Experimental Education*, Vol. 23, December 1954, pp. 179–183.

Gordon, Edmund W., "A Review of Programs of Compensatory Education." *American Journal of Orthopsychiatry*, Vol. XXXV, July 1965, pp. 640–651.

Gordon, Edmund W., "Counseling Socially Disadvantaged Children," pp. 275–282 in Riessman, Frank; Cohen, Jerome; and Pearl, Arthur; eds., *Mental Health of the Poor*. New York: Free Press of Glencoe, Inc., 1964, 648 pp.

Gordon, Edmund W., *Educational Achievement in the Prince Edward County Free School, 1963–64*. New York: Ferkauf Graduate School of Education, Yeshiva University, 1965, 63 pp. Mimeographed.

Gould, Rosalind, "Some Sociological Determinants of Goal Strivings." *Journal of Social Psychology*, Vol. 13, May 1941, pp. 461–473.

Haeusserman, Else, *Developmental Potential of Preschool Children: An Evaluation of Intellectual, Sensory and Emotional Functioning*. New York: Grune & Stratton, Inc., 1958, 285 pp.

Hager, Walter E., "Challenges to Public Higher Education." *School and Society*, Vol. 91, April 20, 1963, pp. 200–201.

Hansen, Carl F., "The Scholastic Performances of Negro and White Pupils in the Integrated Public Schools of the District of Columbia." *Harvard Educational Review*, Vol. 30, No. 3, Summer 1960, pp. 216–236.

Harrington, Michael, *The Other America: Poverty in the United States*. New York: The Macmillan Company, 1962, 191 pp.

Hieronymus, A. N., "Study of Social Class Motivation: Relationships Between Anxiety for Education and Certain Socio-Economic and Intellectual Variables." *Journal of Educational Psychology*, Vol. 42, April 1951, pp. 193–205.

Hilliard, George H., and Troxwell, Eleanor, "Informational Background as a Factor in Reading Readiness and Reading Progress." *Elementary School Journal*, Vol. 38, December 1957, pp. 255–263.

Hunt, Joseph McV., *Intelligence and Experience*. New York: Ronald Press Company, 1961, 416 pp.

Irwin, Orvis C., "Infant Speech: The Effect of Family Occupational Status and of Age on Use of Sound Types." *Journal of Speech and Hearing Disorders*, Vol. 13, September 1948, pp. 224–226.

Jensen, Arthur R., "Learning Ability in Retarded, Average, and Gifted Children." *Merrill-Palmer Quarterly*, Vol. 9, April 1963, pp. 123–140.

John, Vera P., and Goldstein, Leo S., "The Social Context of Language Acquisition." *Merrill-Palmer Quarterly*, Vol. 10, July 1964, pp. 265–276.

Katz, Irwin, "Review of Evidence Relating to Effects of Desegregation on the Intellectual Performance of Negroes." *American Psychologist*, Vol. 19, June 1964, pp. 381–399.

Keller, Suzanne, "The Social World of the Urban Slum Child: Some Early Findings." *American Journal of Orthopsychiatry*, Vol. XXXIII, October 1963, pp. 823–831.

Kendrick, S. A., "College Board Scores and Cultural Bias." *College Board Review*, No. 55, Winter 1964–65, pp. 7–9.

Keppel, Francis, "In the Battle for Desegregation What Are the Flanking Skirmishes, What is the Fundamental Struggle?" *Phi Delta Kappan*, Vol. 46, September 1964, pp. 3–5.

Kirk, Samuel A., *Early Education of the Mentally Retarded: An Experimental Study*. Urbana: University of Illinois Press, 1958, 216 pp.

Klineberg, Otto, "Negro-White Differences in Intelligence Test Performance: A New Look at an Old Problem." *American Psychologist*, Vol. 18, April 1963, pp. 198–203.

Lee, Everett S., "Negro Intelligence and Selective Migration," pp. 669–676, in Jenkins, James J., and Paterson, Donald S., eds., *Studies in Individual Differences*. New York: Appleton-Century-Crofts, 1961, 774 pp.

LeShan, Lawrence L., "Time Orientation and Social Class." *Journal of Abnormal and Social Psychology*, Vol. 47, July 1952, pp. 589–592.

Lopez, Leo, and Thomas, Donald, *Recommendations for Expansion by the California State Legislature of the State Compensatory Education Program Based on the McAteer Act*. Sacramento, Calif.: Advisory Committee on Compensatory Education, 46 pp. Mimeographed.

McGrath, Earl J., *The Predominantly Negro Colleges and Universities in Transition*. New York: Bureau of Publications, Teachers College, Columbia University, 1965, 204 pp.

McKendall, Benjamin W., Jr., "Breaking the Barriers of Cultural Disadvantage and Curriculum Imbalance." *Phi Delta Kappan*, Vol. 46, March 1965, pp. 307–311.

Meister, Morris; Tauber, Abraham; and Silverman, Sidney, "Operation Second Chance." *Junior College Journal*, Vol. 33, October 1962, pp. 78–88.

Montague, David O., "Arithmetic Concepts of Kindergarten Children in Contrasting Socioeconomic Areas." *Elementary School Journal*, Vol. 64, April 1964, pp. 393–397.

Niemeyer, John, "Some Guidelines to Desirable Elementary School Reorganization." *Programs for the Educationally Disadvantaged*. U.S. Office of Education Bulletin 1963, No. 17 (OE-35044). Washington, D. C.: U.S. Department of Health, Education, and Welfare, 1963, pp. 80–85.

Pasamanick, Benjamin, and Knobloch, Hilda, "The Contribution of Some Organic Factors to School Retardation in Negro Children." *Journal of Negro Education*, Vol. 27, February 1958, pp. 4–9.

Plaut, Richard L., *Blueprint for Talent Searching: America's Hidden Manpower*. New York: National Scholarship Service and Fund for Negro Students, 1957, 41 pp.

Plaut, Richard L., "Increasing the Quantity and Quality of Negro Enrollment in College." *Harvard Educational Review*, Vol. 30, No. 3, Summer 1960, pp. 270–279.

Plaut, Richard L., "NSSFNS and Volunteers Create New Program for Disadvantaged Students." ACAC *Newsletter*, Vol. 2, No. 4, October 1964.

Pringle, M. L. Kellmer, and Tanner, Margaret, "The Effects of Early Deprivation on Speech Development: A Comparative Study of Four Year Olds in a Nursery School and in Residential Nurseries." *Language and Speech*, Vol. 1, October–December 1958, pp. 269–287.

Riessman, Frank, *The Culturally Deprived Child*. New York: Harper & Row, Publishers, 1962, 140 pp.

Rockefeller Panel Reports, *Prospect for America*. New York: Doubleday & Company, Inc., 1961, 486 pp.

Rosen, Bernard C., "The Achievement Syndrome: A Psychocultural Dimension of Social Stratification." *American Sociological Review*, Vol. 21, April 1956, pp. 203–211.

Rosenthal, Robert, *Research on Experimenter Bias*. Paper read at the American Psychological Association, Cincinnati, September 1959.

Sells, S. B., "An Interactionist Looks at the Environment." *American Psychologist*, Vol. 18, November 1963, pp. 696–702.

Sewell, William H.; Haller, Archie O.; and Straus, Murray A., "Social Status and Educational and Occupational Aspiration." *American Sociological Review*, Vol. 22, February 1957, pp. 67–73.

Siller, Jerome, "Socioeconomic Status and Conceptual Thinking." *Journal of Abnormal and Social Psychology*, Vol. 55, November 1957, pp. 365–371.

Silverman, Susan B., *Self-Images of Upper-Middle Class and Working Class Young Adolescents*. Unpublished master's thesis, University of Chicago, 1963.

Smith, Sherman E.; Mathamy, Harvard V.; and Milfs, Merele M., *Are Scholarships the Answer?* Albuquerque: University of New Mexico Press, 1960, 89 pp.

Southern School News, Untitled. *Southern School News*, Vol. 7, No. 2, Columns 1–2, August 1960.

Stallings, Frank H., "A Study of the Immediate Effects of Integration on Scholastic Achievement in the Louisville Public Schools." *Journal of Negro Education*, Vol. 28, Fall 1959, pp. 439–444.

Strauss, Alfred A., and Kephart, N. C., *Psychopathology and Education of the Brain-Injured Child. Vol. 2, Progress in Theory and Clinic*. New York: Grune & Stratton, Inc., 1955, 266 pp.

Strodtbeck, Fred L., "The Hidden Curriculum of the Middle Class Home," pp. 15–31, in Hunnicutt, C. W., ed., *Urban Education and Cultural Deprivation*. Syracuse, N. Y.: Syracuse University Press, 1964, 126 pp.

Templin, Mildred C., *Certain Language Skills in Children; Their Development and Interrelationships*. Institute of Child Welfare Monograph Series No. 26. Minneapolis: University of Minnesota Press, 1957, 183 pp.

Templin, Mildred C., "Norms on Screening Test of Articulation for Ages Three through Eight." *Journal of Speech and Hearing Disorders*, Vol. 18, December 1953, pp. 323–331.

Theobald, Robert, *Free Man and Free Markets*. New York: Crown Publishers, Inc., 1963, 203 pp.

Thomas, Dominic Richard, *Oral Language, Sentence Structure and Vocabulary of Kindergarten Children Living in Low Socio-Economic Urban Areas*. Doctoral thesis. Detroit, Mich.: Wayne State University, 1962, 393 pp. Abstract: *Dissertation Abstracts*, Vol. 23, No. 3, 1962, p. 1014.

Trueblood, Dennis L., "The Role of the Counselor in the Guidance of Negro Students." *Harvard Educational Review*, Vol. 30, Summer 1960, pp. 252–269.

Turkewitz, G.; Gordon, E. W.; and Birch, Herbert G., "Head Turning in the Human Neonate: Spontaneous Patterns." *Journal of Genetic Psychology*, Vol. 107, September 1965, pp. 143–158.

Wax, Murray L.; Wax, Rosalie H.; and Dumont, Robert V., *Formal Education in an American Indian Community*. Society for the Study of Social Problems Monograph, Spring 1964, 126 pp.

Directory of Compensatory Practices

The directory which follows consists of an extensive sample of programs and practices that illustrate developments in compensatory education in the United States. The selection of particular programs or practices has in some instances been determined by the desire to illustrate a wide variety of practices and in other instances to reflect geographic distribution. The directory does not pretend to be a complete representation of programs and practices; however, programs that provide innovative and possibly fruitful approaches to educating the disadvantaged are included.

A number of preschool and tutoring programs have been omitted, especially those organized on a volunteer basis. Not only are volunteer programs numerous, but they are often similar in organization, approach, and services offered. Also omitted are a number of programs, usually university-based, devoted entirely to research. Because the directory focuses upon compensatory education programs operating in the public schools, the reader is referred to Chapter 6 for descriptions of programs operating in colleges and universities. The data for the directory were collected largely before the varied innovations stemming from Project Head Start programs could be adequately represented.

It is not surprising that any listing of this nature should be outdated before publication. Developments in this field have been rapid and new organizational forms are constantly emerging. It is hoped, however, that even though a few programs or practices mentioned may have been recently included under a new organizational structure or title, the ideas represented will be of service to the reader, and the contact person available for further details.

We wish to thank the many busy school administrators and project directors who managed to respond to requests for information.

Arizona

Phoenix:

Careers for Youth is a private pupil motivation program designed to help disadvantaged children raise their self-concepts and so motivate them to develop maximally their capabilities.

Date begun: January 1, 1960

Target population: Eight hundred disadvantaged pupils, 400 in two high schools and 400 in 11 elementary schools in inner-city areas, organized into "career clubs." Population roughly one-third each Negro, Mexican-American, and Anglo, selected on basis of principal and teacher judgments that children would profit from opportunity.

Per pupil costs: $75

Sponsoring group: Private solicitations and Choate Foundation (Ford Foundation grant ending 1965 for research).

Staff: School personnel, nonschool personnel, administrator, professional counselor, school coordinator.

Services: Career Clubs organized commencing at seventh grade and continuing through grade 12 with high school clubs organized in four vocational interest areas; extensive contact with successful people from world of work through visiting speakers and field trips to places of work; enrichment program includes field trips to concerts, art galleries, museums, theaters, and so forth; motivation trips to junior colleges and universities, government offices; participation in recreational activities, sports events, picnics, scenic outings, and so forth; in-city day camp summer program and integrated sleep-away camp; educational, vocational, and personal counseling; scholarship aid to purchase high school textbooks or for post-high school education.

Contact person:
John McBride, Executive Director
Careers for Youth
P. O. Box 2326, Phoenix, Arizona

Evaluation: Two year Ford Foundation-financed research study entitled *Phoenix Pupil Motivation Project*, concluded September 1965. Report completed January 1966.

Tucson:

1. The Safford Exploratory Program is a junior high school project aimed at promoting the self-awareness and self-respect of minority group students through helping them to take pride in their dual heritage and by extending their in-school and out-of-school experience to extend their concept of community and their place in it.

Date begun: September 1962

Target population: Five hundred pupils in grades 7 and 8 of one junior high school serving a low socioeconomic status area of Mexican-American and Negro families.

Per pupil costs: $875

Sponsoring group: Local school district.

Staff: Eight classroom teachers (working in two teams), full-time caseworker, secretary.

Services: Team approach at grade level, one team to each grade with four-hour block of time devoted to group work permitting flexibility of scheduling large and small group instruction and field trips; extensive use of speakers, demonstrations, field trips, films, and so forth; specially devised instructional materials and curriculum; parent involvement through home visits.

Contact person:
Thomas L. Lee, Deputy Superintendent
Board of Education
1010 East 10th Street, Tucson, Arizona

2. A Junior High School Pilot Program in Teaching English as a Second Language is designed to provide remedial English instruction, based on linguistic theory and method-

ology as well as on theories involving the culturally disadvantaged, to a group of children from Spanish-speaking homes.

Date begun: September 1963 (pilot group 1962–64)

Target population: Currently, 100 children in grades 7 and 8 in a junior high school serving a relatively low socioeconomic status largely Mexican-American population. Pupils chosen on basis of teacher evaluation that they have greater capacity than test results indicate.

Per pupil costs: $810

Sponsoring group: Local school district.

Staff: Four classroom teachers with part-time consultative help.

Services: Special academic program with extra period of language arts; use of special equipment such as tape recorders, special approaches such as linguistic analysis, and specially developed teaching materials.

Contact person:
Thomas L. Lee, Deputy Superintendent
Board of Education

Evaluation: Pilot study (1962–64) evaluated.

California

Berkeley:

1. The Berkeley City Unified School District Pilot Project in Compensatory Education is designed to reach children at the earliest possible age in school and so enrich their experiences as to prepare them for success in the first grade.

Date begun: February 1964

Target population: Five hundred and seventy-one children in kindergarten classes of five schools, Negro, Caucasian, and Oriental lower socioeconomic status pupils who remain in enriched program through first grade.

Per pupil costs: $65

Sponsoring group: State of California through McAteer Act and local school district.

Staff: Twelve regular kindergarten teachers, four additional resource kindergarten teachers.

Services: Reduced pupil-teacher ratio to allow for small group work; field trips and other cultural enrichment activities; parent conferences and workshops, and additional parental involvement through field trips and helping the teacher.

Contact person:
Neil V. Sullivan, Superintendent
Berkeley Unified School District
1414 Walnut Street, Berkeley, California

2. School Resource Volunteers, Inc., is a program designed to make use of the community's human resources to enrich the educational program, supplement the work of the classroom teacher, and improve school-community relations. All volunteers work under professional supervision.

Date begun: 1960

Target population: Volunteers are supplied on the basis of teacher requests (in classrooms throughout the school districts). The majority of volunteers fill requests in schools with a high proportion of Negro students.

Per pupil costs: Not determined

Sponsoring group: School district.

Staff: Some 550 volunteers, administrative personnel.

Services: Variety of services as needed by teachers, including general classroom assistance, individual and group work with children; after school assistance in study centers and clubs; volunteers also serve as guest speakers, entertainers, or both.

Contact person:
Mrs. Violet Smith
1222 University Avenue, Berkeley, California

Evaluation: Informal—teacher requests for volunteers exceed supply.

Bishop:

The Bishop Union Elementary School District "Study of the Socio-Economic and Anthropologic Impact of the Piute Indian Culture on the Educational Development of the Children" was designed to evaluate the effect of the Indian culture on the learning of their children and by a variety of activities to correct the existing imbalance between their potential and actual achievement.

Date begun: September 1963

Target population: Two hundred Indian children from preschool through eighth grade in three schools.

Per pupil costs: $27

Sponsoring group: State of California through McAteer Act and local school district.

Staff: Seven classroom teachers, guidance counselor, psychologist, physician, and nurse.

Services: Daily preschool classes for four-year-olds; individual and small group remedial work for primary, middle, and upper-grade pupils below grade level in achievement; field trips; individual counseling for seventh- and eighth-graders; monthly parent meetings for all grade levels; organization of community advisory committee.

Contact person:
Sidney L. Gardner, District Superintendent
201 Home Street, Bishop, California

Evaluation: Final report June 1965.

Centinela Valley:

The Pilot Project in Compensatory Education is essentially a teacher-counselor team guidance project designed to increase the self-understanding of and thereby promote improvement in attitude and achievement of a group of secondary school students.

Date begun: September 1963

Target population: Originally, 15 lower socioeconomic status pupils (30 pupils, 1964–65) in the tenth grade of one high school.

Per pupil costs: $482

Sponsoring group: State of California through McAteer Act and local school district.

Staff: Guidance counselor-psychometrist, curriculum coordinator, psychiatrist, nurse.

Services: Core curriculum in English and social studies in special class; extensive individual attention; case studies of each student prepared; inservice training sessions for teachers and counselors; group counseling and individual counseling and guidance.

Contact person:
Laban C. Strite, Project Director
Lennox High School
11033 South Buford
Lennox, California

Evaluation: Completed June 1965.

Central Union (see Kings County)

Chualar (see Monterey County)

Coachella Valley (see Riverside County)

Colusa:

Compensatory Education Program is a pilot project designed to alter the school achievement of disadvantaged children through altering attitudes among themselves, their parents, and the community.

Date begun: September 1963

Target population: Forty-two fourth- and fifth-grade pupils in one rural elementary school, largely lower socioeconomic status and 65 percent Mexican-American.

Per pupil costs: Not available

Sponsoring group: Local school district, County Health Department.

Staff: Guidance counselor, curriculum coordinator, psychologist, psychiatrist, nurse, social worker.

Services: Field trips; special reading program; after school activities; English instruction for non-English-speaking parents, home visits and parent and teacher conferences; social worker and nurse involved in evaluating home situation and consulting in school.

Contact person:
Carol Strifler, Coordinator
Route 1, Box 1890
Colusa, California

Contra Costa County:

The Rodeo-McAteer Pilot Program seeks to examine the feelings, attitudes, and behavior of the "educationally-socially discouraged child" and to adapt teaching methods and curriculum materials in order to improve the student's achievement as well as to increase the student's feeling of self-worth through guidance and counseling.

Date begun: September 1963

Target population: Eighteen seventh-graders who have had difficulty in school learning and 18 first-graders identified in kindergarten as not being "ready" for the usual first grade program.

Per pupil costs: $680 (not including testing and observation)

Sponsoring group: State of California through McAteer Act, County Department of Education, and local school district.

Staff: Four classroom teachers, curriculum and guidance consultants, librarian, shop teacher.

Services: Special guidance help; special curriculum help, modified academic program with extensive study trips, team teaching, shop-crafts program for older children; cooperative teacher effort in program development; special testing for experimental group; parental contacts and investigation of family status; modification of kindergarten program on basis of needs observed in first-grade group; project based on extensive past program of studies, surveys, and experimental activities.

Contact person:
Mary Ellen Maton, Guidance Consultant
Department of Education
Contra Costa County
75 Santa Barbara Road
Pleasant Hill, California 94523

Corcoran (see Kings County)

Fresno:

The Compensatory Education Program for Fresno was a multiphase program for students from preschool to high school which utilized a considerable amount of intraproject mutual help.

Date begun: October 1963

Target population: About 2,015 predominantly Negro pupils in the Fresno schools including 50 preschoolers in two classes, 1,640 pupils in grades K-6 in six elementary schools, and 375 pupils grades 7–12 in one junior and one senior high school in a center city area.

Sponsoring group: State of California through McAteer Act and local school district.

Staff: Coordinator, guidance counselor, teacher education specialists, student teachers, preschool nursery teachers, psychologist, home visitor, nurse, college students and other volunteers, reading adjustment teacher.

Services: Preschool program for three- and four-year-olds, including daily health inspection, with parent participation one morning and one evening per week; two preschools on junior high campuses with underachieving junior high schoolers selected as storytellers, and so forth; field trips for junior high schoolers participating in preschool program; special reading program for underachieving second- and third-graders, and extended day language arts program for second-graders at one elementary school; fifth- and sixth-graders used as tutors; after-school study centers staffed with teachers and sociology students from local college; drama students act plays in study centers; high school study centers include "jazz" room for music appreciation, typing room, and so forth; extensive program of field trips, including field trips to library for elementary pupils having good attendance; split session in elementary schools to permit smaller reading groups; nongraded English program in high school with language laboratory facilities, high school linguistics course, and course in Negro literature; extensive involvement of local state college students and local citizens in study trips, dinners out, "Big Brother" program, and so forth; evening counseling for parents; home visits; concentrated program of inservice teacher training.

Contact person:
Arthur Carlson, Director of Program
305 East Belgravia, Fresno, California

Evaluation: Final report completed and available: *Pilot Project in Compensatory Education.* Fresno City School District, June 4, 1965.

Hanford (see Kings County)

Indio (see Riverside County)

Kings County:

The Kings County Supplementary Experience Program is a wide-ranging compensatory project designed to develop a better understanding of the problems of disadvantaged students among the faculty and the community, to develop appropriate learning experiences for these students and improve student self-concept, and to involve student teachers and so develop future resources for dealing with these students. (This project includes: Central Union Elementary School District, Corcoran Unified School District, Hanford Elementary School District, Lemoore Union Elementary School District, Stratford Union Elementary School District.)

Date begun: September 1963

Target population: Two hundred and seventy pupils in nine elementary schools, 220 in grades K-3, 16 in grade 4, and 34 in grade 7, all from indigent or lower socioeconomic status families, 60 percent of whom are Mexican-American, 20 percent Negro.

Per pupil costs: $44

Sponsoring group: State of California through McAteer Act and local school district.

Staff: Fifteen classroom teachers, guidance counselor, curriculum coordinator, principals, college sociologist, college education teacher, attendance officer.

Services: Weekly teacher inservice training; use of student teachers from local state college to supplement classroom teacher and so provide for individual and small-group learning experiences which encourage language development; use of social welfare students to make home visits and develop project-student social histories; after-school enrichment activities; provision of special experiences, field trips, discussions, special language arts activities for project children.

Contact person:
Robert Bair
Kings County Court House
Hanford, California

N.B. Program expanded into nine school districts during 1966 with the aid of federal Elementary and Secondary Education Act funds.

Lemoore (see Kings County)

Lennox (see Centinela Valley)

Los Angeles:

1. The Supplementary Teaching Program is a seven-part project covering grades K-12 with a variety of activities designed to improve the attitudes toward and the performance in school of selected children having difficulties in their academic work, as well as to involve parents in the school goals.

Date begun: September 1963

Target population: Eight hundred and forty-three children in grades K-6, 907 children in grades 7–9, and 814 pupils grades 10–12 in 28 schools, and 298 adults.

Per pupil costs: $23

Sponsoring group: State of California through McAteer Act and local school district.

Staff: Classroom teachers, reading coordinators and consultants, student teacher-aides, counselors, school-community workers.

Services: In six elementary schools 20 hours per week supplementary teaching time after regular school day for remedial reading, arithmetic improvement, added use of library, individual tutoring, and supervision of homework; use of student aides to assist teachers; coordinated parent education project to enlist parent cooperation in promoting school goals. On secondary level, inservice teacher training; in five schools, reading rooms providing basic reading course for most disadvantaged readers, and reading improvement classes for pupils at least one-and-a-half grades below placement in reading; after-school library with study assistance; evening parental counseling; Child Observation Project involving parents and children in one 3-hour class per week of parent observation and discussion of nursery program for preschoolers; school-community workers to provide new-student orientation and to make contact with families new to area.

Contact person:
George McMullen, Director
Los Angeles Unified School District
    McAteer Project
Los Angeles City Board of Education
450 North Grand Avenue
Los Angeles, California

Evaluation: Completed and available (1964–65).

2. The Saturday School provides a variety of supplementary educational, recreational, and enrichment activities for children in disadvantaged neighborhoods.

Date begun: September 1964

Target population: Twelve hundred pupils in 21 schools for classroom instruction; 4,500 other pupils using recreational and library facilities.

Per pupil costs: Not determined

Sponsoring group: United States Office of Economic Opportunity and local school district.

Staff: Eighty-four teachers, playground directors, other school staff.

Services: Concentrated instruction in reading, arithmetic, language arts, use of library, and homework concepts; special activity programs; playground and library activities; bus trips to cultural events; playgrounds and libraries open to children not in academic program.

Contact person:
Harry Handler, Director
Research and Development
Los Angeles City Board of Education

3. The Student Achievement Center Program offers concentrated remedial work in various academic areas in order to help disadvantaged secondary school pupils achieve academic success, as well as attempting to involve the parents in school goals.

Date begun: September 1964

Target population: One thousand disadvantaged pupils at four junior and three senior high schools.

Per pupil costs: Not determined

Sponsoring group: United States Office of Economic Opportunity and local school district.

Staff: Four teachers, counselor, school-community coordinator at each of seven centers.

Services: Special rooms with specialized resources for remedial work in communications skills, social studies, and mathematics for pupils at each of six secondary school grade-levels; counselor to work with able as well as disadvantaged pupils; school-community coordinator to provide liaison between school, parents, and community.

Contact person:
Harry Handler, Director
Research and Development
Los Angeles City Board of Education

4. In addition to the programs described above, a number of other programs and practices have been developed in the school system to benefit disadvantaged pupils. Among them are:

Assignment of additional teachers to areas serving large numbers of disadvantaged pupils in order to reduce class size, or provide special remedial services. These include special programs for non-English-speaking and foreign students whose ability to read, write, and speak English is inadequate for their participation in the regular school program.

Divided Primary Day provides for staggered school opening and closing in order to reduce the number of pupils in reading classes at one time, and thereby allow for more intensified reading instruction.

The Back-to-School Project, an extension of the nationwide dropout program of the summer of 1963, now operates in two schools, offering extensive individual counseling and an individually designed program of academic and vocational training.

Contact person:
Harry Handler, Director
Research and Development
Los Angeles City Board of Education

5. Among the practices developed by voluntary and community personnel are:

An estimated 100 tutoring projects of various types operate within the geographical boundaries of the Los Angeles City School District.

One major program, the Student Tutorial Education Project (STEP), functions with summer school programs. Others at the primary or secondary level are largely run by various community organizations who recruit tutors from local high schools and colleges, and provide funds, if any, for paying them.

6. Among the practices developed in cooperation with the Youth Opportunities Board of Greater Los Angeles are:

A preschool program in 10 centers which has been in operation since September 1964, serving 200 three- and four-year-olds in classes of 25. One center, located in a Mexican-American neighborhood, teaches English as a second language.

A counseling team approach is used in a "reception room" program to determine proper classroom placement of children new to a school about whom there are insufficient data.

A group counseling program in five junior and five senior high schools in poverty areas involves intensive group and individual counseling for pupils identified as potential dropouts. A related summer program includes enrollment in a summer class of choice or need.

Summer study centers at 24 schools include such activities as a reading clinic, language clinic, library, art, and instrumental music workshops, and so forth, for elementary pupils; while at the secondary level, Summer Opportunity Centers at 10 poverty area schools provide enrichment programs including field trips in such areas as social science, agriculture, industrial arts, mathematics, and so forth.

Extended day programs similar to those under the McAteer program (q.v.) operate in 70 elementary schools and serve about 8,000 children.

Job readiness programs involving counseling,

206

testing, and vocational training for jobless out-of-school youth include one center providing free evening art classes for dropouts.

Contact person:
Joseph P. Maldonado, Director
Youth Opportunity Board of
    Greater Los Angeles
220 North Broadway
Los Angeles, California

Los Nietos:

Experimental Program for Culturally Disadvantaged Children in the Los Nietos School District is an early intervention program designed to help prepare Spanish-speaking children for success in school.

Date begun: June 1963

Target population: Thirty lower socioeconomic status Mexican-American children initially picked up in prekindergarten summer school.

Per pupil costs: $59

Sponsoring group: State of California through McAteer Act and local school district.

Staff: Two classroom teachers, guidance counselor, curriculum coordinator, psychologist, nurse.

Services: Prekindergarten summer school with bilingual teacher; many home visits and parental involvement in school, including classroom observation; substitute teacher to release teacher for work with parents; visiting community workers; field trips; children's books in English and Spanish for parents to read.

Contact person:
Martha S. Hittinger, Director of Curriculum
Box 2006, Los Nietos, California

Merced:

Teaching Spanish to Mexican-American Students is a program designed to stress the cultural and academic advantages of bilingualism for the Mexican-American pupil in terms

of his future academic and vocational achievement, and to help Spanish-speaking pupils to learn correct Spanish.

Date begun: 1963 (preceded by a pilot, September 1962–63)

Target population: One hundred and eighty seventh- and eighth-grade lower socioeconomic status Mexican-American pupils.

Per pupil costs: $55

Sponsoring group: State of California through McAteer Act and local school district.

Staff: Two classroom teachers, special language teacher, core teacher, curriculum coordinator, guidance counselor, principal.

Services: Daily Spanish classes with Spanish-speaking pupils grouped according to ability to read, write, and speak Spanish; study of Hispanic culture reinforced by program with school in Mercedes, Uruguay; use of audiovisual materials; Spanish clubs; parental involvement; guidance and counseling including information on bilingual job opportunities.

Contact person:
William C. DeSimone, Principal
Tanaya School
2821 Tahoe Drive, Merced, California

Evaluation: Students tested before and after a year of study. Program description including special testing materials available for $1 from Mr. DeSimone.

Monterey County:

The Compensatory Education Program in the Chualar Union Elementary School District is designed to enrich the experience of Spanish-speaking children in order to improve their language skills, to involve their parents and the community in the school program, and to instill in parents and children pride in their cultural heritage.

Date begun: October 1963 (ended June 1965)

Target population: Fifty-six seventh- and

eighth-grade Mexican-American and Filipino students in one elementary school.

Per pupil costs: $36

Sponsoring group: State of California through McAteer Act and local school district.

Staff: Classroom teachers, language arts teacher, special teacher familiar with Mexican customs.

Services: Language-arts teacher provides individual remedial work and Spanish teaching; field trips; Spanish-English newsletter to go to the home; community music programs; adult education classes in Spanish and English; establishment of library in Chualar fire house—first in community.

Contact person:
Mrs. Esther M. Bird, Project Director
Compensatory Education Project
Box 188, Chualar, California

Oakland:

1. The Interagency School Project, Oakland Public Schools, is a broad-scale program designed to prevent future learning disabilities among primary children and to provide enrichment and counseling services to overcome existing learning disabilities at the higher grade levels.

Date begun: March 1962

Target population: Approximately 120 preschoolers, 1,800 pupils in two elementary schools, 900 pupils in one junior high school, 3,900 pupils in two senior high schools. All schools drawing from a lower socioeconomic status population, 80 percent plus Negro. (Twelve additional elementary schools, three junior highs, and three high schools have after-school study programs enrolling 2,000 pupils and 250 paid school-age tutors.)

Per pupil costs: Not available

Sponsoring group: Ford Foundation, local school district.

Staff: Sixteen classroom teachers, guidance counselors, attendance supervisors, reading specialists, psychologist, librarians, elementary and secondary counselors, research assistant, curriculum development specialists.

Services: At preschool level, enrichment and language and cognitive development; parent aides involved in daily activities and in parent education classes. At primary level, language development classes using new methods and materials; individual and group conferences with pupils and parents; inservice teacher education; increased library services including during summer. At junior high school level, team approach with English teachers and reading specialists concentrating on language-arts skills; counseling and guidance with parental involvement; after-school study centers at all levels using volunteer and paid tutors; field trips; summer teacher workshops. At high school level, intensive counseling and guidance services to the potential dropout; extended vocational testing and career guidance services, work experience programs, and special combinations of employment and school attendance; adjustment center for re-entry of dropouts. For teen-age pregnant girls, instructional, counseling, guidance, medical, and recreational services to enable students to continue their education and ultimately return to school.

Contact person:
Andrew J. Viscovich, Director
Interagency School Project, School Programs
1025 Second Avenue
Oakland, California 94606

2. The Willow Manor Oral Language Project is a program which attempts both to broaden the experiential background of disadvantaged children and to increase their opportunities to use language within the school day.

Date begun: July 1963 (preceded by a pilot, September 1962-June 1963)

Target population: The entire school population at Willow Manor School (350 children).

Per pupil costs: Not determined

Sponsoring group: Local school district.

Staff: Fourteen teachers, parent aides, teacher assistant, principal, remedial reading teacher, instructional clerk, guidance consultant, nurse, librarian.

Services: Examination of all activities and curriculum areas for opportunities to increase use of language; teacher assistant to develop materials, such as listening tapes, for teacher use; parent aides in each classroom for two hours a day to assist teacher in variety of activities; extensive use of audiovisual materials, dramatics, storytelling, singing, and materials which enable children to hear speech well used; trips into community and visits with adults who have interesting occupations.

Contact person:
Edward Cockrum, Assistant Superintendent
Oakland Public Schools
1025 Second Avenue
Oakland, California 94606

N.B. The Willow Manor program has served as an effective pilot leading to a Language Development Project sponsored by the Oakland Public Schools and the United States Office of Economic Opportunity for 1965–66, during which services were expanded to four additional Oakland schools. Among the additional resources were four language specialists, 80 parent aides, a research assistant, data processing, and equipment. Both the Willow Manor and Language Development Projects have recently become beneficiaries of the Oakland's EASE Program of Compensatory Education, a program serving 11,000 children in 11 elementary schools.

3. The Remedial Reading Centers project is designed to provide intensive remedial work through the establishment of workshops and to combat the characteristic slowing of the rate of achievement in disadvantaged children, thereby improving the general achievement, and extending the educational careers.

Date begun: 1964

Target population: About 8,700 lower socio-economic status children in 10 elementary schools.

Per pupil costs: Not determined

Sponsoring group: Local school district and federal government.

Staff: Ten remedial reading teachers, research associate, and clerk.

Services: Entire faculty, assisted by the reading specialist, will identify pupils with reading difficulty. Reading specialist then undertakes remedial activities, working with children as individuals and in small groups. Pupils are released from the remedial activities when they have developed strength enough to operate successfully in the regular classroom situation.

Contact person:
Alden W. Badal, Assistant in Research
Oakland Public Schools

4. Centers for Academically Talented Children is a program designed to offer the kind of program provided for gifted children to culturally disadvantaged pupils whose IQ scores do not qualify them for admission to such classes, but whose potential is judged to be high.

Date begun: 1964

Target population: Two classes of 25 students entering sixth grade, 60 percent Negro, 10 percent Oriental, 5 percent Mexican, and 25 percent Caucasian, referred by teachers and principals.

Per pupil costs: Not determined

Sponsoring group: Local school district.

Staff: Two teachers, principals of participating schools, psychologists as needed.

Services: Class size limited to 25; instructional program includes regular sixth-grade subjects plus opportunities to pursue individual projects; supplementary books and materials; rewriting or revising of instructional materials.

Contact person:
Donald G. Anderson, Director of Elementary Education
Oakland Public Schools

5. The Ten Schools Project is a program aimed at improving the academic achievement, at raising the self-image of disadvantaged pupils, and at involving their parents in the school program.

Date begun: 1963

Target population: Pupils at 10 elementary schools enrolling large numbers of disadvantaged children.

Per pupil costs: Regular school budget

Sponsoring group: Local school district.

Staff: Classroom teachers, teachers' aides.

Services: General emphasis on raising academic standards for all grades; home visits by room mothers and classroom teachers; parent aid enlisted for library work, field trips, nurses helpers, and so forth; teacher-formed Uplift Committee concerned with help with academic and personal habits.

Contact person:
Alden W. Badal, Assistant in Research
Oakland Public Schools

6. Other programs and practices have been instituted by the Oakland Public Schools for the improvement of education for the disadvantaged. Among them are:

Extensive inservice education to increase staff understanding of the disadvantaged, including 28 half-hour television showings for course credit on teaching the culturally deprived.

A compensatory education program at Gold-en Gate Elementary School involves 94 pupils, grades 1–6, in a program of intensive counseling and remedial work in special classes.

Contact person:
Alden Badal, Assistant in Research
Oakland Public Schools

Oasis (see Riverside County)

Oxnard:

The McAteer Program is designed to help overcome the cultural and language-related handicaps of the Spanish-speaking children of the community.

Date begun: September 1963

Target population: About 365 elementary, 180 junior high, and 65 senior high school pupils, 75 percent of whom are Mexican-American.

Per pupil costs: $36

Sponsoring group: State of California through McAteer Act and local school district.

Staff: Language resource teacher, teacher's aides, subject supervisors, guidance counselors, psychologists, attendance officers.

Services: Use of language experience approach to teaching of reading at first-grade level; special English instruction and help in other subject areas by language resource teacher for non-English-speaking students; teacher aide to help in preparation of instructional materials; work-study center with special instructional materials for all grades; parent interviews.

Contact person:
Alvin E. Robinson, Assistant Superintendent
255 Palm Drive, Oxnard, California

Palo Alto:

1. Increasing the Receptivity of Culturally Deprived Children to School Learnings through Home-School Contacts is a program devoted to improving home-school interre-

lationships in order to promote improved school motivation and performance.

Date begun: November 1964

Target population: Three hundred and thirty-seven lower socioeconomic status Negro pupils in grades 1–6 of one elementary school.

Per pupil costs: $22

Sponsoring group: State of California through McAteer Act and local school district.

Staff: Twenty-two classroom teachers, guidance counselor, curriculum coordinator, social workers.

Services: Inservice teacher preparation for home visits; released time for teachers to visit homes, with follow-up consultation for evaluation.

Contact person:
Alfred J. Villa, Director, Pupil Personnel Services
Ravenswood City School District
2160 Euclid Avenue, Palo Alto, California

Evaluation: Completed in July 1965.

2. An Automated Primary-Grade Reading and Arithmetic Curriculum for Culturally Deprived Children is designed to identify through detailed analysis those areas in reading and mathematics curriculums which present particular difficulties for culturally deprived children, and, by eliminating them, to prevent early failure.

Date begun: July 1964

Target population: One hundred and eighty children, grades preschool through 4, mainly non-Caucasian, selected from a disadvantaged population.

Per pupil costs: Not determined

Sponsoring group: United States Office of Education.

Staff: Two teachers, two specialized teachers, psychologists, project directors.

Services: Summer school project involving computer-assisted instruction and continuous rewriting of curriculum as difficulties are encountered by children; use of audiovisual techniques in computerized environment; on-line use of computer-controlled teaching terminals is one of essential characteristics of project.

Contact person:
Patrick Suppes
Richard C. Atkinson, Co-Directors
Stanford University, Palo Alto, California

Pasadena:

1. The Compensatory Education program in Pasadena is a broad-scale program aimed at improving pupil self-image and achievement, expanding pupil horizons, and involving parents in the school-child goals.

Date begun: September 1963

Target population: Approximately 1,089 pupils in grades K-6 at one elementary school.

Per pupil costs: $43

Sponsoring group: State of California through McAteer Act and local school district.

Staff: Classroom teachers, enrichment teacher, orientation teacher, teacher-librarian, community volunteers serving as teacher aides, school-community coordinator, reading teacher.

Services: Extensive language program involving tapes for listening, encouragement of reading, writing, speaking; remedial reading program; reduced pupil-teacher ratio for selected classes; Lincoln library with filmstrips, pictures, tapes, records, as well as books for teacher and pupil use; enrichment through trips, musical events, art museum scholarships; orientation teacher to introduce each new child to some community youth group; psychological counseling; inservice training for teachers; cooperation with community assistance agencies to provide counseling and assistance to families.

Contact person:
Edward Shutman
Department of Intergroup Education
Pasadena Public Schools
351 South Hudson Avenue
Pasadena, California

2. Other practices: A Higher Horizons sort of program involving cultural enrichment, curriculum revision, and guidance has operated in Pasadena under the name of HOPE (Higher Opportunities in Pasadena Education) since 1961. It now functions in eight elementary schools, one junior high, and two senior high schools.

A reading laboratory staffed by a reading specialist and volunteer graduate assistants operates in one junior high school. A P.T.A.-school sponsored after-school study center operates in another junior high school.

Contact Person:
George W. Norene, Superintendent
Pasadena Public Schools

A special art program jointly sponsored by the Pasadena Art Museum and the schools is designed to explore the effectiveness of an after-school program of special art education in improving general attitudes toward learning.

Contact person:
Grace McFarland
Assistant Superintendent of
  Elementary Schools
Pasadena Public Schools

Pittsburg:

The Compensatory Education Program attempted to reorganize the science curriculum in order to provide for more experimentation and make science more meaningful and interesting to disadvantaged children.

Date begun: November 1963

Target population: One hundred predominantly white lower socioeconomic status seventh- and eighth-grade pupils from one school.

Per pupil costs: $36

Sponsoring group: State of California through McAteer Act and local school district.

Staff: Guidance counselor, curriculum coordinator, three classroom teachers, attendance officer.

Services: Special practical science curriculum directed toward gardening and practical botany; reduced reading and text activities with emphasis on direct experiences in garden plots, experimental raising of plants; special classroom and laboratory activities in mathematics, home economics, woodshop, and language.

Contact person:
Douglas Usedom, Project Director
Mt. Diablo McAteer Project
611 Pacifica Avenue
Pittsburg, California

Pleasant Hill (see Contra Costa County)

Ravenswood (see Palo Alto)

Redwood City:

The Sequoia Union High School District Compensatory Education Program, initially a teacher retraining project, now includes curriculum revision in the areas of social studies and English.

Date begun: October 1963

Target population: Seventy-five students in grades 10 and 11 of one high school.

Per pupil costs: Not determined

Sponsoring group: State of California through McAteer Act and local school district.

Staff: Two classroom teachers, consultants, psychologist, principal.

Services: Concentration on continuing in-service retraining of teachers and on reworking of curricular offerings with particular attention to differences in cognitive processes of pupils involved; group counseling sessions with students.

Contact person:
Elizabeth Van Dalsem,
  Director Guidance and Research
Sequoia Union High School District
480 James Avenue
Redwood City, California 94062

Riverside County:

The Coachella Valley McAteer Pilot Project for Spanish-Speaking Culturally Disadvantaged Children involves six school districts in a program to raise the educational achievement, aspirational level, and community acceptance image of local Spanish-speaking children.

Date begun: September 1963

Target population: Three hundred and sixty children in grades 1–3; 50 sixth-graders; 50 eighth-graders; 40 eleventh-graders, all of them Spanish-speaking Mexican-Americans of lower socioeconomic status, many of them children of agricultural migrants.

Per pupil costs: $36

Sponsoring group: State of California through McAteer Act and local school district.

Staff: Curriculum coordinators, psychologists, speech consultant.

Services: In three general areas—increasing total language facility, particularly at primary level, with special sound training program and special reading program with language experience approach; expanded school libraries; study halls; bilingual teacher aide program; at upper grade levels attempts to measure self-image of population with interviews and project-devised self-concept scale; use of high school students from same population as interpreter aides in teaching and counseling; interviews with "successful" children to determine elements of their success; involvement of parents in project

through Spanish festival celebrating opening of school; positive emphasis on Mexican-American heritage.

Contact person:
William D. Stocks, Director of Instruction
Riverside County Schools
82-675 Avenue 46
Indio, California

Rodeo (see Contra Costa County)

Sacramento:

1. Neighborhood Study Centers is a study hall program for children whose own homes do not provide a place, the materials, and the personal help for effective study.

Date begun: September 1963

Target population: Some 2,000 children, half minority group (Mexican and Negro) in 27 study centers throughout the city.

Per pupil costs: Not determined

Sponsoring group: Community Welfare Council of the Greater Sacramento Area, Inc., funded by United States Office of Economic Opportunity, 1965–66.

Staff: Six hundred volunteer tutors, college and high school students, and community volunteers, paid supervisory personnel from various agencies, coordinating staff.

Services: Study centers in churches, schools, neighborhood centers, union hall, juvenile detention center—all containing reference books, writing materials, and tutors to provide assistance when needed; coordination with schools to encourage attendance and meet student needs; involvement of various community agencies and neighborhood people in providing facilities, supervisory personnel, materials, refreshments, and so forth.

Contact persons:
Marion Joseph, Director, or
  Leah Chase, Coordinator
Community Welfare Council
1010 24th Street, Sacramento, California

2. Two special adult education projects conducted by the local school district were designed to improve the competence of disadvantaged parents and thereby improve the prospects for their children. The Parent-Child Observation Classes for Mothers Receiving Aid to Needy Children involves mother and child participation in mutual learning experiences. Classes are given five days a week.

Date begun: February 1963

Target population: Parents of culturally disadvantaged children—260 children, 13 classes.

Per pupil costs: Not determined

Sponsoring group: Local school district, United States Office of Economic Opportunity.

Staff: Thirteen teachers for parents' class, 13 teacher-aides, 13 male work-experience high school students (often of lower socioeconomic status), nurse, school social worker, psychometrist, clerk coordinator.

Contact person:
Mrs. Jeanada Nolan, Coordinator
Sacramento City Unified School District
Sacramento, California

Evaluation: Agnes S. Robinson, *A Progress Report on Adult Special Education Projects, October 22, 1963.* Continuing evaluation.

The Literacy Program for Culturally Deprived Dependent Parents involves six classes in basic academics, reading, mathematics, discussion of family and school problems, and home and family management courses. At present 150 adults are enrolled.

Contact person:
Tom Weems, Director
Adult Education
Sacramento City Unified School District

San Bernardino:

1. Training Natural Talent is a program to identify underachievers and provide them with enrichment and counseling in order to raise their aspiration level and their achievement.

Date begun: January 1959

Target population: One hundred and thirty predominantly Negro and Mexican-American students in five elementary schools (sixth-grade only), one junior high, and one senior high school. Two-thirds of the group rank over 110 in IQ.

Per pupil costs: $100

Sponsoring group: Local school district (Ford Foundation carried 50 percent from 1959 to 1963).

Staff: Ten classroom teachers, guidance counselors, reading specialist, subject supervisor, curriculum coordinator, psychologist, art consultant, music consultant, social worker, nurse, dean.

Services: Extensive field trip program; cultural activities; new classroom materials; teacher reorientation; individual and group counseling and guidance; parent meetings and home visits; summer school program with reading improvement emphasis.

Contact person:
John D. Gathings
1290 Muscott Street
San Bernardino, California

Evaluation: Completed and available, *A Minority of One.* San Bernardino City Schools Publication, San Bernardino, California, 1964.

N.B. Program expanded in 1965 to one junior high, one high school, and 14 elementary schools, with federal Elementary and Secondary Education Act funds; plans for 1966 call for serving all children in all schools.

2. San Bernardino City Schools Compensatory Education Project is an early intervention program emphasizing oral language work and enrichment activities as a means

of overcoming deficiencies of experience, vocabulary, and language among disadvantaged children.

Date begun: September 1963

Target population: Approximately 1,500 children, largely Negro and Mexican-American, in grades K-3 in 10 schools.

Per pupil costs: $37

Sponsoring group: State of California through McAteer Act and local school district.

Staff: Classroom teachers, teacher aides.

Services: Seminars to orient teachers and project personnel to new techniques and to an understanding of the disadvantaged; specially planned experiences for language opportunity; field study trips and tours; use of aides to provide more small-group conversation; parent-teacher home conferences.

Contact person:
Ethel Johnson, Project Director
San Bernardino City Unified School District
799 F Street, San Bernardino, California

San Diego:

Pilot Project in Compensatory Education hopes to raise student aspiration and achievement by enriching school experiences, increasing teacher acceptance, and helping parents develop realistic goals.

Date begun: October 1963

Target population: Seven hundred and fifty children from three elementary schools and 750 children from two junior high schools. Extended program including two primary, four elementary, two junior high, and two senior high schools to begin September 1965 with aspects of program extended to a total of 31 schools.

Per pupil costs: $36

Sponsoring group: State of California through McAteer Act and local school district.

Staff: Sixty classroom teachers, guidance counselor, reading specialists, curriculum coordinator, speech teacher, psychologist, home visitors, physician, nurses, social worker.

Services: At elementary level: use of teacher assistants to allow for more individualization of instruction; academic emphasis on language arts and number concepts; enrichment through field trips, and so forth; counseling; after-school reading rooms; use of substitutes to allow teacher time to meet with parents. At secondary level: basic skills classes; extensive curriculum revision with program enriched and extended through use of resource teachers and volunteer college student tutors; inservice teacher reorientation; field trips; group counseling.

Contact person:
William H. Stegemen,
    Assistant Superintendent
Curriculum Services, Education Center
San Diego City Schools
Park and El Cajon Boulevards
San Diego, California

Evaluation: In progress (but see *Pilot Project in Compensatory Education*, San Diego City Schools, January 1965).

San Francisco:

1. San Francisco's McAteer project is essentially a field-trip program designed to broaden the experiential base of minority group children.

Date begun: September 1963

Target population: About 1,518 second-graders in 12 schools, and 1,384 eighth-graders in four junior high schools. Children are predominantly of Chinese, Negro, and Spanish-speaking background.

Per pupil costs: $36

Sponsoring group: State of California through McAteer Act and local school district.

Staff: Thirty-six elementary classroom teachers, and a comparable number of junior high school teachers.

Services: Entire project devoted to trips into community combined with pre-trip and post-trip activities related to the experiences, including resource visitors to school, panel discussions, written compositions, and so forth; trips included theater and ballet, museums, aquarium, dairy ranch, bridges, and so forth; some trips vocationally oriented; parent participation in trips.

Contact person:
Isadore Pivnick, Supervisor,
    Compensatory Education
Board of Education
135 Van Ness Avenue
San Francisco 2, California

2. The School-Community Improvement Program is the outgrowth of a pilot project which was devoted to developing solutions to the reading and language problems of disadvantaged children with attention to their relevance to later employability or college placement.

Date begun: February 1961 (pilot ended June 1964—has been extended under a Supervisor of Compensatory Education)

Target population: Pilot served 1,400 pupils in two elementary schools, 150 pupils in one junior high school, and 3,000 pupils in three senior high schools—all predominantly Negro of lower-middle or lower socioeconomic status. Extended program involves a total of 47 schools.

Per pupil costs: $40 (pilot)

Sponsoring group: Ford Foundation and local school district.

Staff: Eighty-four classroom teachers, guidance counselors, reading specialists, home visitors, social worker.

Services: Remedial and developmental reading classes; extensive testing and evaluation of new materials, cultural enrichment activities; volunteer-staffed study centers; field trips and camping experiences; resource teachers to work with children and other teachers; demonstration and observation lessons; teacher training in reading and human relations; summer teacher workshops; recruitment and training of volunteer storytellers; counseling; career clinics, jobs for youth; home visiting.

Contact person:
Isadore Pivnick, Supervisor,
    Compensatory Education
Board of Education

3. The Superintendent's Compensatory Program is designed to provide special help, particularly in the language arts area, to enable disadvantaged children to compete successfully in school.

Date begun: September 1961 (preceded by pilot February–June 1961)

Target population: Pupils residing in areas heavily populated by Negro, Oriental, and Spanish-speaking families. Pupils identified for help had severe reading problems.

Per pupil costs: $150

Sponsoring group: Local school district.

Staff: Supervisor and three resource teachers give service to 58 classroom teachers.

Services: Special help in language arts skills in reading and language laboratory; introduction of special materials, equipment, and techniques to facilitate learning; wide use of field trips; inservice training; study centers.

Contact person:
Isadore Pivnick, Supervisor,
    Compensatory Education
Board of Education

4. The Drama Demonstration Project is a pilot study which attempts to demonstrate that drama can be used to motivate pupils to stay in school and can help provide them with the skills necessary to succeed. Program cooperates closely with four community agencies.

Date begun: September 1963

Target population: Seventy-two pupils attending school in a low socioeconomic area.

Per pupil costs: $110

Sponsoring group: Rosenberg Foundation and local school district.

Staff: An in-school and out-of-school coordinator, plus nine teachers assigned part time

Services: Pupils travel in groups of 18 to mathematics, social studies, English, and physical education; electives consist of drama, shop, home economics, art, and music; special attention given to use of drama throughout entire day and in after-school program in four centers.

Contact person:
Isadore Pivnick, Supervisor,
  Compensatory Education
Board of Education

5. A Family School Program for Bilingual Families with Preschool Children is designed to provide help to young families, recent immigrants from non-English-speaking countries.

Date begun: September 1964

Target population: Disadvantaged and/or bilingual families with young children, recent immigrants from Latin America, the Caribbean, the Far East, and some European countries.

Per pupil costs: Not determined

Sponsoring group: United Community Fund, Bothin Helping Fund.

Staff: Teachers, social workers, psychologists.

Services: Concurrent classes for mothers and children in same building, but with separate rooms and teachers, continued for a year or two after arrival in the United States; mothers' classes involve English language and introduction to the culture of the United States; nursery school program involves language instruction, enrichment, socialization.

Contact person:
Irving Kriegsfeld
Mission Neighborhood Center
2595 Mission Street
San Francisco, California

Santa Fe Springs (see Los Nietos)

Sausalito:

scope, the Sausalito School District Compensatory Education Program, is designed to improve student performance through enrichment and counseling, and through increasing teacher understanding and educational effectiveness, as well as to encourage mutual school-home-community interrelationships.

Date begun: October 1963

Target population: Approximately 511 children in grades K-8.

Per pupil costs: $58

Sponsoring group: State of California through McAteer Act and local school district.

Staff: Remedial reading teachers, psychologist, social worker, pupil personnel counselor.

Services: Counseling and guidance; extensive inservice teacher reorientation; home visits; field trips; after-school recreation and clubs; outdoor science and conservation education school; tutoring centers.

Contact person:
Charles Nagel, Coordinator
Civic Center, Marin County
San Rafael, California

Sequoia (see Redwood City)

Stanford University (see Palo Alto)

Stockton:

Stockton Program of Education for Enrichment for Disadvantaged Youth (speedy) is an elementary school program which seeks to improve the self-image, attitudes, and achievement of disadvantaged children.

Date begun: October 1963

Target population: Six hundred and ninety lower socioeconomic status pupils in three elementary schools, predominantly of minority group origin, Negro, Mexican-American, or Asian.

Per pupil costs: $34

Sponsoring group: State of California through McAteer Act and local school district.

Staff: Forty-four classroom teachers, resource teachers.

Services: Broad attack on remedial reading; extensive program of trips to cultural and other enrichment experiences, often with parents involved; inservice teacher reorientation; development of special vocabulary-building and other original teaching materials, study hall and library programs.

Contact person:
Jeff B. West, Assistant Superintendent
Elementary Education
Board of Education
701 North Madison Street
Stockton, California

Stratford (see Kings County)

Thermal (see Riverside County)

Tulare:

Preschool Program is designed to provide opportunities to deprived children for improved language development and to further provide an avenue for parent education.

Date begun: October 1964

Target population: Twenty-four preschool children, predominantly Negro and Mexican-American.

Per pupil costs: Not determined

Sponsoring group: Rosenberg Foundation, local school district.

Staff: Two preschool teachers, volunteer, psychologists, principal, Assistant Superin-

tendent of Schools, Executive Secretary, Rosenberg Foundation.

Services: Preschool program including language arts, social studies, science, art, and music; use of audiovisual techniques; field trips, often with volunteer adult participation for individualization of experience; pupil and parental counseling and guidance; health care.

Contact person:
Glena Crumal, Principal
Lincoln School
Tulare, California

Willowbrook (P. O. Los Angeles)

The Willowbrook Extended Learning Program (WELP) is designed to improve the academic performance, the social adjustment, and the motivation of a group of intermediate students through enrichment activities, with emphasis in the language arts area, and through extension of the school day.

Date begun: January 1964

Target population: Two hundred and fifty pupils in grades 4 and 5 of five elementary schools, predominantly Negro and Mexican-American recent migrants. (Equal number in control group.)

Per pupil costs: $24

Sponsoring group: State of California through McAteer Act and local school district.

Staff: Ten classroom teachers, curriculum coordinators, psychologist, director of special services, nurse, attendance officer.

Services: Sixty-minute enrichment and developmental reading class after school each day; class size held to 25; field study trips and assembly speakers; inservice teacher training; group and individual parent conferences; parent workshops for parents to assemble materials needed for project.

Contact person:
Mrs. Doris Jean Austin, Project Director
Curriculum Consultant for Willowbrook
  School District
1623 East 118th Street
Los Angeles, California

Evaluation: Various tests listed.

Colorado

Denver:

1. The Pilot Program for the Disadvantaged is a program designed to upgrade the social and educational development of disadvantaged pupils.

Date begun: September 1962

Target population: About 1,700 elementary pupils in 17 schools, 510 junior high school pupils in two schools, and 360 high school pupils in two schools.

Per pupil costs: Not determined

Sponsoring group: Local school district.

Staff: Eighty-four elementary, 17 junior high, and 11 high school teachers, coordinators.

Services: Team teaching at elementary level with two teachers assigned per class for work on reading and language development for half the day; junior high school has similar program for two periods a day; special teacher selection and training; emphasis on using child's own experiences in teaching activities and on appropriate materials selection; full hour of arithmetic per day.

Contact person:
Dorothy S. Raynolds, Supervisor
Department of General Curriculum Services
414 14th Street, Denver, Colorado

2. Various other practices have been put into effect in the Denver Public Schools many of them designed to implement the recommendations of a Special Study Committee on Equality of Educational Opportunity. Among them are:

An Orientation Room program is designed to provide individualized instruction to transient students whose achievement is below grade level. Pupils remain in these special classes for periods from two to eight weeks and are then transferred to a regular school class.

Various approaches to the improvement of reading include a pilot program which initiates reading instruction in kindergarten; a summer vacation reading program in cooperation with the Denver Public Library; and a summer reading improvement program for pupils below grade in reading achievement.

Study hall programs are school sponsored at the primary level and community sponsored for older children.

Summer workshops and curriculum writing centers prepare materials for the early reading program and train kindergarten and intermediate teachers for follow-up activities.

Connecticut

Hartford:

The Fred D. Wish School Higher Horizons Program is a broad-spectrum project designed to help a group of disadvantaged children attain their maximum potential.

Date begun: September 1962

Target population: About 934 predominantly lower socioeconomic status Negro pupils, representing the entire student body, kindergarten through eighth grade, in one elementary school. (Extended to a second school 1964–65.)

Per pupil costs: $55

Sponsoring group: Local school board.

Staff: Guidance counselor, pupil adjustment worker, reading consultant, psychologist, remedial reading teacher, speech therapist, librarian, helping teacher, special music, art, French, woodworking, home economics and physical education teachers, teachers for mentally retarded, physician, nurse, dental hygienist, social worker, attendance officer.

Services: Ungraded primary sequence in early grades; emphasis on language arts with special attention to reading, verbal, and auditory perceptual skills; extensive audio-visual program; class size reduced to 25; group and individual guidance; enrichment activities such as field trips, cultural events, glee club, student council, activity clubs; study center; parent conferences; involvement of community in providing enrichment opportunities.

Contact person:
Elizabeth M. Dennehy, Principal
Fred D. Wish School
350 Barbour Street
Hartford, Connecticut

Evaluation: Evaluation of reading program completed.

New Haven:

Community Progress, Incorporated (cpi), is a community action program designed to coordinate the work of various community institutions in a massive attack on poverty and to help secure funds for such an attack. There are more than 50 programs in the areas of education, employment, and neighborhood services in which cpi has had a role, either in coordinating and planning, in staffing, or (as in the educational programs developed and run by the Board of Education), in obtaining and allocating available federal and foundation funds. Some of the current Board of Education programs include:

1. The Preschool Program is designed to involve both parents and children in a structured program of activities which will increase the children's opportunities to develop skills and attitudes necessary for school achievement.

Date begun: September 1963 (preceded by a pilot, 1962–63)

Target population: Four hundred and fifty preschoolers from three years-eight months to four years-eight months of age, and their parents, in 17 centers, 75 percent Negro, 25 percent Caucasian. (Project has served 1,035 preschoolers since its inception.)

Per pupil costs: Not determined

Sponsoring group: Ford Foundation (7 centers) and United States Office of Economic Opportunity (10 centers).

Staff: Sixteen teachers, 17 teachers' aides, parent supervisor, parent counselors, secretaries, custodians, baby attendants, part-time curriculum coordinators.

Services: Nursery school program two hours per day, four days a week for groups of 15 children, morning or afternoon sessions; centers located in churches, housing developments, schools, within walking distance of families served; parent program on fifth day involving discussions of home and family problems, child-rearing techniques, school activities, and so forth; baby program for younger siblings one year to three years-eight months; coordination with elementary school teachers—records and information passed on to kindergarten teachers; follow-up with parents and children's teachers through grade 3.

Contact person:
Mrs. Adelaide Phillips, Director
Pre-Kindergarten Program
31 Webster Street
New Haven, Connecticut

2. The Reading Program is a project in the primary and junior high school grades designed to improve reading through improvement of teacher techniques and materials as well as through an extensive remedial reading program. Program emphasizes prevention of reading problems in the primary grades.

Date begun: September 1963

Target population: Thirteen thousand pupils

from 33 elementary schools and one junior high school, 60 percent Caucasian, 40 percent Negro.

Per pupil costs: Not determined

Sponsoring group: Ford Foundation and local school district.

Staff: Twelve reading teachers.

Services: Developmental reading program to establish good basic reading skills in grades 1-4; emphasis at intermediate and secondary levels on developing reading-study skills; individualized reading programs at all levels; remedial program for pupils in need of special help; revised instructional materials including new basal reading series; extensive pupil testing to determine reading levels; inservice teacher education through workshops, conferences, demonstrations, participation in experimental programs; classroom demonstration and individual assistance for teachers in the teaching of reading; pupil and parental counseling.

Contact persons:
Josephine Williams, Nicholas Criscuolo,
   Mrs. Henrietta Fagan
Davis School
35 Davis Street
New Haven, Connecticut

3. The Summer School Program is designed to provide opportunity not only for needed remedial work, but for exploration of new fields of knowledge in courses not generally available during the school year.

Date begun: July 1963

Target population: Approximately 6,165 pupils from grades 4-12 since 1963.

Per pupil costs: Not determined

Sponsoring group: Ford Foundation, local school district, United States Office of Economic Opportunity.

Staff: Staff of 130, including teachers, building leaders, principals.

Services: Six-week summer sessions at 11 elementary schools and four junior high schools from 8:30 a.m. to 12:30 p.m. five days a week; wide variety of course offerings in such areas as map-making, folk music, cooking, puppetry, as well as refresher courses in reading, mathematics, and other academic areas; no tuition, no marks, no credits; encouragement of teacher experimentation in new teaching methods, new units of work, new subject-matter organization, new materials.

Contact person:
Mrs. Beverly M. Keener, Principal
New Haven Summer School Program
Strong School
69 Grand Avenue
New Haven, Connecticut 06513

4. The Tutorial Program is designed to provide inner-city youth with a personal successful educational experience through the services of tutors working in small groups, or on a one-to-one basis.

Date begun: September 1963

Target population: Students in inner-city schools (5,000 have been served since inception of program).

Per pupil costs: Not determined

Sponsoring group: United States Office of Economic Opportunity (since September 1965).

Staff: Volunteers from community, 70 teachers as tutorial supervisors.

Services: Supervised study halls; group tutoring and one-to-one tutoring sessions; library facilities; emphasis on development of close personal relations between tutors and students.

Contact person:
Ralph M. Goglia
Director Community Schools
New Haven Public Schools
200 Orange Street, New Haven, Connecticut

5. The Unified Curriculum Services Program is designed to provide major assistance to 14 inner-city elementary schools faced with special educational problems as a result of poverty impaction, as well as providing some general assistance to other schools with less severe problems.

Date begun: September 1965 (This program has superceded the Helping Teacher and Higher Horizons programs which began in 1963.)

Target population: About 7,900 pupils and 264 teachers in 14 elementary schools.

Per pupil costs: Not determined

Sponsoring group: State of Connecticut Disadvantaged Youths Grants.

Staff: Supervisor, 15 curriculum service teachers, one secretary, part-time curriculum service teacher.

Services: Aid provided to teachers in creation of appropriate curriculum approaches and materials specifically designed for disadvantaged children; concentrated curriculum help, personnel, equipment, and materials provided in such areas as: language arts, science, art, music, audiovisual education, mathematics, social studies, and in such enrichment activities as field trips, cultural activities, and use of special resource personnel; special curriculum service teachers help to organize and staff seminars for inservice education.

Contact person:
Mrs. Beverly Keener
Unified Curriculum Services
Strong School
69 Grand Avenue
New Haven, Connecticut

6. Program to Improve Teacher-Pupil Ratios and Provide Teacher Education is an attempt to improve education in 14 inner-city schools (see 5) by providing additional personnel to these schools in order to reduce teacher-pupil ratios, and by providing all teachers with additional special services and materials.

Date begun: September 1965

Target population: Sixty-five hundred pupils and 236 teachers.

Per pupil costs: Not determined

Sponsoring group: State of Connecticut Disadvantaged Youths Grant.

Staff: Three assistant principals-coordinators, 51 teachers, 26 indigenous community-school relations workers.

Services: Each school may hire one full-time professional educator, social worker, counselor, or other needed specialist for every six teachers assigned to the school; schools each receive, in addition, up to two community-school relations aides, funds for extra materials, books and classroom equipment, and transportation for cultural enrichment field trips.

Contact person:
Sam Nash
Director of Administration
New Haven Public Schools

7. The Grade 9 Work-Study Program is designed to encourage potential dropouts to remain in school by providing them with the opportunity to discover the relationships between academic achievement and job success, as well as to earn money while still in school.

Date begun: September 1964

Target population: Ninth-grade pupils in four junior high schools.

Per pupil costs: Not determined

Sponsoring group: United States Office of Economic Opportunity, Community Action Program.

Staff: Four full-time teacher advisers.

Services: Morning school program including four academic courses and daily session with teacher-adviser; group guidance sessions devoted to discussing job and school progress, grooming, occupational information; students work in school they attend or one convenient to it for maximum of 15 hours per week at 85 cents per hour.

Contact person:
Robert Zaorski, Director
Work-Training Program
55 Audubon Street
New Haven, Connecticut

8. There are various other work training programs designed to help pupils who are unlikely to continue on in school or to seek further training after school. These include a high school pretechnical program designed to prepare eleventh- and twelfth-graders for higher education in electronics, a prevocational program designed to provide industrial skills to pupils in the same age group, and a business education program providing training to high school students and adults in the use of modern business machines. A high school work training program under the Neighborhood Youth Corps provides work after school or during study hall periods as well as needed financial supplements to pupils from low-income families.

Contact persons:

John McGavack, Director
Pre-Technical Program, or

Frederic Rossomando, Director
Business Education Program
Wilbur Cross High School
181 Mitchell Drive
New Haven, Connecticut

Robert Zaorski, Director
Work-Training Program, or

Edward Harris, Director
Pre-Vocational Program
55 Audubon Street
New Haven, Connecticut

9. As a result of the recommendations of a 1961 school building study, seven inter-

mediate schools in New Haven are currently operating as community schools. The community school concept is potentially the most far-reaching approach to school-neighborhood involvement. It views the school as an educational center, a recreational center, a service center, and as a center for neighborhood and community life—initiating and conducting programs, and coordinating programs conducted by a variety of community agencies. Twelve-month administrators (the principal and two assistant principals) head the staff of each school, and in addition, various community agencies such as the Park and Recreation Department, CPI Neighborhood Services Division, the YMCA and YWCA, Dixwell Community House, and the Boy Scouts have assigned full-time professional workers to work in the development of community school programs. Teachers work as part-time staff during evenings, weekends, and summer, and volunteers from universities, junior chamber of commerce, and the community at large are involved in the various counseling, club, classroom, sports, cultural, and other activities.

Contact person:
Ralph Goglia
Director of Community Schools
New Haven Public Schools

10. Other programs designed to help disadvantaged pupils: A full-time research and evaluation team investigates the effectiveness of special programs tried in the schools and conducts research on various educational tactics.

Contact person:
Albert Myers
Psycho-Educational Clinic
295 Crown Street
New Haven, Connecticut

A proposed Program to Improve Planning and Curriculum for Disadvantaged Students in Middle Schools is designed to develop prototype programs for the improvement of both attitude and academic achievement among the most severely disadvantaged pupils.

Contact person:
Mrs. Elizabeth S. Wright
Director of Curriculum
New Haven Public Schools

South Norwalk:

Project #3, Potential Dropouts is part of the overall Norwalk School Improvement Program. It is designed to keep potential dropouts in school through providing successful academic experiences, establishing positive attitudes toward work, raising educational and vocational aspirations, and improving self-image.

Date begun: September 1963

Target population: Thirty-nine predominantly lower socioeconomic status Negro pupils in grades 7, 8, and 9 of one junior high school (matched by an exactly balanced control group).

Per pupil costs: $500

Sponsoring group: Ford Foundation and local school board.

Staff: Academic teachers, guidance counselors, social workers, principal-director.

Services: Special academic classes including remedial reading and training in auditory perception, with emphasis on "concrete" projects and extensive use of audiovisual aids; cultural, occupational, and recreational field trips; group and individual guidance; social worker referrals of parents and students to appropriate community agencies; extensive interpretation of program to community.

Contact person:
Joseph C. De Vita, Principal
Benjamin Franklin Junior High School
Flax Hill Road
South Norwalk, Connecticut

Evaluation: Continuously evaluated.

Delaware

Wilmington:

The Wilmington Public Schools engaged in a project from 1959-1962 entitled The Three-Year Experimental Project on Schools in Changing Neighborhoods, a project sponsored by the National Conference on Christians and Jews. A number of features of the project are being continued—teacher reeducation and improved community cooperation are permanent benefits of the project. Various specific programs have grown either directly or indirectly from the three-year program.

1. The North East School Language Project is designed to help the school staff understand the vernacular of the children with whom they are concerned, to broaden the children's experiences in order to increase their opportunities to use language, and to improve their language skills in both oral and written communication.

Date begun: September 1962 (preceded by a pilot, March-June 1962)

Target population: Seven hundred and sixty pupils in one school serving a disadvantaged neighborhood.

Per pupil costs: $1.50

Sponsoring group: Wilmington Board of Education.

Staff: Classroom teachers, special teachers, helping teachers, language consultant, volunteer aides.

Services: Emphasis on oral language development as approach to reading and writing; general enrichment to provide added opportunities to use language.

Contact person:
Grace Crawford
North East Elementary School
Claymont Street and Todds Lane
Wilmington, Delaware

2. Project Boys is a program designed to lift the aspiration level of a group of boys in a slum neighborhood through contact with successful members of the community.

Date begun: September 1963 (preceded by pilot, August 1959-September 1962)

Target population: Boys in Pyle School attendance area.

Per pupil costs: $2

Sponsoring group: Volunteers and local school board.

Staff: Regular school staff and numerous individuals and groups of men from greater community.

Services: Social therapy for project boys by neighborhood settlement house group workers during regular school hours; high school graduates from community brought in to speak and talk about their own childhood and present lives and work. Assemblies featuring talks on job opportunities by successful men whose formal education ended with high school graduation. Men's Day Luncheons where business and professional men join the boys.

Contact person:
Mrs. August F. Hazeur
Pyle School
5th and Lombard Streets
Wilmington, Delaware

3. Family Life is a program designed to motivate both parents and children by making them aware of the new opportunities for full citizenship and to assist parents in providing a home atmosphere satisfying to the children and conducive to school success.

Date begun: September 1961

Target population: Families of 800 elementary school pupils.

Per pupil costs: 75 cents

Sponsoring group: Local school district and Stubbs School p.t.a.

Staff: Principal and faculty of school, volunteers from various community agencies, hired consultants on family life and children's literature.

Services: Parental workshops and individual conferences on family problems; guidance and information through assemblies and small-group conferences; reading materials on special problems made available to parents; special enrichment trips; Fun with Books library project.

Contact person:
Eldridge J. Waters, Principal
Frederick D. Stubbs School
11th and Pine Street, Wilmington, Delaware

District of Columbia

Washington:

1. The Language Arts Project, a Great Cities Program for School Improvement, is a pilot program designed to improve the oral and written language facility and the comprehension skills of early primary grade children.

Date begun: January 1961

Target population: Seventy-four hundred lower socioeconomic status predominantly Negro pupils in 14 elementary schools, grades K-3.

Per pupil costs: $23

Sponsoring group: Local school district.

Staff: Two hundred and twenty classroom teachers, 14 language arts teachers, language arts supervisor, director.

Services: Structural language development; intensified experiences in listening, speaking, reading, and writing, with emphasis on "literature"; use of tape recorders and tele-trainers, puppetry, creative dramatics; field trips; study hall programs; after-school creative dramatics program; Saturday field trips; parent programs and parental involvement in setting up libraries, book fairs, class field trips; teacher workshops; summer school program for entering kindergartners and first-graders to provide enrichment experiences as preparation for school experience, and for weak kindergartners and first-graders who have demonstrated need for additional enrichment; teacher assistance and training by language arts personnel; demonstration lessons.

Contact person:
Louis H. Kornhauser, Director
Language Arts Project
10501 Pinedale Drive
Silver Spring, Maryland

2. MacFarland-Roosevelt Guidance Project is a longitudinal study providing intensive personal attention over a six-year period to a group of disadvantaged students in order to determine whether such a concentration of guidance, remedial work, and enrichment can help them fully develop their talents.

Date begun: September 1959

Target population: One hundred and fifty students, predominantly Negro, who were graduated from high school in June 1965.

Per pupil costs: Unknown

Sponsoring group: Eugene and Agnes E. Meyer Foundation and local school district.

Staff: Counselor, social worker, remedial reading and mathematics teachers, psychiatrist, psychologist, therapist.

Services: Remedial reading and mathematics; individualized developmental reading program; cultural enrichment; clinical program to help pupils analyze their abilities and improve their own adjustment; intensive and individualized guidance; parent education program.

Contact person:
John Koontz, Assistant Superintendent
Junior and Senior High Schools
Franklin Administration Building
Washington, D.C.

Evaluation: Final report completed and available.

3. The Model School System is an attempt to set up a group of center-city schools as a relatively self-contained system within which flexibility and innovation in developing approaches to educating the disadvantaged can be encouraged and long-range programs of instructional improvement can be undertaken.

Date begun: October 1964

Target population: Some 18,000 children from five preschool centers, 13 elementary schools, three junior high, one senior high, and one vocational high school.

Per pupil costs: Not determined

Sponsoring group: United Planning Organization and local school district.

Staff: Teachers, teacher-aides, other staff as program develops.

Services: Extensive innovation planned involving structural rearrangements such as team teaching and ungraded units, development of original teacher techniques and teaching materials; utilization in elementary schools of techniques of "Language Arts Project"; extensive inservice teacher training, partly to permit recruitment from broader group of applicants, in programed instruction, remedial reading, and so forth; use of teacher aides—often indigenous—in tutorial and counseling programs; summer school programs.

Contact person:
Norman W. Nickens,
    Assistant Superintendent
Model School Division
Franklin Administration Building

4. The Urban Service Corps is one of the earliest and most extensive of the volunteer-staffed programs designed to help prevent juvenile delinquency by improving educational opportunity for disadvantaged young

people through a variety of voluntary services provided to the schools.

Date begun: July 1961

Target population: Student bodies of all the inner-city schools of Washington, D. C., and their parents.

Per pupil costs: Not determined

Sponsoring group: Eugene and Agnes E. Meyer Foundation.

Staff: Volunteers (2,328) from all professions, supervisory staff of 6.

Services: A variety of programs, all volunteer staffed, to augment the work of the schools; parent counseling; job placement and counseling for students, dropouts, older youths; homework study centers; library aide program to expand use of library facilities; recreation and club activities; summertime educational tours of Washington; counselor-aide program to provide assistance to professional school guidance counselors; remedial reading aides working in school reading clinics to aid regular reading teachers; Saturday school for mothers and preschoolers; English teaching for the foreign-born; extended day program aimed at developing community school with variety of activities for parents, children, and other community adults; other programs as need determined in consultation with school administrators.

Contact person:
Benjamin J. Henley,
    Assistant Superintendent
Urban Service Corps
Franklin Administration Building

Florida

Dade County (see Miami)

Gainesville:

An Interdisciplinary Approach to Improving the Development of Culturally Disadvantaged Children is a projected program to provide intensive health care and tutorial services to a group of disadvantaged children as a means of improving their physical health, their self-image, and their attitudes toward school.

Date begun: September 1964

Target population: Sixty children (20 each from three schools) grades 1-8, two-thirds Caucasian, one-third Negro. Population selected as being culturally disadvantaged but not requiring special education.

Per pupil costs: Not determined

Sponsoring group: United States Office of Education.

Staff: Six classroom teachers, testing psychologist, physicians, 15 student nurses, education faculty from University of Florida, 60 volunteer education majors as tutors.

Services: Twenty hours individual tutoring per student (one hour per week); five hours consulting health care per student after physical examination by physician; nursing and education students supported by professional consultation.

Contact person:
Ira J. Gordon, Professor of Education
University of Florida
Gainesville, Florida

Evaluation: In progress with United States Office of Education support.

Hillsborough County (see Tampa)

Miami (Dade County)

1. The Miami summer-reading program is designed to improve reading achievement among disadvantaged youngsters and to narrow the gap between predominantly Negro schools and other schools in the county.

Date begun: July 1962

Target population: Fourteen thousand five hundred Negro pupils from grades 3–6 in 29 school centers (1964).

Per pupil costs: $17

Sponsoring group: Local school district.

Staff: Teachers, principals, librarians, reading clinic teachers.

Services: Six-week summer session with intensive reading program and recreational activities; personalized language charts and stories; training sessions for teachers; house-to-house canvass to explain program to parents; parent meetings to encourage parent encouragement of children; weekly "report cards" to parents scoring attendance, promptness, reading of library books, completed homework, and so forth.

Contact person:
Howard D. McMillan,
   Director of Special Programs
Dade County Public Schools
1410 N. E. 2nd Avenue
Miami, Florida

2. The John F. Kennedy Memorial Program is a mutual cooperation program in which high school graduates from disadvantaged neighborhoods help preschool children in those neighborhoods in return for free junior college tuition and expenses.

Date begun: September 1964

Target population: Sixty high school graduates from disadvantaged neighborhoods and 993 five-year-olds in 53 preschool classes in the same neighborhoods.

Per pupil costs: $70

Sponsoring group: Local school district.

Staff: Psychology and education faculty at Miami-Dade Junior College, three "Kennedy Consultants" from public school staff serving as directors and instructors of preschool teachers, kindergarten television teacher.

Services: Sixty John F. Kennedy Community Service Awards to high school graduates providing free tuition at Miami-Dade Junior College and cash payments of $500; training for awardees by Junior College and Kennedy Consultants; student-conducted daily two-and-one-half hour preschool classes; daily tele-lessons for student teachers.

Contact person:
Howard D. McMillan,
   Director of Special Programs
Dade County Public Schools

Tallahassee:

Making the Content of Basal Readers More Meaningful by Using the Content of the Real Life Drama of Pupils is a program designed to enrich the experiential backgrounds of disadvantaged children, build their self-esteem, and thereby improve their academic performance.

Date begun: 1964

Target population: Thirty-four Negro second-graders.

Per pupil costs: None

Sponsoring group: Bond Elementary School.

Staff: Teacher, assistant principal, librarian, volunteer aides.

Services: Emphasis on "sharing" periods which provide motivation and content for materials prepared for project; children encouraged to talk about experiences, and supplementary experiences, both first-hand and vicarious, provided to enrich their informational background.

Contact person:
Mrs. Doris N. Alston, Project Director
3210 Hastie Road, Tallahassee, Florida

Tampa (Hillsborough County)

1. The Work-Study Program is a project which tries to give the potential dropouts a realistic work-study experience to encourage them to continue their education or, if they do drop out, to assist them in making the school to job transition and avoid unemployment.

Date begun: September 1963 (preceded by pilot program, January–June 1963)

Target population: Forty-five hundred junior high school pupils at least 14 years of age identified as nonacademically talented child-misfits and potential dropouts.

Per pupil costs: $305

Sponsoring group: Hillsborough County School System.

Staff: Team of teacher, principal, guidance counselor, and work-study coordinator for each group of 20 to 25 students.

Services: Teacher works directly with approximately 25 children in morning study curriculum concluding with hot lunch; work-study coordinator liaison between school, employer, and parents, and finding student jobs; maximum student work five hours a day, five days a week; students protected by insurance and work in nonhazardous occupations. On-the-job visiting, job counseling.

Contact person:
Richard G. Roland, Coordinator,
   Work-Study Program
Hillsborough County Schools
P. O. Box 3408, Tampa, Florida 33601

2. Preschool Program for Culturally Disadvantaged Children in Tampa will provide preschool experiences for culturally disadvantaged children based on evaluation of existing community services, practices, and needs.

Date begun: August 1965

Target population: Approximately 500 preschool children.

Per pupil costs: $666

Sponsoring group: Tampa Commission of Community Relations, Hillsborough County School System, University of South Florida, United States Office of Economic Opportunity.

Staff: Twenty certified teachers, supervising

principal, assistant supervising principal, 20 noncertified teachers' assistants, secretary.

Services: Medical examinations and treatment; free lunch; regular preschool programs; testing and research on population, transportation (if needed).

Contact person:
L. E. Swatts, Assistant Superintendent
   for Instruction
Hillsborough County Schools

Georgia

Atlanta:

The Education Improvement Project (EIP) is a long-range, broad-scale project involving a number of colleges in states throughout the South in a program to upgrade the level of instruction in southern schools and to provide a generally improved educational opportunity for young people in the South.

Date begun: February 1964

Target population: Boys and girls from preschool to precollege age, from socially deprived situations.

Per pupil costs: Not determined ($9 million total for five-year program)

Sponsoring group: Southern Association of Colleges and Secondary Schools, Ford and Danforth Foundations, local school districts, universities and colleges.

Staff: A central staff associated with the Southern Association of Colleges and Secondary Schools in Atlanta, including a director and two associate directors. The staff of the centers is selected by the schools and cooperating colleges.

Services: Six centers in which two or more colleges or universities will participate in providing assistance to the primary and secondary schools in the area; three centers now in operation in Nashville, Durham, and Atlanta; proposed additional centers will be in Huntsville, New Orleans, and Houston; services will include inservice and preservice innovations, model laboratory schools, constructional innovations, summer programs and institutes, and special patterns of research and evaluation. A second program under EIP, Project Opportunity, involves 11 schools and 16 colleges in a cooperative program to identify potential college students at the seventh-grade level and to provide innovations, particularly counseling, throughout the additional years prior to college. Program involves some $350,000 per year.

Contact person:
Donald Agnew, Director
Education Improvement Project
Southern Association of Colleges and Secondary Schools
795 Peachtree Street, N. E., Suite 592
Atlanta, Georgia 30308

Illinois

Chicago:

1. The Special Summer Schools program is designed to explore new approaches to teaching the culturally disadvantaged pupil and through the involvement of parents and the provision of the best possible teaching situation to maximize learning and promote a more advantageous relationship between school and home.

Date begun: Summer 1960

Target population: Six hundred children in classes of 25, grades 1–6 in each of 30 summer schools, selected to participate by teachers and principals. Classes for prekindergartners, three-and-a-half and four-year-olds provided by district in summer 1964, absorbed by Head Start Project, summer 1965.

Per pupil costs: Not determined

Sponsoring group: Local school district.

Staff: Director, assistant director, classroom teachers, principals, adjustment teachers, resource teachers, teacher-librarians, teacher-nurses, parent coordinators, consultants, psychologists.

Services: Classes from 9 a.m. to 2 p.m. during eight-week summer period; groupings into four levels at each grade on basis of reading achievement with grade level groups frequently combined for various activities; curriculum emphasizing reading and mathematics with remaining two-fifths of day devoted to special integrated teaching units correlating such subject areas as music, art, science, social studies; 50 minutes daily inservice training period for teachers; extensive use of audiovisual and other new instructional materials; field trips; lunch period shared by teachers and pupils as social learning experience; parent involvement through special coordinator in each center.

Contact person:
Mrs. Evelyn F. Carlson,
    Associate Superintendent
Department of Curriculum Development
Chicago Board of Education
228 North LaSalle Street
Chicago, Illinois 60601

Evaluation: Special Summer School Reports, 1963, 1964, 1965.

2. Education and Vocational Guidance Centers have been set up as a special facility for overage pupils still in elementary school and likely to drop out when they reach school leaving age.

Date begun: February 1962

Target population: Eighteen hundred youths in eight centers, one or more years overage for grade and still in elementary school.

Per pupil costs: Not determined

Sponsoring group: Local school board.

Staff: Teachers, counselors.

Services: Classes of not more than 20 pupils each, housed in separate school facilities housing no more than 350; pupils transferred to centers with parental consent beginning with most overage; individual attention to reading and arithmetic skills to promote rapid completion of elementary school work and advancement into high school; extensive guidance and counseling; provision for 15-year-olds to participate in work-study program under Vocational Act of 1963 to orient student to world of work; cooperative education programs for 16-year-olds unable to reach sixth-grade reading level and unable to continue education in general or vocational high school program; continued counseling for this group to assist in adjustment to world of work after they leave school.

Contact person:
Arthur Lehne, Assistant Superintendent
Vocational and Practical Arts Education
Chicago Board of Education

3. Carver Demonstration Center for the Education of Gifted Children offers a program designed to provide early school experiences to the able but culturally disadvantaged primary pupil which will enrich his cultural background and develop in him positive attitudes toward school in his early years.

Date begun: January 1964

Target population: Primary pupils identified as "relatively able" (top 10 or 15 percent of their classes) through teacher judgments and various tests—some project-devised.

Per pupil costs: Not determined

Sponsoring group: Illinois Plan for Program Development for Gifted Children and local school district.

Staff: Full-time director, principal, selected classroom teachers, psychologist.

Services: Speech development activities; parental involvement; emphasis on positive attitude development and discovery learning; teacher teaming.

Contact persons:
Robert Todd
Department of Curriculum Development
Chicago Board of Education
or
Mrs. Irene Z. Hagan, Principal
Carver Primary School
909 East 132nd Street
Chicago, Illinois 60627

4. The Kelley High School Demonstration Center for the Gifted is a program emphasizing cultural enrichment as a way of upgrading the achievement of able students from less culturally advantaged, though not severely disadvantaged, circumstances.

Date begun: April 1964

Target population: Students identified as academically able, who live in an area populated mostly by industrial and manual service workers, with some semiskilled workers and unskilled manual laborers.

Per pupil costs: Not determined

Sponsoring group: Illinois Plan for Program Improvement for Gifted Children and local school district.

Staff: Full-time director, principal, classroom teachers.

Services: Special English 7X program involving team teaching; tutorial English contract plan involving series of articulated learning experiences aimed at developing effectiveness in written and oral expression; cultural enrichment through a Student Academy of Arts and Sciences to develop appreciation of humanities and the arts (studies of, and visits to plays, concerts, museums; guest artists invited to perform at school); Junior Great Books program.

Contact persons:
Mrs. Mary C. Knaus, Principal
Kelley High School
4136 South California Avenue
Chicago, Illinois 60632
or

Robert Todd
Department of Curriculum Development
Chicago Board of Education

N.B. In addition to these state aided demonstration centers, a number of programs for "gifted" pupils function in areas serving a disadvantaged population. Chicago makes a practice of including the relatively able, the top 10 percent or 15 percent of pupils in a given school, in programs for the gifted. Guidance and counseling are also provided for the gifted at the elementary level. At the high school level, the "100" program identifies the 25 top scholars in the ninth, tenth, eleventh, and twelfth grades in each high school, and provides them with special guidance in long- and short-term planning. Curriculum guides have been designed to meet the varying needs of students, including the gifted and talented disadvantaged, from kindergarten through grade 12.

Contact person:
Mrs. Ruth Hoffmeyer, Consultant
Department of Curriculum Development
Chicago Board of Education

5. The After-School Reading Improvement Program provides short-term intensive reading help for pupils of normal intelligence who are at least one year retarded in reading.

Date begun: May 1962

Target population: Over 25,000 pupils from all grade levels in 222 schools predominantly located in disadvantaged areas.

Per pupil costs: Not determined

Sponsoring group: Local school district.

Staff: Reading teachers.

Services: In spring 1965, 1,394 classes each enrolling 15 to 20 pupils met from 3:15 p.m. to 4 p.m. twice a week; emphasis on determining individual deficiencies and on utilization of specifically appropriate techniques to overcome these deficiencies; variety of techniques, materials, and equipment. Plans for expanding program to 36-week, four-day-a-week program under Elementary and Secondary Education Act.

Contact person:
Mrs. Evelyn F. Carlson,
   Associate Superintendent
Department of Curriculum Development
Chicago Board of Education

6. The Chicago Project: District 11, is a multifaceted program designed to help a variety of pupils from elementary through post-high school to achieve their own maximum development.

Date begun: September 1960

Target population: Originally aimed at pupils in one school district who were 14 years of age or older and still in elementary school; extended in 1961 to cover both older and younger pupils with various services.

Per pupil costs: Not determined

Sponsoring group: Local school board and Ford Foundation through Great Cities Program for School Improvement.

Staff: District superintendent, principals, classroom teachers, plus special project staff including an assistant director, counselors, and clerical staff.

Services: For 14- to 17-year-old elementary pupils, special classes in at least 11 schools for overage pupils in grades 5–8; in-school reading clinic; special core program in urban-oriented social studies; educational and vocational guidance center; services of part-time psychologist, social worker, and counselors; various afterschool clubs and classes including Urban 4-H clubs and reading program, and after-school vocational, pre-employment, cultural, and reading improvement classes at one high school. For 16- to 21-year-olds, school to work transition classes from 4 p.m. to 6 p.m. at one high school under project auspices; cooperative occupational training classes; evening vocational high school program; job placement service.

For parents, involvement with school program through clubs and meetings; fathers' clubs; cooking, sewing, nutrition classes, and field trips for mothers.

Contact person:
Mrs. Louise Daugherty,
District Superintendent (11)
Chicago Project: Great Cities Program
for School Improvement
3000 South Parkway
Chicago, Illinois 60616

7. The Urban Youth Program is designed to provide counseling, training, and job-placement to unemployed and unemployable youth in order to fit them for employment and responsible citizenship.

Date begun: Summer 1961

Target population: Youth between 16 and 21 who are out of school and out of work.

Per pupil costs: Not determined

Sponsoring group: Local school board and MDTA funds (prior to 1965, school board only).

Staff: Director, principals, teachers, counselors.

Services: Three-part program which includes: Double C (Census and Counseling), aimed at locating dropouts, contacting them, and bringing them into either a school or a work situation; Double E (Education and Employment), a work-study program involving 12 hours of classes and 24 to 32 hours of on-the-job experience in clerical or merchandising work; and Double T (Training and Transition), a program which provides short-term pre-employment training for such occupations as hospital aide, needle-trades work, service-station attendant, and so forth; follow-up by counselors to age 21. Multi-occupations program established March 1965 subsequent to federal grant. Training in various vocational areas, from power-woodworking to pressing, provided with supportive literacy courses.

Contact person:
Director, Urban Youth Program
Division of Work Experience and
Post-High School Guidance
64 East Lake Street, Room 1008
Chicago, Illinois 60601

8. The Free Bus Program is designed to compensate children in disadvantaged areas for their meager backgrounds and lack of experience outside their homes.

Date begun: September 1965

Target population: Children at any school in a disadvantaged area.

Sponsoring group: Local school board.

Per pupil costs: Not determined

Services: Funds allotted in budget (from $1,000 in 1956 to $12,000 in 1965) to permit teachers to take on field trips pupils who are without funds of their own. Trips to museums, zoos, parks, planetarium, aquarium, industrial plants, farms. Funds allocated by central committee of district superintendents on basis of need determined by such factors as size of school, number of students in need of enriched experience, and so forth.

Contact person:
George Balling
District Superintendent (10)
3300 South Kedzie Avenue
Chicago, Illinois 60623

9. The Prekindergarten Program is designed to provide the disadvantaged child with experiences at the preschool level which will help develop his potential, as well as to provide parents with skills and insights which can be incorporated into the general family pattern.

Date begun: March 1965

Target population: Children living in areas of need who will be eligible for the kindergarten program in following school year.

Per pupil costs: Not determined

Sponsoring group: Local school board and United States Office of Economic Opportunity.

Staff: Director, teachers, teacher-assistants, teacher aides, curriculum consultants, adjustment teachers, parent-coordinators, teacher-nurses, clerical staff.

Services: Classes of 25, meeting in morning or afternoon sessions of two-and-a-half hours each; curriculum providing language experiences, opportunity for creative responses to nature, art, and music; parent involvement and coordination of school-parent effort toward common goal; field trips; health program involving health education and nutrition, physical examination for each child.

Contact person:
Helen Bradley, Director
Prekindergarten Centers
Chicago Board of Education

10. In addition to the programs listed above, the Chicago Board of Education has sponsored or participated in a number of other programs of compensatory education. Among them are the following:

The Value Sharing Project, originally known as the Doolittle Project which was in operation for five years at five pilot elementary schools in a disadvantaged area of the city. A cooperative activity of the National College of Education and the Chicago Board of Education (financed through the Wieboldt Foundation), the project aimed to maximize the social values of the pre-adolescent child through a planned program of value shaping and sharing. By helping each child, parent, and teacher to fulfill his social needs, the project aimed to free energies to develop abilities. Pilot study currently being evaluated.

Contact person:
Marie Frank
Director of Value Sharing Project
Bureau of Research Development and
  Special Projects
Chicago Board of Education

A project at the Howland Elementary School serves pupils in grades K-6. Its program emphasizes curriculum modification in relation to pupil ability, with emphasis on the language arts, as a way of making classroom experiences more stimulating and more relevant to disadvantaged pupils.

Contact person:
Joseph Rosen, Principal
Howland Elementary School
1616 South Spaulding Avenue
Chicago, Illinois

Day School and After-School Reading Clinics serve more than 1,000 pupils with an extensive and intensive program of remedial reading involving the services of special reading teachers who provide small-group instruction. In addition the clinics utilize numerous specialized reading materials and mechanical devices to facilitate reading progress.

Contact person:
Reading Supervisor
Bureau of Child Study
Chicago Board of Education

The regular Summer School Program offers tuition-free classes in all regular academic and some vocational high school subjects to pupils in grades 9 through 12 who wish to attend. The program includes special remedial classes in reading and mathematics for grades 6–8, honors classes for gifted students, and extensive counseling. In 1965, 69,959 pupils were enrolled; of these, 23,362 registered for the special classes in reading and mathematics.

Contact person:
Director, Summer School Division
Chicago Board of Education

I see Chicago was initiated in 1965 as a summer enrichment program designed to give culturally disadvantaged students a richer experiential background as well as greater facility in the use of oral and written language. Eighth-grade graduates from disadvantaged areas of the city are taken on tours to places of civic interest. Emphasis is placed on the art of listening and recording what is seen and heard through subsequent preparation of research booklets and oral reports.

Contact person:
Mrs. Ruth Hoffmeyer
Department of Curriculum Development
Chicago Board of Education

A similar summer program, Project Apex, provides counseling, group guidance, parent meetings, and various recreational and creative activities to pupils from culturally disadvantaged areas who are of average or above-average ability and who will be moving into the eighth or ninth grade in the fall. The program is designed to improve motivation to pupils prior to high school.

Contact person:
Mrs. Blanche B. Paulson, Director
Bureau of Pupil Personnel Services
Chicago Board of Education

Various cooperative education programs, which provide supervised on-the-job training are increasingly prominent features of the regular educational program. Among the programs are Distributive Education (merchandising and sales), Office Occupations, Industrial Cooperative Education, Interrelated Instructional Program, Home Economics Related Occupations, and Cooperative Work Training. These programs include a minimum of 15 hours a week on the job plus a substantial amount of time devoted to job-related academic work.

Contact person:
Arthur Lehne, Assistant Superintendent
of Schools
Vocational and Practical Arts Education
Chicago Board of Education

The IMPACT (Improvement of Attendance and Curtailment of Truancy) Program was initiated in 1963 in five districts as an approach to dealing with cases of chronic truancy and nonattendance among boys under 14 years of age. Home visits by the school attendance officer and head attendance officer are supplemented by conferences, utilization of such consultative personnel as nurses, social workers, and psychologists, and ultimately, failing solution of the problems, assignment of children needing further help to special classrooms similar to social adjustment rooms, called IMPACT rooms.

Contact person:
Mrs. Blanche B. Paulson, Director
Bureau of Pupil Personnel Services
Chicago Board of Education

11. Additional practices have been instituted by the school system for the benefit of pupils in disadvantaged areas. Among them are the following: Use of master teachers who provide aid to inexperienced teachers and special service teachers assigned to work with small groups of children wherever existing number of classrooms will not permit city-wide average class size. These personnel functions grew out of experience gained through implementation of the High Transiency Formula, an approach to improving education in disadvantaged schools, first instituted in 1955. It provided for reduction in class size, assignment of extra personnel, increase in clerical services and in per capita appropriation for textbooks, instructional materials and educational supplies at schools having among other problems, a high rate of pupil and teacher turnover. Current practice calls for planned progressive decrease in class size for all schools and assignment of extra personnel and funds on a per school basis rather than on basis of formula.

Special guides and supplements are supplied by the Department of Curriculum including materials to help teachers working with less academically-able groups. An inservice training program developed especially for teachers working with overage pupils, is based on the guides.

The Continuous Development Plan, a nongraded program initiated in 1957, operates in all elementary schools, predominantly in what would be grades K–3, but in some cases in grades 4–6. Primary pupils are placed in one of eight or nine achievement levels, grouped separately according to ability in reading and mathematics.

In Opportunity Rooms, teachers with a knowledge of the problems of the non-English-speaking child provide instruction in English language to facilitate participation in the regular classroom. Such activities as music, art, physical education, and assembly are taken with a regular class and pupils are moved into the regular school program when their proficiency warrants it.

Contact person:
Mrs. Evelyn F. Carlson,
  Associate Superintendent
Department of Curriculum Development
Chicago Board of Education

The Adult Education Center provides a 12-month program of literacy education for adult relief recipients with provision made in the curriculum for the adult to study, discuss, and understand the role of the contemporary parent.

Contact person:
Edward C. Bennett, Assistant Director
Division of Basic Adult Education
Chicago Board of Education

The Urban Gateways Program of the Institute for Cultural Development (in cooperation with the Board of Education) provides opportunities for attendance at cultural events for children from selected schools in disadvantaged areas. With funds available under the United States Economic Opportunity Act, the program has been expanded from 23 to 50 schools and two programs have been added: a carrousel art project which circulates art exhibitions among the schools and provides visiting artists to speak to groups in the schools. A second project involves three performing units available to provide an

"Orientation to the Performing Arts" at special school assemblies.

Contact persons:
Mrs. James H. Woods, Executive Director
Institute for Cultural Development
1425 South Racine Avenue
Chicago, Illinois 60608
or
Philip Lewis, Director
Bureau of Research, Development and
  Special Projects
Chicago Board of Education

A cultural resource consultant, first appointed in 1962, coordinates opportunities for cultural enrichment for public school children, especially in disadvantaged areas, arranging for special reduced rate performances of theater, movies, concerts, and so forth, or for free tickets to various cultural events.

Contact person:
Gertrude Guthman
Department of Curriculum Development
Chicago Board of Education

12. In Chicago, as in a number of other large urban communities, various private and public organizations, churches, settlement houses, community centers, clubs, and other groups are conducting programs outside of the regular school program, to aid disadvantaged children and their parents. These include tutoring and study centers, nursery schools, adult education programs, and club programs which provide academic classes, social life, recreation, and enrichment to disadvantaged neighborhoods and serve to integrate newcomers into the community. Many of these programs supplement the school program with remedial classes, tutoring, field trips, home visits, job placement, and so forth. Many of them are virtual schools outside of school, providing regular academic (including programed) instruction, enrichment, counseling, and library projects during after-school, Saturday, and summer hours. Some other programs are: The Tutoring

Project for Mothers which utilizes graduate students and faculty wives to tutor mothers receiving Aid to Dependent Children, in order to help these women in better preparing their preschoolers for formal education. Work is given in reading, writing, and arithmetic.

Contact person:
Mrs. J. Michael Porteus
1163 East 54th Place
Chicago, Illinois 60615

The Preschool Education Project at Firman House and a related Parents' School Readiness Program are aimed at raising the educational level of a group of disadvantaged preschoolers in order to enable them to make better use of the public schools. The parent program is designed to show the parents how they can participate in this goal. Parents participate in the preschool classes, in parent discussion groups to share experiences with other parents, and in guidance sessions.

Contact persons:
Dorothy Jones
Firman House
37 West 47th Street, Chicago, Illinois
or
William J. Neal, Executive Director

Quincy:

Prevention of School Problems of Culturally Handicapped Children is a longitudinal study designed to determine whether modifying and enriching the early school experience of disadvantaged children can substantially alter their level of achievement.

Date begun: January 1961

Target population: Two hundred predominantly lower socioeconomic status white kindergarten children in four elementary schools. Children entered kindergarten in 1961, were followed through grade 3.

Per pupil costs: $150

Sponsoring group: National Institute of Men-

tal Health (through Quincy Youth Development Commission).

Staff: Eight classroom teachers, curriculum coordinator, home-school liaison persons, psychologist, principals, associate superintendent of schools.

Services: Modified classroom methods including use of volunteer community personnel as teacher helpers, special art and science classes, reading program, field trips, summer day-camp, prekindergarten summer experience (continued for all entering kindergartners since 1961), parent meetings, and interviews.

Contact person:
Gordon P. Liddle, Associate Director
Interprofessional Research Commission on
    Pupil Personnel Services
College of Education
University of Maryland
College Park, Maryland

Evaluation: In progress. Preliminary evaluation available through United States Office of Education, Pub. OE-35044, pp. 57–69, "Programs for the Educationally Disadvantaged."

Indiana

Indianapolis:

1. Program of Intensified Education is a compensatory program involving teacher training and a general upgrading of the curriculum for students in areas of the community identified as disadvantaged.

Date begun: September 1964

Target population: Ninety-two hundred elementary school children identified as culturally deprived, 60 percent Caucasian, 40 percent Negro.

Per pupil costs: Not determined

Sponsoring group: Private foundation, local

school district, Mayor's Committee on Human Rights.

Staff: Seventy-two specialized teachers, psychologists, 50 to 60 paid college student tutors, research supervisor, superintendent of schools, supervisor of schools.

Services: General academic enrichment, remedial reading, after-school tutoring by paid college student tutors in any academic subject.

Contact person:
Joseph Payne, Chairman,
   Identification Subcommittee
   Research Supervisor
Indianapolis Public Schools
150 North Meridian, Indianapolis, Indiana

2. Wood High School is a center-city school, serving a largely disadvantaged population, which has made use of extensive curriculum revision and innovation in order to provide an opportunity for education for students of varying ability.

Date begun: 1953

Target population: Students at the Wood High School.

Per pupil costs: Not determined

Sponsoring group: Local school district, civic groups.

Staff: Occupational training teachers, counselors, principal.

Services: Extensive attention to providing instruction suited to individual abilities and needs of students; variety of occupational courses, some developed in cooperation with local industries; choice of academic-vocational or pure vocational training; orientation is toward providing for success in a job which may lead to return to academic program.

Contact person:
Richard E. Emery, Principal
Wood High School
501 South Meridian Street
Indianapolis 25, Indiana

Kansas

Topeka:

Project Assurance is a program to provide special services to areas of the city identified as having a high percentage of children with environmental handicaps to successful learning.

Date begun: 1964

Target population: All pupils in six elementary, two junior high, and two high schools.

Per pupil costs: Not determined

Sponsoring group: Local school district.

Staff: Classroom teachers, including those with special qualifications for teaching culturally deprived children; librarian, visiting nurse, superintendent of schools, and deputy superintendent of instruction.

Services: Reduced pupil-teacher ratio; in-service teacher training workshops and importation of special teachers; special learning materials; reading projects; guidance; home economics teas; study centers.

Contact person:
Merle R. Bolton, Superintendent
The Public Schools of Topeka
414 West Eighth Street
Topeka, Kansas

Kentucky

Berea:

The Appalachian Volunteers is a program designed to utilize volunteer college students and local community residents to improve the quality of education in Appalachian mountain schools and to encourage self-help among the residents of Appalachia.

Date begun: December 1963

Target population: School children and townspeople in isolated rural areas of eastern Kentucky.

Per pupil costs: Not available

Sponsoring group: Federal grant and volunteers.

Staff: Over 1,000 eastern Kentucky college students and a similar number of local people.

Services: Volunteers work in eastern Kentucky's one- and two-room schools and their communities conducting programs of remedial work and curriculum enrichment with an emphasis on personal attention and individual help. Additional work with community adults in school renovation and general community improvement. A "Books for Appalachia" drive conducted in spring 1965 had a goal of putting 400 libraries into rural schools.

Contact person:
Milton Ogle, Executive Director
Appalachian Volunteers
College Box 2307, Berea, Kentucky

Louisville:

1. Higher Aspirations for Living is a program designed to raise the self-concept and motivation of disadvantaged students in order to help them attain a higher level of academic and social achievement.

Date begun: February 1963 (preceded by pilot guidance project, 1961–62)

Target population: Pupils of one junior high school, Negro, predominantly lower socio-economic status.

Sponsoring group: National Council of Jewish Women, Louisville Branch and Links, Inc.

Staff: Guidance counselor, principal, school staff, volunteers from sponsoring service groups.

Services: Reading clubs; cultural enrichment through trips to museums, libraries, concerts, choral groups, with preliminary orientation for pupils; field trips to factories,

offices, plants; visits to homes of adults with whom students work; student discussion groups dealing with personal and social problems, job opportunities, and special interests; parent counseling.

Contact person:
Austin Edwards
Jackson Street Junior High School
Jackson and Breckinridge Streets
Louisville, Kentucky

Evaluation: Guidance program evaluated.

2. The Roosevelt Format is a program to provide remedial reading teaching and materials in a school through the involvement of local service groups.

Date begun: 1960

Target population: Pupils at one elementary school, reading one year or more below grade, IQ 80 or above.

Per pupil costs: Not determined

Sponsoring group: Civic groups, volunteer contributions.

Staff: One reading teacher, volunteer aides.

Services: Remedial reading program utilizing special remedial reading room equipped through community contributions and volunteer aides to provide individual attention. Program serves as model for Louisville area.

Contact person:
A. B. Harmon
Roosevelt High School, Louisville, Kentucky

Evaluation: Evaluations completed each semester and available.

Maine

Jay:

A Practical Arts Course for Potential Dropouts is a high school-level program for unsuccessful junior high school students aimed at either reinstating them in a regular high school program or in preparing them for work.

Date begun: September 1960

Target population: Thirteen pupils in one junior high school.

Per pupil costs: $375

Sponsoring group: International Paper Company Foundation.

Staff: Guidance counselor, one classroom teacher.

Services: Special classes for two years with middle-grade level work, special related reading material, plus supervised work experience. At end of two years some students able to enroll in regular Track III freshman or sophomore work in high school. Others have half-time work for junior and senior years; counseling with parents; local merchants involved in providing work experience.

Contact person:
Mary E. York, Guidance Counselor
Jay High School, Jay, Maine

Livermore Falls:

Livermore Falls Program for the Less Academically Talented Student is a multigrade program designed to keep potential dropouts in school through providing an adequate academic program combined with work preparation and experience. The project has served as a pilot model for the rest of the state.

Date begun: September 1960

Target population: Fifteen elementary school and 13 high school pupils with IQ scores between 40 and 82 who have experienced repeated school failure.

Per pupil costs: Approximately $430

Sponsoring group: Local school board.

Staff: Subject supervisor, psychologist, home visitor, psychiatrist, physician, nurse, attendance officer.

Services: Individualized academic program with emphasis on practical approaches such as letter writing as a way of upgrading skills; mathematics; social studies; industrial arts training; homemaking courses; field trips; work experience program with half-time work junior and senior years for 10 academic credits; guidance and counseling.

Contact person:
Mrs. Patricia Rowe
10 Millet Street, Livermore Falls, Maine

Evaluation: Informal.

Maryland

Baltimore:

1. Early School Admissions Project (Project HELP) is a three-year program designed to determine the kinds of learning experiences needed to overcome the academic handicaps with which disadvantaged children often enter school, and to provide experiences to overcome those handicaps.

Date begun: September 1962

Target population: Four centers each serving approximately 30 children are located as follows: two in Negro neighborhoods, one in a predominantly white neighborhood, and one in a racially integrated neighborhood. Children are chosen according to criteria which assure that they come from families with multiple problems.

Per pupil costs: $917

Sponsoring group: Ford Foundation and local school district.

Staff: Primary school teachers, teachers' aides, volunteer mothers, project coordinator, curriculum coordinator, physicians, nurses, social workers, psychologist, counselors.

Services: Daily preschool classes; daily health examinations; field trips; parental involvement through observation and participation in one-day-a-week voluntary classroom work.

Contact person:
Mrs. Catherine Brunner, Coordinator
  Early School Admissions Project
Baltimore Public Schools
2519 North Charles Street
Baltimore, Maryland 21218

2. Other practices: Both the elementary and secondary divisions of the public schools have instituted changes designed to help disadvantaged children. Among these are:

Twenty-three reading centers throughout the city where children whose IQs are 95 or over may receive remedial reading instruction. Each child becomes a member of a homeroom class operating at his own grade level, but is given instruction in reading in the Reading Center for approximately an hour a day.

Twenty-six schools are now operating on a nongraded system, primarily for children who would have been in grades 1 through 3 under the graded system.

Thirteen schools are involved in team-teaching projects, all of them in disadvantaged neighborhoods.

Summer school programs at the elementary school level have been sponsored by the P. T. A.s of various center-city schools, staffed in some cases by unpaid volunteers and in others by teachers paid out of nonschool funds.

Modified curriculums and flexible scheduling to allow for part-time employment have been offered to returned and potential dropouts at the high school level, including in some cases the option of taking a program which does not lead to graduation.

Contact person:
Orlando F. Furno, Director of Research
Baltimore Public Schools

Ken-Gar (see Montgomery County)

Montgomery County:

The Home Study Programs, Inc., is a broad-scale program which seeks to help children in low-income, mostly Negro communities, bridge the educational gap between themselves and the middle-class children of the surrounding communities. Emphasis is placed upon community contribution and parent and young adult participation.

Date begun: Originated in 1958 as the Ken-Gar program and expanded into the Home Study Programs, Inc., in 1960

Target population: Children in seven neighborhoods in Montgomery County and two neighborhoods in Prince George County.

Per pupil costs: Not determined

Sponsoring groups: Churches, Public Welfare Foundation, the Junior League, and volunteer contributions.

Staff: Each community has a board, composed of representatives of both residents and volunteers. The Central Board of Directors includes representatives of all nine communities, a part-time executive director, adult tutors, parents, two professional preschool teachers, language enrichment teachers, home visitors, and numerous volunteers.

Services: In-home tutoring where one grade group meets in the home of a community resident (if possible) with several adult tutors and a parent present for one to one-and-a-half hours a night, two nights a week; an Honors Program in which each child participating in Home Study is awarded a carefully selected age and reading level appropriate book; supervised study halls; in-school tutoring as requested by school authorities; preschool programs; provision of scholarships for sending children to already existing nursery schools outside the community; summer and recreation programs; and field trips. Each community plans and conducts its own programs. The Central Board of Directors is responsible for coordination, cross-fertilization of ideas, the acquisition of resource materials, development of a library, training of tutors, and so forth.

An Infant Education Program, in conjunction with the National Institute of Health, is a newly begun research-demonstration project designed to enrich the verbal competency of children 12 to 24 months of age who are from educationally deprived families. Adult volunteers visit the homes of these children for one hour daily.

Contact person:
Mrs. Ann Leonard, Executive Director
Home Study Program, Inc.
8814 Kensington Parkway
Chevy Chase, Maryland 20015

Rockville:

The Projects of the Community Coordinators of the Montgomery County Schools are designed to provide improved social, educational, and cultural opportunities to children and their parents existing in pockets of poverty in a predominantly privileged area.

Date begun: November 1961

Target population: Some 4,000 children, predominantly Negro, from preschool to high school age in rural and urban areas of the county.

Per pupil costs: Not determined

Sponsoring group: Foundation, social agency, local contributions, board of education.

Staff: Three Community Project coordinators, resource person.

Services: Program serving county involves total population: nursery school programs with mothers participating; study sessions with volunteer tutors in children's homes, schools, other public buildings, churches; field trips and other cultural, recreational, and educational excursions away from community; counseling discussions for older pupils; summer program; encouragement of

parental involvement in promoting academic endeavor through using homes for tutoring sessions. Elementary school program involving several schools includes variety of enrichment activities—puppet shows, dancing, folk singing, after-school classes—some conducted by volunteers, often community professionals or parents, and aimed at enlarging children's experience as a way of stimulating increased and improved language usage; parent luncheon meetings and home visits.

Contact person:
James C. Craig, Assistant Superintendent
    for Instructional and Personnel Services
Montgomery County Public Schools
Rockville, Maryland

Massachusetts

Boston:

1. Operation Counterpoise is a program designed to increase motivation, improve self-image, effect changes in attitudes and behavior, and develop the latent talents of disadvantaged children through an approach emphasizing a strong language arts and arithmetic program.

Date begun: September 1963 as a pilot program

Target population: About 8,800 children, predominantly lower socioeconomic status in grades K-6 in 12 school districts.

Per pupil costs: $49

Sponsoring group: Boston School Committee.

Staff: Master teachers, auxiliary teachers, pupil adjustment counselors, special art teacher, special music teachers, research assistant.

Services: Team teaching as basic educational design; master teachers to supervise, assist, and coordinate work of regular teachers; junior grade 1 and junior grade 4; remedial reading; phonetic approach to teaching of reading and heavy emphasis on listening skills and diction; field trips and assemblies; in-service teacher training and orientation; special advanced work class for ablest pupils, grades 5 and 6; enrichment programs in music, art, and literature; parent meetings.

Contact person:
Marguerite G. Sullivan,
    Deputy Superintendent
Boston Public Schools
15 Beacon Street, Boston, Massachusetts

Evaluation: Pilot has been evaluated: *Operation Counterpoise*. Initial evaluation. Boston Elementary Schools, September 1964.

2. Action for Boston Community Development, Inc., is one of the Ford Foundation Great Cities Gray Areas Programs aimed at combating a wide array of urban problems. The school program is designed to eliminate the deficiencies in the backgrounds of disadvantaged children which retard their school progress.

Date begun: October 1963

Target population: Eighty preschoolers in two centers, 824 pupils in grades 4, 5, and 6 of seven elementary schools, and 710 eighth- and ninth-graders in three junior high schools. Eighty percent of the pupils are of lower socioeconomic status.

Per pupil costs: $180

Sponsoring group: Ford Foundation and local school district.

Staff: Reading consultants, pupil adjustment counselors, guidance counselors, preschool teachers.

Services: Developmental reading programs for grades 4–9 utilizing reading consultants as resource persons in materials and techniques for classroom teachers; cross-grade homogeneous grouping based on reading ability with weekly enrichment literature program for ablest readers; emphasis on improving reading skills in all subject areas; four prekindergarten classes emphasizing de-velopment of social skills and various cognitive functions; extensive preservice orientation and inservice training and curriculum refinement for preschool program, plus parental involvement activities; pupil adjustment program covering grades K–9 for children with serious emotional, behavioral, or environmental problems; adjustment program involves work with home, school, and social welfare agencies by school adjustment counselors; guidance adviser program in grades 7–9 with guidance counselors working individually with students and teachers with goal of improving academic performance.

Four additional programs are projected under joint ABCD and school board sponsorship: a work-study program for selected potential dropouts utilizing a teacher-coordinator to supervise on-the-job training and related classroom activities; a tutoring program involving tutors specially trained by classroom teachers to administer individualized programs of after-school tutoring; ability identification and development, an in-school, after-school, and weekend program of enrichment designed to follow up and explore student interests in music, science, and so forth; a home-school liaison program which will establish a Bureau of Home-School Liaison to centralize and increase home-school interactions.

Contact person:
Marguerite G. Sullivan,
    Deputy Superintendent
Boston Public Schools

Evaluation: Extensive evaluation in progress.

There are in addition to the eight programs jointly planned by the public schools and ABCD a number of other ABCD programs planned or functioning. These include a Youth Training and Employment Program largely financed through the United States Department of Labor which aims to help out-of-school out-of-work youth toward employment through providing testing, counseling, training, and remedial education services as well as through opening up job opportunities through cooperation with employers and labor unions.

Contact person:
Leo C. Renaud, Director and Coordinator
Youth Training and Employment
Action for Boston Community
    Development, Inc.
18 Tremont Street
Boston, Massachusetts

There are also several camp programs operating under ABCD auspices. Among them:

Agassiz Village Program, financed by the United States Office of Education which provides remedial reading and other academic activities in a summer camp setting; a camp jointly sponsored by YMCA and the Office of Education (through ABCD) will attempt to effect changes in academic achievement through regular camp activities.

Contact person:
Stanley F. Overlan, Program Specialist III
Summer-Camp, ABCD
18 Tremont Street
Boston, Massachusetts

A third camp functions on weekends and holidays and provides a program of physical work and recreation for delinquent boys.

Contact person:
Aura L. Monahan, Research Assistant
Week-end Rangers, ABCD
18 Tremont Street, Boston, Massachusetts

3. The Diversified Shop Program is designed to provide a special work-oriented curriculum to a group of boys who are considered probable dropouts.

Date begun: October 1962

Target population: Boys attending high school who are judged likely to drop out on basis of attendance and achievement records.

Per pupil costs: Not determined

Sponsoring group: Local school district.

Staff: Shop and regular teachers.

Services: Eighty percent of school day devoted to shop—20 percent to basic academic subjects; field trips and guest lecturers; job placement.

Contact person:
Thomas Roche, Director
Department of Vocational Education and
    Industrial Arts
Boston Public Schools

Springfield:

Parent-Teacher Discussion Groups is a pilot study designed to explore the effects of involving parents with each other and with the school in order to improve home-school relationships and provide for home reinforcement of school learnings.

Date begun: January 1964

Target population: Parents of 1,000 children in grades K–6, equally divided between Caucasian, Negro, and Puerto Rican families, 80 percent of whom live marginally.

Per pupil costs: None

Sponsoring group: Board of education.

Staff: Staffs of two elementary schools involved.

Services: Weekly parent and teacher meetings for one-and-a-half hours in evening in small groups based on parent interest, by grade, or subject; each group includes at least one teacher, special class teacher, Spanish interpreter, reading specialist; informal atmosphere for discussions of common needs, concerns, and problems, successful child-rearing practices shared by parents, discussion of ways in which home can reinforce school learning.

Contact person:
Thomas J. Donahoe, Principal
Hooker School-Carew Street School
Franklin Street
Springfield, Massachusetts

Michigan

1. The Detroit Great Cities Project for School Improvement is a broad-scale city-wide program designed to promote the development of academic and social competence in disadvantaged children.

Date begun: September 1964 (preceded by a pilot project 1961–64)

Target population: Approximately 32,250 pupils and their families in 27 schools.

Per pupil costs: $42

Sponsoring group: Local school district (pilot sponsored by Ford Foundation and local school district) and federal government through Economic Opportunity Act.

Staff: Twelve hundred and fifty school personnel including approximately 950 classroom teachers, 27 coaching teachers, 27 visiting teachers, 27 school-community agents. Project staff includes director, language arts coordinator, school-community agent coordinator.

Services: Numerous organizational innovations, team teaching, ungraded primary sequences, block-time programing; academic emphasis on reading, developmental and remedial; development and use of new series of interracial city-oriented primers (The *Jimmy* Series) and other special reading materials; extensive field trip program; camping out experiences; extensive inservice training; teacher workshops structured around individual school problems; diagnosis and referral of disturbed children by visiting teachers to appropriate social agencies; school-community agents to involve parents and larger community in adult education and recreation programs; Community School concept with after-school classes and clubs, use of community personnel, young and old, as baby sitters, teacher aides, after-school assistants in academic and recreational programs; comprehensive summer program including enrichment, remedial work, and recreation.

Contact person:
Louis D. Monacel, Director
Detroit Great Cities School Improvement
  Project
453 Stimson Street
Detroit, Michigan 48201

Evaluation: Pilot has been evaluated.

2. The Extended School Program is a broad-spectrum project, working in cooperation with the Great Cities Program (q.v.) and attempting to provide within local areas the components of a total community program, involving both adults and school pupils in community and school planning, and motivating them toward education.

Date begun: February 1965

Target population: Ten thousand pupils and 3,500 adults in 51 schools in the inner-city area.

Per pupil costs: Not determined

Sponsoring group: United States Economic Opportunity Act and Detroit Public Schools.

Staff: Classroom teachers, librarians, counselors, volunteers, local youth, and adults.

Services: After-school, evening, Saturday morning, and summer classes in remedial and adult education; small class size and individualized instruction; expanded library facilities with libraries open for browsing and study; job-oriented adult education courses; counseling and guidance.

Contact person:
James Neubacher, Program Director
Extended School Program
Detroit Public Schools
5057 Woodward, Detroit, Michigan 48202

3. Preschool Child and Parent Education Program is designed to provide early school experience for preschoolers from areas of

poverty and to improve the quality of parent-child interaction through a specially designed parent program.

Date begun: July 1, 1965

Target population: Two hundred three- and four-year-old children and 190 adults from inner-city areas.

Per pupil costs: Not determined

Sponsoring group: United States Economic Opportunity Act and Detroit Public Schools.

Staff: Six teachers, six assisting teachers, preschool aides, clerks, language development and parent education specialists.

Services: Therapeutic children's program designed to "fill in the gaps" in the experiential background of disadvantaged preschoolers; program oriented toward cultivating curiosity in order to encourage children to become self-motivated learners; parent education program using group-dynamics techniques for improving parent self-esteem and parent competence.

Contact person:
Bert B. Pryor, Director
Preschool Child and Parent Education
  Program
Detroit Public Schools

4. The Job Upgrading Program is a long-established program designed to help disadvantaged young people become employable, find jobs and/or return to school.

Date begun: April 1949

Target population: Each year, approximately 1,000 youths aged 16 to 21 who are out of school and unemployed, 70 percent Negro.

Per pupil costs: Not determined

Sponsoring group: Local school district, foundation, city groups.

Staff: Eleven teacher-coordinators, supervisor, project director.

Services: Classroom instruction involving re-medial reading, general enrichment and job-oriented subject matter: counseling and guidance; subsidized and supervised work experience; placement in full-time jobs with follow-up service.

Contact person:
David Dombey, Director, Job Upgrading
  Program
Detroit Public Schools

Flint:

1. School and Home: Focus on Achievement was a program designed to raise the achievement level of primary children largely through involvement of the parents as motivators of such achievement.

Date begun: April 1961–June 1963

Target population: Twenty-three hundred children in three elementary schools, predominantly Negro lower socioeconomic status, 70 percent recent migrants.

Per pupil costs: $3.50

Sponsoring group: Local school district.

Staff: Seventy-two classroom teachers, reading specialists, curriculum coordinator, home visitors, home counselors, attendance officers.

Services: Special multilevel reading materials; expanded library service; Bookworm Club to motivate children's reading; extensive involvement of parents in encouraging them to read to their children and to otherwise motivate reading and study for their children; dictionaries for home use.

Contact person:
Mildred Beatty Smith, General
  Elementary Consultant
Administration Building
Flint Public Schools, Flint, Michigan

Evaluation: Has been evaluated.

2. The Mott Program is a community-wide project utilizing the public schools as recreational, educational, and enrichment centers and attempting to provide, through the

widest use of community resources, opportunities for all the citizens of the community to develop their potential.

Date begun: 1935 (initiated as a summer recreation program)

Target population: Program available to all children and adults in city.

Per pupil costs: Not determined

Sponsoring group: Mott Foundation through Flint Board of Education.

Staff: Seven hundred teachers, teachers' aides, social workers, psychologists, clinical psychologists, remedial teachers, part-time volunteers.

Services: Classes in any subject available on request of 12 people; after-school and summer-school programs of recreation, general enrichment, art, music, job retraining; pupil and parental counseling and guidance; inservice teacher training; adult high school; adult basic reading program; children's health program; other experimental programs.

Contact person:
Peter L. Clancy
Associate Superintendent for the Mott Program
Flint Public Schools

Grand Rapids:

The Program for Inner-City Schools is designed to provide to disadvantaged children experiences to compensate for impoverished experiential backgrounds, which are seen as a hindrance to learning.

Date begun: November 1964

Target population: Approximately 45,242 children in the inner-city schools.

Per pupil costs: Summer school $70, other programs not determined.

Sponsoring group: Local school board.

Staff: Coordinator, secretary, 11 instruc-

tional assistants, two prekindergarten teachers, eight summer school teachers, volunteer college students, and community volunteers.

Services: Remedial and enrichment program with emphasis in language arts area; prekindergarten program; instructional assistants (coaching teachers) for grades 1–6; summer school grades 1–6; volunteer tutorial and remedial programs.

Contact person:
Mrs. Jacquelyn Nickerson, Coordinator
Program for Inner-City Schools
Grand Rapids Public Schools
143 Bostwick Avenue, N.W.
Grand Rapids, Michigan 49502

Pontiac:

Experimental Program for Learning Readiness in Seven Pontiac Experimental Schools is a multifaceted program designed to improve the school performance of culturally deprived elementary school pupils through a program of enrichment and curriculum modification.

Date begun: September 1962

Target population: Approximately 3,972 children attending eight elementary schools.

Per pupil costs: Not determined

Sponsoring group: Local school district.

Staff: Staffs of eight elementary schools.

Services: Modifications and revisions of instructional materials; special teacher selection and inservice training; enrichment activities including field trips; tutorial projects; pupil counseling and visiting teachers for parent counseling; special reading teachers; health services; library services.

Contact person:
William J. Lacy, Assistant Superintendent
School District of the City of Pontiac
40 Patterson Street
Pontiac 15, Michigan

Ypsilanti:

Intervention in the Cognitive Development of the Culturally Deprived and Functionally Retarded Negro Preschool Child is a program designed to assess the effect of a school and home based program upon a group of preschool children, to develop specific techniques and curriculum for operation of such a program, and to contribute to basic research.

Date begun: January 1964 (preceded by a pilot project 1962–63)

Target population: Twenty-four 3-year-old Negro preschoolers testing at IQ levels under 90, all of whom come from lower socioeconomic status families. Matched control group. New group starts each year in the two-year program.

Per pupil costs: $1,500

Sponsoring group: United States Office of Education Cooperative Research Program, local school district, Michigan Department of Public Instruction, Washtenaw County.

Staff: Four preschool teachers, social workers, psychologists.

Services: Daily morning preschool program structured to promote specific learnings in concept formation, use of symbols, and so forth; very low pupil-teacher ratio with consequent extensive individual attention; extensive field trip program to broaden experiential base; children permitted to take nursery school equipment home; weekly two-hour home visits by teachers, bringing nursery school equipment, to continue teaching in mother's presence; monthly group meetings between teachers and mothers; semimonthly fathers' meetings including such activities as making toys for school.

Contact person:
David P. Weikart,
Division of Special Services
Ypsilanti Public Schools, Ypsilanti, Michigan

Evaluation: Progress report through 1964 available. Evaluation of each group as data become available.

Minnesota

Minneapolis:

1. The Youth Development Demonstration Project is a comprehensive network of programs jointly planned and carried out by various community agencies under the auspices of the Community Health and Welfare Council of Hennepin County, Inc., and designed to provide a number of compensatory services to youth in two disadvantaged areas of the city.

Date begun: August 1964

Target population: Infants through precollege youth in two target areas.

Per pupil costs: Not determined

Sponsoring group: President's Committee on Juvenile Delinquency and Youth Crime and contributions from local public and private agencies through the Community Health and Welfare Council of Hennepin County, Inc.

Staff: Director, school services coordinator, research director, community services coordinator, youth employment coordinator, research consultants in administration and research. Other paid and volunteer personnel for various specific programs.

Services: There are some 22 small and large programs. Among those in which the schools have been most involved are: Development of a service-station attendants course at one high school under the Youth Employment Program; an Elementary Reading Materials Development Program involving 217 children in seven classes of one elementary school in an exploration of methods and materials in teaching reading; a junior high school curriculum development program involving 44 eighth- and ninth-graders in a special basic curriculum and vocational program in a nonschool setting (project operates out of an old print shop located near the junior high school); a family counseling program utilizing caseworkers from the Family and Children's Service; a one-to-one tutoring and motivation program involving university students; a reading program for second-graders who are taken to the library and read to by volunteers from a local church; a visiting program where two-man teams of businessmen visit elementary school classrooms; and a Youth Opportunity Program with the local chapter of the National Council of Jewish Women providing a higher horizons type of enrichment program to one group of children and a remedial reading program to another. A Comprehensive School Readiness Program sponsored by the Junior League works with preschoolers, their mothers, and younger siblings in the area of one elementary school.

Contact person:
Larry Harris, Director,
   Washington Elementary School
Chicago at 6th Street
Minneapolis, Minnesota

Evaluation: All programs being evaluated by research unit.

2. In addition to programs under the YDP, the Minneapolis schools have instituted various practices to benefit disadvantaged youth. Among them are:

Staffing on the basis of socioeconomic index provides for lower pupil-teacher ratios in schools serving disadvantaged populations.

Programs of inservice education for principals, teachers, counselors, and other school personnel have been offered in the area of the education of disadvantaged children.

An ungraded cooperative work program for dropped-out or potentially dropped-out tenth-graders provides help in finding and holding a job or in re-enrolling in classes.

Contact person:
Nathaniel Ober, Assistant Superintendent
Minneapolis Public Schools
807 Northeast Broadway
Minneapolis, Minnesota 55413

Missouri

Kansas City:

1. The Kansas City Work-Study Program to Reduce Juvenile Delinquency is a longitudinal study designed to test the hypothesis that boys vulnerable to delinquency will become less delinquent if they are given a systematic work experience commencing as early as age 13.

Date begun: September 1961

Target population: Four hundred boys (200 as controls) 50 percent white and 50 percent Negro from four high schools, identified in the seventh grade (one-half in 1961, one-half in 1962) as potential delinquents.

Per pupil costs: $500 (operating costs only, research additional)

Sponsoring group: Ford Foundation, local school district, Kansas City Association of Trusts and Foundations.

Staff: Classroom teachers, work supervisors, assistant work supervisors, director, research associates, employment supervisors.

Services: Work-study Stage I (boys 13 to 15) half-day academic program, half-day "socially useful" work in groups, primarily around school doing furniture repair, yard work, and so forth; Work-study Stage II (boys 15 to 17), part-time school, part-time individual employment under supervision; Work-study Stage III (boys 16 to 18) are placed in full-time paid job.

Contact person:
Ralph Berry, Director Work-Study Program
Board of Education Building
1211 McGee Street, Kansas City, Missouri

Evaluation: *Third Progress Report*, July 1964, available.

2. The Lincoln Plus Project is designed to elevate the aspirations of disadvantaged children, to discover latent talent, and to raise achievement levels.

Date begun: September 1963

Target population: Forty preschoolers from two centers, 4,980 pupils from eight elementary schools and 2,113 pupils from two secondary schools. Pupils are 95 percent Negro and approximately 52 percent test below 90 in IQ.

Per pupil costs: $20

Sponsoring group: Local school district (nursery schools sponsored by Council of Jewish Women and Midtown Preschool Foundation, Inc.).

Staff: Two hundred and twenty classroom teachers, 10 reading teachers, general grade consultants, home-school coordinators, psychologists, nurses, volunteers.

Services: Remedial reading and speech improvement; general enrichment with emphasis on language arts, small reading groups; use of volunteers for enrichment and after-school recreation programs; study centers; home visits and other parental involvement; visits to community including preschoolers; pupil and parental counseling.

Contact person:
John A. Clair,
    Director Compensatory Education
2012 East 23rd Street
Kansas City, Missouri

St. Louis:

1. Efforts in the Banneker District to Raise the Academic Achievement of Culturally Disadvantaged Children is primarily a motivation program designed to improve the achievement of children in the predominantly Negro Banneker District through attitudinal change on the part of pupils, teachers, and parents, rather than through specific curriculum modification.

Date begun: September 1957

Target population: Some 15,000 predominantly Negro pupils from 23 schools, grades K-8 in one elementary school district, and 60 preschoolers in four groups.

Per pupil costs: No additional funds (Preschool program sponsored by National Council of Jewish Women, St. Louis Section)

Sponsoring group: Local school district.

Staff: Five hundred classroom teachers, administrators, 25 volunteers for nursery school.

Services: Parent meetings at which parents are shown low standing of their school district and inspired to rise above discrimination to help their children succeed through education; ungraded primary with heavy emphasis on reading so that every child will be reading at grade level; pep rallies, honor assemblies, contact with successful people to prove education can lead to success; home visits, staff reeducation; panel programs with successful young people describing their jobs and how they got their start to parents and eighth-grade pupils; two-day-a-week preschool program, volunteer staffed, with training for volunteers.

Contact person:
Samuel Shepard Jr.
Assistant Superintendent in charge of
    Banneker District
Board of Education
St. Louis, Missouri

2. National Council of Jewish Women Remedial Reading Program is a program using volunteers as a means of assisting the staffs of public school reading clinics in order to serve a larger group of children.

Date begun: 1963

Target population: Pupils in need of remedial reading throughout St. Louis School District, grades 1–12, 75 percent boys.

Per pupil costs: None over regular reading clinic costs

Sponsoring group: National Council of Jewish Women, St. Louis Section.

Staff: Six specialized teachers, full- and part-time volunteers who receive special training.

Services: Volunteers are all specially trained to teach regular school remedial reading program; tutorial basis with not more than three pupils to one teacher; six clinics serving pupils from neighboring schools.

Contact person:
Mrs. Robert Sidel, Chairman
Remedial Reading Program
St. Louis Section, National Council of
    Jewish Women
8129 Delmar, Suite 203
St. Louis, Missouri 63130

Evaluation: Reading tests given regularly.

3. In addition to the programs listed, there are a number of other programs and practices in the St. Louis schools designed to benefit disadvantaged pupils. Among them are:

Combat Teams of guidance counselors, social workers, and administrative assistants are used to combat absence and tardiness by providing concentrated attention to cases of persistent absenteeism.

A Primary School Guidance Program has been instituted at some schools to allow for early identification of children with behavior patterns likely to lead to later school problems in order to provide help for these children.

Since 1943 special Reading Clinics have provided for diagnosis and treatment of reading disabilities. Children are scheduled for 45-minute periods, three times a week, for periods ranging from a few weeks to two years, in five clinics. A sixth clinic, established in 1963 is a laboratory for training future teachers. The NCJW Reading Program functions in these clinics (q.v.).

4. In addition to the preschool program sponsored by the local section of the NCJW, there are a number of other voluntary preschool programs functioning. These have been organized informally as a Volunteer Preschool Council.

Contact person:
Mrs. J. Peter Schmitz, Research Chairman,
    Junior Kindergarten Committee
Junior League of St. Louis
6800 Kingbury Boulevard
St. Louis, Missouri

New Jersey

Newark:

The Newark Plan: A Program of Expanded Opportunities, is a secondary school project aimed at raising the vocational, educational, and cultural sights of disadvantaged pupils and their parents and at improving the relationship between the school-community and the greater city.

Date begun: September 1962

Target population: Originally, 700 seventh-graders in a selected junior high school. In 1964–65, all 1,750 pupils, a lower socioeconomic status population, 98 percent Negro, were involved.

Per pupil costs: $70

Sponsoring group: Local school district.

Staff: Eighty-five classroom teachers, reading specialists, project coordinator, teacher coordinator, cultural resources coordinator, principal, social workers, guidance counselors, psychologist.

Services: Direct classroom instruction by reading specialists; remedial reading; extra resource materials; field trips and guest speakers; cultural program including visits to World's Fair; individual counseling; group guidance; after-school supervised study period; club program; teacher inservice training including reading workshops; weekly parent meetings; parental counseling; parent newsletters.

Contact person:
Seymour Puckowitz, Project Coordinator
301 West Kinney Street
Newark, New Jersey

Trenton:

Junior Five Project is a pilot program involving children of preschool through junior high in an attempt to determine the nature of the special needs of education in a depressed area and the possible answers to those needs.

Date begun: September 1963

Target population: Fifty preschoolers in three classes, 537 elementary pupils, and 521 junior high school pupils—all housed in one junior high school building in a district marked for urban renewal. Population is predominantly lower socioeconomic status Negro or Puerto Rican.

Sponsoring group: New Jersey State Department of Education.

Staff: Two preschool teachers, 47 classroom teachers, helping teacher, consultants, guidance counselor, reading specialist, curriculum coordinator, psychologists, physician, nurse, social workers, attendance officer, community coordinator.

Services: Inservice training and action research as means of improving teaching-learning process; consultant visits in classrooms; emphasis on teacher reorientation and skill development; de-emphasis on formal reading, emphasis on child-centered creative writing and reading; enriched in-school club-activity program; after-school tutorial program; cultural visits; parent involvement in school and classroom activities; nursery school parent education program; School and Community Association instituted.

Contact person:
Theodore C. Lynch, Project Coordinator
Junior Five School
North Montgomery Street
Trenton, New Jersey

New York

New York State:

There are four separate state-sponsored compensatory programs operating in New York State. Two of them, the Project Able programs and the Project Talent Search programs are listed in this directory under the communities in which they operate since the Able programs, in particular, vary considerably from community to community. Two of the programs, the School to Employment Program (STEP) and the Project Re-entry program are substantially the same in the various communities in which they are in operation.

1. Since September 1961, Project Able programs have been initiated in the following communities (q.v.):

Albany	Rochester
Buffalo	Roosevelt
Hartsdale (Green-	Schenectady
burgh #8)	Suffern (Hillburn)
Hempstead	Syracuse
Kingston	Utica
Mount Kisco	White Plains
Newburgh	Windsor
New York City	Yonkers
Oppenheim-	
Ephratah	

In addition the following communities have Project Able programs which began in September 1965, and are not separately described:

Amsterdam	Jamestown
Brentwood	Long Beach
Freeport	Mount Vernon
Goshen	Niagara Falls
Ithaca	South New Berlin

Evaluation: *Able: An Appraisal*. Theodore Bienenstok and William C. Sayres, Albany.

2. Since March 1960, Talent Search Projects have been initiated in the following communities (q.v.):

Akron
Altmar-Parish-
  Williamstown
  (Parish)
Arcade
Bellport
Canajoharie
Deposit
Dunkirk
East Syracuse
Gloversville
Harpursville

Hornell
Hudson
Mamaroneck
North Tonowanda
Nyack
Rensselaer
Springfield (East
  Springfield)
Uniondale
West Hempstead
Wyandanch

In addition, the following communities began Talent Search Projects in September 1965, which are not separately described:

Baldwin
Carthage
Centereach
Galway
Gowanda
Great Neck
Huntington
Liberty
Manhasset
Mineola
Monroe-Woodbury
Monticello
New York Mills

Niagara-Wheatfield
Ossining
Oswego
Peekskill
Perth
Ravenna-Coeymans-
  Selkirk
Salamanca
Salmon River
Southampton
South Kortright
Selkirk
Troy

3. The School to Employment Program (step) is a work-study program designed to help potential dropouts stay in school or, if they do leave school, to help them to become more successfully employed.

Date begun: Spring 1961

Target population: Approximately 1,000 potential high school dropouts 15 years of age or older in the following communities: Albany, Brentwood, Clarence, Glens Falls, Greece, Hempstead, Ithaca, Levittown, Maine-Endwell, Medina, Monticello, New York, North Babylon, North Tonowanda, Nyack, Port Byron, Rochester, Sewanhaka, South New Berlin, Spring Valley, Syracuse, Watertown, and Yonkers. For the school year 1965–66 the following communities will also have step programs: Amsterdam, Colonie, Endicott, Glen Cove, Mineola, and Vestal.

Per pupil costs: Average $340 per pupil in 1964–65 (from $210 in New York City to $700 in Maine-Endwell)

Sponsoring group: State Education Department and local school districts.

Staff: Teacher-coordinators, one for each group of 20 to 25 potential dropouts.

Services: Regular school classes in morning plus at least one daily session with teacher-coordinator for general work orientation and counseling; 15 to 20 periods per week at work station with teacher-coordinator responsible for job placement; stipends provided to pay students for work in tax supported agencies —upstate employment primarily in public agencies, New York City employment predominantly in private agencies; parental counseling, parent consent to participation.

Contact person:
Bernard A. Kaplan, Project Coordinator,
  Bureau of Guidance
The University of the State of New York
State Education Department
Albany, New York 12224

Evaluation: step, *An Appraisal*. Theodore Bienenstok and William C. Sayres, Albany, March 1964. *Cases in Point*. Albany, March 1964.

4. Project Re-entry is a summer and fall program, modeled after the 1963 Summer Dropout Campaign sponsored by President Kennedy, and designed to encourage the return to school in the fall of recent and potential dropouts.

Date begun: Spring 1964

Target population: Seventeen hundred pupils (1964) in the following eight school districts: Albany, Buffalo, Mount Vernon, New Rochelle, Niagara Falls, Schenectady, Syracuse, Yonkers. The program was repeated in these communities in the summer of 1965 with 14 more communities added to the program.

Per pupil costs: Approximately $9

Sponsoring group: NDEA, Title V-A Funds through Bureau of Guidance, State Education Department.

Staff: Counselors, teachers, administrators, clerical staff.

Services: Spring identification of potential and recent dropouts; summer home-visits or phone contact with pupils by counselors; follow-up of returned pupils in fall; return of some pupils to evening school, MDTA training, and so forth, rather than to regular school program.

Contact person:
Bernard A. Kaplan, Project Coordinator,
Bureau of Guidance

Akron:

Talent Search is a program designed to survey the educational, vocational, and motivational needs of a group of reservation Indian students and their parents and to develop guidance approaches, techniques, and activities to improve their motivation and achievement.

Date begun: January 1962

Target population: Forty-two Seneca Indian pupils from the Tonawanda Indian Reservation enrolled in grades 7–10 at a local junior-senior high school.

Per pupil costs: $75

Sponsoring group: NDEA, Title V-A, funds through Bureau of Guidance, State Education Department, local school district, and county Board of Cooperative Educational Services.

Staff: Coordinator-counselor, guidance counselor, teacher-advisers, school social worker, school psychologist.

Services: Educational and cultural trips; small group discussions and intensive individual counseling; provision of special reading materials; home visits and parent meetings; use of "successful" Indians as models; survey of former Indian students for information and comparison.

Contact person:
Ellsworth L. Brown, Director of Guidance
Akron Central School
47 Bloomingdale Avenue
Akron, New York 14001

Albany:

1. Project Able is a program emphasizing curricular and cultural enrichment to improve the education achievement and the attitudes of disadvantaged primary children.

Date begun: September 1961

Target population: Nine hundred and twenty-five children in grades 3–6 in three elementary schools and one junior high school. Population is lower socioeconomic status and 75 percent Negro.

Per pupil costs: Not determined

Sponsoring group: State Education Department and local school district (1966–75 local school district only).

Staff: Thirty-four classroom teachers, two guidance counselors, five remedial reading specialists, professional clerk aid, home-school coordinator, four librarians, curriculum team (helping teachers and supervisors), outside consultants.

Services: One-half day per week team teaching for enrichment in cultural and social areas; remedial reading and arithmetic; extensive field trip program and guest speakers; curriculum enrichment with films, TV, radio, foreign languages, and so forth; home visits, parent meetings, after-school tutoring.

Contact person:
David Bray, Assistant Superintendent of
  Schools and Director of Guidance
School Administration Building
Albany, New York

2. STEP (see New York State)

3. Re-entry (see New York State)

Altmar-Parish-Williamstown (see Parish)

Amsterdam:

Identification and Guidance of Talented
Youth from Lower Socio-Economic or Culturally Impoverished Areas is essentially a
guidance program aimed at identifying underachievers, potential dropouts, and pupils
with unrealistic goals; and providing guidance aimed at improving their self-concept
and motivation.

Date begun: November 1962

Target population: Fifty-seven underachieving eighth-grade pupils of one junior high
school. Population is of average IQ, primarily
from lower socioeconomic status families.

Per pupil costs: $75

Sponsoring group: NDEA, Title V-A funds
through Bureau of Guidance, State Education Department. Funded 50 percent through
Project Able after September 1965.

Staff: Fourteen classroom teachers, guidance
counselors, reading specialist, psychologist,
coordinator, attendance officer, county welfare officer (Child Guidance Unit).

Services: Individual and group guidance directed toward improving self-concept and
helping students with appropriate course
selection; field trips; home visits with vocational and educational counseling of parents.

Contact person:
William Tecler, Director of Pupil
  Personnel Services
Board of Education
41 Division Street
Amsterdam, New York

Arcade:

Talent Search is primarily a motivation program designed to raise the aspirations of students of better than average ability, through
exposing them to a variety of experiences.

Date begun: September 1962

Target population: Twenty-three predominantly lower socioeconomic status pupils in
grades 7, 8, and 10 of one high school.

Per pupil costs: Not determined

Sponsoring group: NDEA, Title V-A funds
through Bureau of Guidance, State Education Department.

Staff: Guidance counselors.

Services: Field trips to colleges, junior colleges, museums, local factories; after-school
discussion groups including use of visual aids;
talks by armed forces recruiters.

Contact person:
Richard E. McAdoo
Arcade Central School
Arcade, New York 14009

Bedford (see Mount Kisco)

Bellport:

Talent Search is a guidance oriented project
aimed at improving academic achievement,
self-confidence, and social competence and at
promoting a positive vocational and educational outlook.

Date begun: September 1964 (preceded by
a pilot 1962–63)

Target population: Twenty-eight eighth-
grade children of predominantly lower socioeconomic status in one junior high school.

Per pupil costs: $238

Sponsoring group: NDEA, Title V-A funds
through Bureau of Guidance, State Education Department.

Staff: Five classroom teachers, guidance
counselor, reading specialist, psychologist,

librarian, physical education instructors, nurse, attendance officer.

Services: Flexible curriculum organization for remedial development; "fifth" day curriculum for field trips and other enrichment activities; group and individual counseling; parent-teacher workshops; parental counseling.

Contact person:
Edward A. McHugh, Principal
Bellport Junior High School
Bellport, New York

Brentwood:

1. The Talent Search project is essentially a guidance program designed to improve the academic achievement of secondary school students by improving their motivation and self-concept.

Date begun: January 1963

Target population: One hundred and twenty-four largely lower socioeconomic status pupils from three junior high and two senior high schools.

Per pupil costs: $275

Sponsoring group: NDEA, Title V-A funds through Bureau of Guidance, State Education Department, and local school district. Funded 50 percent through Project Able after September 1965.

Staff: Guidance counselors, project consultant, project director.

Services: Remedial reading and mathematics; intensive individual and group counseling; vocational guidance; field trips and guest speakers; parental counseling; tutoring in summer by former students.

Contact person:
Gerard E. Smith
Director of Guidance
Brentwood Public Schools
Brentwood, New York

Evaluation: *Operation Challenge, Interim Report for Administrators and Teachers,* 35 cents per copy.

2. Operation Aladdin is a STEP program designed to help reduce the number of unemployed dropouts.

Date begun: February 1964

Target population: One hundred and forty dropouts, either those eligible to take the high school equivalency examination or recent dropouts.

Per pupil costs: $150

Sponsoring group: New York State and local school district.

Staff: Work coordinators, counselor-coordinators, and project director.

Services: Courses to prepare older dropouts to take high school equivalency examination; placement in regular night high school classes for younger dropouts; counselor-coordinator assigned to each group of five students for counseling on local employment prospects; job placement.

Contact person:
Gerard E. Smith, Director of Guidance
Brentwood Public Schools

Evaluation: Continuing.

Buffalo:

1. The Guided Talent Project, one of the Project Able programs, is designed to identify and encourage potential ability among able culturally disadvantaged pupils through a program of enrichment and remedial work conducted before and after school, and to provide intensive educational and vocational counseling to encourage such pupils to complete an educational program consistent with their ability.

Date begun: September 1962

Target population: Five hundred and eighty-one pupils in grades 7–12 in five schools (one elementary school grades 7–8, two junior high schools, one academic and one vocational high school). Pupils are predominantly lower socioeconomic status Negro, selected on the basis of potential ability in various areas, including music, art, and so forth.

Per pupil costs: $54

Sponsoring group: State Education Department and local school district.

Staff: Project director, guidance counselors, psychologists, social workers, 57 teachers paid as tutors and group leaders, volunteers for enrichment program.

Services: Before and after school classes providing enrichment in academic and cultural areas, and, when needed, remedial work in subject areas; intensive individual counseling in vocational and educational areas; parental involvement through home visits and school meetings; extensive use of community personnel in "Better Citizenship" programs featuring successful Negroes and in one-to-one contacts between representatives of local industries and project pupils for inspiration and academic enrichment; numerous trips to concerts, cultural programs with frequent community participation through provision of tickets.

Contact person:
Jonah Margulis,
   Project Able Coordinator
Board of Education
City Hall, Buffalo, New York

2. Great Cities Program for School Improvement: The Buffalo Project seeks to promote the total development of a child living in a substandard environment.

Date begun: September 1962 (preceded by a pilot 1961–62)

Target population: About 2,913 lower socioeconomic status children, including a number of recent southern Negro migrants in five elementary schools. Pilot involved 545 pupils.

Per pupil costs: $30

Sponsoring group: Buffalo Board of Education (pilot largely financed by Ford Foundation).

Staff: Director, educational coordinator, psychologist, community coordinator, reading consultant, remedial reading teacher, speech therapist, extra art and music teachers, arithmetic coaching teacher, social worker.

Services: Special classroom reading materials, remedial reading classes, arithmetic coaching, and remedial speech instruction; weekly speech lessons for all classes; special art and music classes; grade-level music performance groups; parent conferences and home visits; field trips with parent participation; "demonstration" program in original "pilot" school to train new teachers throughout system.

Contact person:
Claude D. Clapp,
   Assistant Superintendent of Schools
Board of Education

3. Project Re-entry (see New York State)

Canajoharie:

Develop Potential is essentially a guidance program designed to improve the motivation among high-potential, low-achieving students and to provide vocational and educational information to such students and their parents.

Date begun: September 1965

Target population: Eleven eighth-grade pupils, lower to middle socioeconomic status white, in one junior high school. Program will eventually include grades 7–12 with about 12 students added each year.

Per pupil costs: $117

Sponsoring group: NDEA, Title V-A funds through Bureau of Guidance, State Education Department.

Staff: Guidance counselors.

Services: Saturday trips to college campuses, museums, plays, factories with pre- and post-trip planning; group counseling and guidance exploring attitudes, study habits, manners, and so forth.

Contact person:
Robert J. Cornell, Director of Guidance
Canajoharie High School
Canajoharie, New York 13317

Evaluation: In progress.

Deposit (see also, Windsor)

Talent Search is a combined program with Project Able in Windsor, New York, the combined goals of which are to enlarge the experience, improve communications skills, and thus increase the motivation and competence of rural high school students.

Date begun: 1962

Target population: Initially, average and above-average high school students with observed social restriction. Eventually total high school population.

Per pupil costs: Approximately $195

Sponsoring group: NDEA, Title V-A funds through Bureau of Guidance, State Education Department, and local school district.

Staff: Psychologists, counselors, tutors, academic instructor, approximately 20 guest lecturers from university, industry, and government.

Services: University lecturers; IBM mathematics program; group and individual counseling; social-interest groups in theater, music, and athletics; field trips with resource personnel.

Contact person:
Denis I. Donegan
Deposit Central School, Deposit, New York

Evaluation: Available.

Dunkirk:

The Talent Search Program is designed to improve communications skills, to improve the motivation and raise the aspiration level of disadvantaged pupils, and to increase their interest in completing high school.

Date begun: 1964

Target population: Thirty-six pupils, predominantly Puerto Rican, in grades 7–12 of one school.

Per pupil costs: $175

Sponsoring group: NDEA, Title V-A funds through Bureau of Guidance, State Education Department, and local school district.

Staff: Classroom teachers, home-school liaison teacher, Spanish-speaking resource teacher, attendance officer, program coordinator.

Services: Individual counseling at least once monthly with additional time for students who need it; group guidance for children and parents; establishment of faculty fund to assist with school supplies; occupational information; parental involvement through home visits and school meetings; special class for Spanish-speaking pupils; community involvement through financial assistance to school and homes, provision of part-time work, and one-to-one contact with members of Industrial Club.

Contact person:
Joseph Parlato, Director of Guidance
Dunkirk Public Schools
525 Eagle Street
Dunkirk, New York

East Springfield:

Talent Search is a program designed to increase the self-awareness of and to provide educational and vocational guidance to a group of secondary school students and their parents.

Date begun: February 1964

Target population: Twenty pupils in one eighth-grade class in a rural community. Children are predominantly middle-class.

Per pupil costs: $7.50

Sponsoring group: NDEA, Title V-A funds through Bureau of Guidance, State Education Department, and local school board.

Staff: Guidance counselor, psychologist.

Services: Evaluation of student aptitudes; provision of educational and vocational information; field trips including trips to schools and colleges; guidance.

Contact person:
James M. Brayden, Guidance Counselor
Springfield Central School
East Springfield, New York

East Syracuse:

Talent Search attempts to identify and improve the achievement of bright, underachieving secondary school students of lower socioeconomic background.

Date begun: March 1962

Target population: Fifty lower socioeconomic status underachieving white pupils with IQs over 110 from two junior and two senior high schools.

Per pupil costs: $80

Sponsoring group: NDEA, Title V-A funds through Bureau of Guidance, State Education Department, and local school board.

Staff: Guidance counselors, psychologists, nurses.

Services: Individual and group counseling with emphasis on providing information about advanced education and local cultural and vocational opportunities; reading help; visiting speakers; field trips; evening parent counseling.

Contact person:
Mrs. Harriet Brown, Guidance Coordinator
East Syracuse-Minoa Central Schools
East Syracuse, New York

Gloversville:

Talent Search is a talent discovery program

designed to identify and provide enrichment for talented students.

Date begun: May 1962

Target population: Twenty eighth-grade lower socioeconomic status pupils in one junior high school with IQs of 110 or over.

Per pupil costs: $75

Sponsoring group: NDEA, Title V-A funds through Bureau of Guidance, State Education Department, and local school board.

Staff: Guidance counselor, librarian, psychologist.

Services: Special library facilities and instructional projects; extra guidance sessions; free admission to all school cultural events; field trips; evening counseling with parents.

Contact person:
F. C. Woodworth,
    Director Pupil Personnel Services
Board of Education, Gloversville, New York

Greenburgh (see Hartsdale)

Harpursville:

Talent Search is a program designed to improve the academic achievement and raise the goals of underachieving secondary school students.

Date begun: June 1961

Target population: Sixty white students, culturally deprived and/or underachieving, of one junior and one senior high school.

Per pupil costs: $15

Sponsoring group: NDEA, Title V-A funds through Bureau of Guidance, State Education Department, and local school board.

Staff: Three classroom teachers, guidance counselors, reading specialist, psychologist, study skills teacher, speech specialist.

Services: Remedial reading; training in study skills; counseling, field trips, including cultural activities and college visits; work with parents and pupils in educational and vocational planning; three-week summer session for project pupils.

Contact person:
Robert Euker, Coordinator-Counselor
Harpursville Central School
Harpursville, New York

Hartsdale:

Greenburgh School District #8 Project Able is a longitudinal study which attempts to alter the early school program in ways that will make it more appropriate for disadvantaged children as well as provide compensatory education and thus prevent their future school failure. Emphasis is upon genuinely integrating previously desegregated schools.

Date begun: 1961

Target population: Initially, 180 kindergarten, first- and second-grade pupils in two elementary schools serving lower-class or indigent largely Negro families; subsequently all pupils in grades 1–6.

Per pupil costs: $52

Sponsoring group: New York State Education Department, local board of education.

Staff: Elementary supervisor, psychologist, language consultant, social workers, psychiatrist, professional volunteers.

Services: Special kindergarten language development program; language and reading program in first grade; social work counseling; heterogeneous class-grouping, with flexible ability-grouping within class sections; parental counseling.

Contact person:
Sinai M. Waxman,
    Supervisor of the Elementary Schools
Warburg Campus, Hartsdale, New York

Hempstead:

1. Improving the Experiential Background of Culturally Disadvantaged Children by Means of an Enriched Prekindergarten Program and Associated Services is a Project Able program designed to increase readiness for kindergarten.

Date begun: October 1964

Target population: All pupils eligible for kindergarten in a given area were permitted to participate—32 preschoolers enrolled, predominantly Negro.

Per pupil costs: $971

Sponsoring group: State Education Department and local school district.

Staff: Two full-time teachers, nurse, social worker, psychologist.

Services: Preschool classes; parent education meetings at three-week intervals; home visits by teachers and, as necessary, by nurse and social worker.

Contact person:
Thomas Sheldon, Superintendent of Schools
Hempstead Public Schools
185 Peninsula Boulevard
Hempstead, New York

2. STEP (see New York State)

Hillburn:

Project Able is a program designed to give individual direction and help to disadvantaged children and their families in order to improve the children's school achievement and help them to find better lives for themselves.

Date begun: September 1961

Target population: Four hundred and forty-five pupils from grades K–3 in one elementary school and grades K–6 in a second. Both schools serving a depressed rural area.

Per pupil costs: $31.50

Sponsoring group: State Education Department and local school district.

Staff: Nineteen classroom teachers, music teachers, art teacher, psychologist, nurses, principals, director and assistant director of elementary education.

Services: Emphasis in curriculum on "doing" activities; one-half day per week devoted to nonacademic curriculum enrichment—dancing and music, science experiments, dramatics, field trips; group counseling; parent conferences.

Contact person:
William Lathrop, School Psychologist
Ramapo Central School District #1
Mountain Avenue, Hillburn, New York

Hudson:

The Talent Search Program is designed to help a group of children from experientially deprived backgrounds to improve their school achievement, make wise use of their leisure time, and an intelligent choice of vocational pursuit.

Date begun: August 1962

Target population: Fifteen students, half nonwhite in the eighth grade of one school, selected on the basis of underachievement and average or better than average intelligence.

Per pupil costs: $80

Sponsoring group: NDEA, Title V-A funds through Bureau of Guidance, State Education Department.

Staff: Twenty classroom teachers, three counselors.

Services: Group and individual counseling of parents and students; introduction to educational and vocational experiences and to cultural opportunities.

Contact person:
Harold W. Golding, Coordinator
Hudson High School
Hudson, New York 12534

Kingston:

Project Able is a program designed to increase self-understanding, to raise the educational and aspirational levels of disadvantaged students, and to prevent dropouts.

Date begun: March 1961

Target population: One hundred and ninety-two lower socioeconomic status pupils of one elementary, one junior high, and one high school, predominantly Caucasian.

Per pupil costs: $180

Sponsoring group: State Education Department and local school district.

Staff: Guidance counselors, reading specialist, subject supervisor, home visitor, psychologist, attendance officer.

Services: Intensive reading program including remedial reading; flexible scheduling; increased individual and group guidance; parental involvement through home visits and school meetings; field trips and guest speakers; adult evening school programs.

Contact person:
Robert Corcoran, Coordinator
Myron J. Michael School
Andrew Street
Kingston, New York

Long Beach:

1. Curriculum Assistance Reinforcing Education (the CARE program) is designed to improve the learning experiences of disadvantaged children.

Date begun: September 1964

Target population: Fifth- and sixth-grade children from one elementary school selected as disadvantaged by teachers and principal.

Per pupil costs: $1,000

Sponsoring group: Local school district.

Staff: Two volunteer teachers who are guidance oriented.

Services: Small class size; specially selected teachers, and emphasis on individual relationships; special learning activities; selected field trips; extra guidance to promote better home-school relationships.

Contact person:
Jerome P. Oberman
Central School, Long Beach, New York

2. Prekindergarten Programs for Socially Disadvantaged Children is a research program designed to evaluate preschool programs for socially disadvantaged children in terms of their success in increasing learning capacity.

Date begun: September 1965 (preceded by a pilot September 1964–June 1965)

Target population: Children eligible for kindergarten the following year whose parents are of low occupational status.

Per pupil costs: Not determined

Sponsoring group: State Education Department.

Staff: Two teachers, director-psychologist, part-time school social worker, teacher aides, and secretary. Physician and dental hygienist available.

Services: Preschool classes; medical and dental services.

Contact person:
Joseph Sturm
Blackheath Road School
Long Beach, New York

Mamaroneck:

Operation Candle is a pilot program designed to provide remedial and enrichment activities to disadvantaged children in order to motivate them to operate up to potential.

Date begun: January 1965

Target population: Eleven eighth-grade pupils, lower socioeconomic status, nine white, two Negro.

Per pupil costs: $150

Sponsoring group: NDEA, Title V-A funds

through Bureau of Guidance, State Education Department, and local school district.

Staff: Eleven teachers, coordinator, counselor, psychologist, reading consultant.

Services: Individual and group guidance; tutoring, remedial reading, psychological counseling, educational trips.

Contact person:
Henry Baldera, Coordinator
Mamaroneck Junior High School
Mamaroneck, New York

Mount Kisco:

Person to Person Project is a Project Able program designed to improve the attitudes and achievement of school children from small depressed areas in a generally upper socioeconomic status suburban community.

Date begun: September 1961

Target population: Twenty preschoolers, 57 children from one elementary school, and 18 children from one junior high school, all lower socioeconomic status children who demonstrate average to superior ability but have difficulty meeting the prevailing academic standards of the community.

Per pupil costs: $250

Sponsoring group: New York State Education Department and local school district.

Staff: Guidance counselor, reading specialist, curriculum coordinator, psychologist, project teacher, home visitor, physician, nurse.

Services: "Interpersonal interaction" on a variety of levels; individual assistance with reading and homework, field trips, cultural experiences, study clubs, individual and group guidance with children and parents, emphasis on teacher sensitization.

Contact person:
George Bondra,
    Director of Research-Psychologist
369 Lexington Avenue
Mount Kisco, New York

Mount Vernon:

1. Talent Search is essentially an after-school program of cultural enrichment for pupils of unrealized potential from culturally deprived backgrounds.

Date begun: September 1961

Target population: Forty pupils in four elementary schools and 90 pupils in three junior high schools, predominantly lower socioeconomic Negro.

Per pupil costs: $148

Sponsoring group: For elementary program, local school district; for secondary program, NDEA, Title V-A funds through Bureau of Guidance, State Education Department, and local school district (funded 50 percent through Project Able starting September 1965).

Staff: Thirteen classroom teachers, counselors.

Services: Extensive field trip program with trips to New York City area; tutoring; counseling; home visits and joint activities with parents; special programs in nonacademic areas; projects emphasizing service to others.

Contact person:
George Cohen, Director of Guidance
165 North Columbus Avenue
Mount Vernon, New York

2. Re-entry (see New York State)

New Rochelle:

1. New Rochelle Talent Search is a guidance program which attempts to identify able but underachieving students and to improve their motivation for achievement, partly through influencing parental attitudes.

Date begun: March 1960 (preliminary study 1959–60)

Target population: Forty elementary, 60 junior high, and 60 senior high school pupils, 65 percent of them Negro and 50 percent with IQs over 110.

Per pupil costs: $50

Sponsoring group: NDEA, Title V-A funds through Bureau of Guidance, State Education Department.

Staff: Guidance counselors, psychologist, assistant principal.

Services: Extensive initial investigation of needs and attitudes of population; evening counseling and guidance for both pupils and parents; field trips; group discussions of available community resources with parents.

Contact person:
I. Zweibelson, Senior Psychologist,
   Office of Psychological Services
New Rochelle Public Schools
515 North Avenue, New Rochelle, New York

Evaluation: Available.

2. Team Teaching and Flexible Grouping in the Junior High School was a demonstration project designed to test the effectiveness of a new structural approach to the teaching of social studies without a revision of the curriculum.

Date begun: September 1963 (completed 1964)

Target population: Approximately 100 students in each of grades 7, 8, and 9 of one junior high school.

Per pupil costs: Not determined

Sponsoring group: Local school district.

Staff: Team leaders and classroom teachers, chairman of social studies department, guidance counselor, psychologist, principal.

Services: Four-teacher team at each grade level; heterogeneous grouping in large and small groups for three-fifths of time for such activities as lectures, panels, demonstrations, films, and so forth; pupils grouped homogeneously two-fifths of time for remedial help, skill building, enrichment, individual study, and so forth; study designed to determine whether achievement would remain the same and attitudes toward other students and toward social studies would improve under heterogeneous team-teaching approach.

Contact person:
I. Zweibelson, Senior Psychologist
New Rochelle Public Schools

Evaluation: Completed and available.

3. Re-entry (see New York State)

New Rochelle also has a federal and state-sponsored experimental long-range preschool program designed to test the effects of varying conditions on the subsequent achievement of disadvantaged children.

Contact person:
Thelma Wolman, Coordinator
New Rochelle Public Schools

New York City:

1. The Higher Horizons Program is a broad-spectrum program which intends to raise the educational, vocational, and cultural sights of children who represent varying degrees of disadvantage, through a program which applies the principles of compensatory education, differential utilization of services in curriculum and guidance, and inspirational features. Parental and community involvement and teacher training are inherent in the philosophy and practice.

Date begun: September 1959

Target population: Total population of 50 elementary and 13 junior high schools on all grade levels. Schools are located in Manhattan, Bronx, Brooklyn, and Queens.

Per pupil costs: $62

Sponsoring group: Board of Education, New York City.

Staff: All classroom teachers plus supplementary program teachers and guidance counselors for each Higher Horizons school.

Services: Small-group and half-class instruction in reading, mathematics, and other cur-

riculum areas where there is an indicated need; cultural enrichment activities involving music and art instruction as well as field trips; teacher-training conferences and workshops; demonstrated lessons by program teachers, as well as assistance with planning and special activities; curriculum adaptation; individual and group counseling for children and parents; *Higher Horizons Newsletter*; involvement with local community agencies and cultural resources of the city; parent participation through workshops; committees and trips.

Contact person:
Carmela Mercurio
Coordinator, Higher Horizons
Board of Education
110 Livingston Street
Brooklyn, New York 11201

Evaluation: *Evaluation of the Higher Horizons Program for Underprivileged Children* (CRP No. 1124), prepared by the Bureau of Educational Research and financed by the United States Office of Education.

2. Mobilization for Youth is a wide-ranging community-improvement project designed to investigate and develop approaches to combating juvenile delinquency. The World of Education involves a cooperative approach with the Board of Education in a number of projects ranging from teacher training to preschool classes in various schools in the city.

Date begun: September 1962

Target population: Pupils in 16 elementary schools, five junior highs, two "600" schools, and two high schools; pupils more than half Puerto Rican, 19 percent Negro.

Per pupil costs: Not determined

Sponsoring group: Federal government, City of New York, Ford Foundation.

Staff: Curriculum coordinators, reading teachers, reading clinicians, social workers, coordinators, supervisors, guidance counselors, high school student homework helpers.

Services: Inservice teacher education including courses in early childhood education; school-community relations courses involving home and neighborhood visits; pre-service teacher training in cooperation with teacher training institutions; extensive work in curriculum planning and development with curriculum coordination working with teachers in schools to plan course modifications and help with use of new materials; resource collection of curriculum materials for teacher use; provision of supplementary corrective reading personnel to elementary schools to work with children seriously retarded in reading and their parents; homework helper program pays tenth- and eleventh-grade neighborhood children trained as tutors to work on one-to-one basis with middle elementary grade children, two tutoring sessions a week, training sessions for tutors, tutors walk children they have tutored home; early childhood and preschool programs involving inservice training and coordinator assistance for preschool, kindergarten, and first grade teachers in MFY's target areas; guidance program involves intensive work with small pupil-groups in grades 1–6 with inservice guidance counselor training; attendance program has special school-based Attendance Teacher in each target area junior high school to visit homes, counsel with pupils and parents on short term or intensive basis; school social work program in which social workers assigned to elementary schools and junior highs train teachers for home visits, work with guidance and other school personnel, and conduct individual and group consultations; educational guidance and tutoring program encourages return to school and provides needed tutoring for dropouts in MFY work programs; summer program providing some continuation of year-long activities, reading clinics, workshops for teachers, and so forth.

Contact person:
Paul Bisgaier
Mobilization for Youth, Inc.
271 East 4th Street, New York, New York

Evaluation: In progress by Research Center, Columbia University School of Social Work.

3. All-Day Neighborhood Schools is a program designed to provide for children who would otherwise be largely unsupervised an after-school facility on the school grounds. In addition, the extra personnel provide an enriched and personalized program of instruction during the school day.

Date begun: 1936

Target population: Seven thousand children in 14 special service schools.

Per pupil costs: Not determined

Sponsoring group: Board of Education plus contributions of volunteer groups.

Staff: Six teachers, administrator.

Services: Special staff works in curriculum and guidance with classroom teachers from 10:40 a.m. until 3 p.m., giving direct help in classroom, conducting workshops, working with groups of children; same staff conducts after school program, cocurricular and recreational, from 3 p.m. to 5 p.m., including story telling, dramatics, singing, rhythms, painting, clay, and so forth; inservice teacher training and workshops for group teachers in clay, music, creative dramatics, and so forth; Saturday theater program to bring live performances to schools on Saturdays; extensive field trips and cultural excursions.

Contact person:
Adele Franklin, Director
All-Day Neighborhood Schools
130 West 55th Street
New York 19, New York

Evaluation: Extensive evaluation conducted under grant from United States Office of Education, completed and available.

4. The More Effective Schools program combines a flexible team-teaching organization with a strong emphasis on academic achievement in an attempt to provide quality inte-

grated education for disadvantaged children starting at the early primary level, with the ultimate goal of preventing later school problems.

Date begun: September 1964

Target population: Twenty thousand children in 21 schools, prekindergarten through sixth grade.

Per pupil costs: $400

Sponsoring group: Board of Education.

Staff: Teams of four teachers for every three classes; special art, music, science, corrective reading, library teachers; audiovisual coordinators, guidance counselors, psychologists, social workers, community relations expert, auxiliary teachers, speech teacher, and English language resource person.

Services: Team teaching organization with classes of no more than 22 (15 at prekindergarten level); heterogeneous grouping with flexible subgroupings by ability; extensive testing to evaluate individual needs; special art, music, science classes; tutoring, remedial work, and guidance; schools open 8:30 a.m. to 3 p.m.; daily preparation period for teachers; community relations activities; a built-in teacher training program is part of this operation.

Contact person:
Mrs. Elizabeth C. O'Daly,
    Assistant Superintendent
Director, More Effective Schools Program
Board of Education

5. The School Volunteer Program is designed to utilize the talents of volunteer adults to provide remedial and enrichment work to individual children and to provide assistance on request to teachers, guidance counselors, and other personnel.

Date begun: February 1956

Target population: Children in 30 elementary schools, 6 junior high schools, 2 high schools, where School Volunteer units have been established at the request of the principal.

Per pupil costs: Not determined

Sponsoring group: Board of Education, New York City, and Public Education Association.

Staff: Seven hundred volunteers, eight coordinators, three secretaries.

Services: Orientation, training, and inservice work for volunteers; enrichment activities in music, art, dance, drama, creative writing, crafts, science, social studies; volunteers are requested by principals and teachers, work in schools not attended by their own children; assistance to guidance personnel; volunteers provide special reading help to individuals or small groups through the School Volunteer Reading Help Program, and help with oral language development in Puerto Rican children through the School Volunteer Conversational English Program where volunteers work on a one-to-two basis with non-English-speaking children; help in establishment of school libraries.

Contact person:
Mrs. Marcia Shalem, Acting Director
School Volunteers
125 West 54th Street
New York, New York

Evaluation: Informal.

6. The N.E. Program (non-English-speaking program) is a program growing out of the recommendations of the Ford Foundation-sponsored Puerto Rican study and out of earlier, more limited programs of similar purpose. It seeks to develop bilingualism through the services of N.E. coordinators.

Date begun: 1953

Target population: About 24,200 pupils in 34 junior high schools.

Per pupil costs: Not determined

Sponsoring group: Board of Education.

Staff: Thirty-four non-English coordinators, two administrative coordinators, one coordinator assigned to the Spanish-science Project.

Services: Spanish-speaking pupils assigned to regular classes, but classroom teachers receive help from N.E. coordinators in methods of teaching English as a second language; teacher-training; demonstration teaching; special daily language program for pupils with severe language difficulty; science project conducted entirely in Spanish to instill motivation for learning; special instructional materials for N.E. pupils; guidance for pupils and parents; Puerto Rican P.T.A.; after-school Spanish clubs.

Contact person:
Virginia Costadasi, Divisional Coordinator
Board of Education, Junior High Division

N.B. As a further attempt to improve instruction for the Puerto Rican population of New York City, the Board of Education has cooperated with the Department of Instruction in Puerto Rico in a program of teacher interchange, Operation Understanding, which this year was expanded to include exchange of supervisory personnel.

7. Project Able: The Effectiveness of Full-Time Coordinated Guidance Services in the High School, is a program designed to evaluate the usefulness of guidance services in identifying disadvantaged but able pupils and determining effective enrichment programs for them.

Date begun: September 1961

Target population: Twenty-three hundred pupils from three high schools, 75 percent Caucasian, in disadvantaged areas of the city (one control school).

Per pupil costs: $38.66 (1964–65)

Sponsoring group: State Education Department and local school board.

Staff: Twenty-seven coordinators for each

school, three full-time secretaries, one part-time research coordinator.

Services: Concentration of services on group of 150 students in each school identified as culturally deprived; guidance services available to entire school population; intensive individual guidance, small group counseling, and tutorial services; homework center; parent workshops; field trips; outside speakers; improved articulation procedures between feeder junior high school and experimental schools.

Contact person:
Paul Driscoll, Project Able Coordinator
    and Principal
Tottenville High School
Staten Island
New York, New York

8. After-School Study Centers for elementary pupils provide small-group remedial work in reading and mathematics, library services, and homework help.

Date begun: December 1963

Target population: Pupils, primarily from grades 2–6 in over 250 elementary schools designated as special service and transitional schools.

Per pupil costs: $68

Sponsoring group: Board of Education of the City of New York and the federal government.

Staff: One supervisory position and seven teachers for each school participating, plus volunteers from various groups.

Services: Remedial reading, remedial mathematics, library services, and homework help; rooms for homework help available Tuesday through Thursday, 3 p.m. to 5 p.m., to all children who wish to use them.

Contact person:
Truda T. Weil, Assistant Superintendent
Elementary Division
Board of Education

9. Summer Vocational High School Program is designed to prevent dropouts by providing for makeup of failed classes—and hence graduation on time—to vocational high school students.

Date begun: 1954

Target population: Forty-nine hundred vocational high school students in grades 10–12 who wish to make up subject failures.

Per pupil costs: $25

Sponsoring group: Board of Education.

Staff: Ninety-six teachers, seven counselors.

Services: Summer school program in five schools offering a variety of trade, shop, and academic courses; regular vocational-school day does not provide a free or study period to allow for class makeup.

Contact person:
Harry Wolfson, Assistant Superintendent
High School Division (Vocational)
Board of Education

10. Job Counseling Center of the Board of Education is an experimental program of job counseling using a school setting, licensed school counselors, and job developers in day and evening centers.

Date begun: 1964

Target population: Some 2,500 out-of-school boys and girls of high school age, 16 to 21, or unemployed high school graduates.

Per pupil costs: $140

Sponsoring group: Office of Manpower, Automation, and Training of United States Department of Labor.

Staff: Counselors, administrative counselors, job developers, vocational education teachers, basic education teachers, project historian, secretaries.

Services: One-to-one tutoring in remedial reading; prevocation orientation counseling to direct pupils back to school full-time or part-time with job; early job placement, tryout shops. Continued support of counseling and remedial reading; tryout shops, referred into various training programs.

Contact person:
Richard Greenfield, Program Director
Job Counseling Center of the Board of
  Education
Metropolitan Vocational and Technical
  High School
78 Catherine Street
New York, New York 10038

11. Project III (orientation to work) is designed to provide opportunities to potential dropouts either for continued education or preparation for the world of work.

Date begun: 1965 (present format)

Target population: Students approaching ages 16 to 17 who wish to leave school for full-time employment and whose records indicate poor attendance, low reading grades, lack of scholastic success, and poor adjustment to school.

Per pupil costs: Not determined

Sponsoring group: Board of Education.

Staff: Teachers, counselors.

Services: A daily one-period class entitled Project III (orientation to work) is offered for a full semester. Subject matter focuses upon school retention and pre-employment needs. Course may be counted for graduation and pupils are required to take concurrently three major courses. Certification of completion of course or its equivalent a prerequisite for release of student from school. Supportive assistance for pupil retention through counseling with students and their parents emphasized. Among the alternatives to the student's leaving school after certification of completion of Project III (orientation to work) are part-time work, enrollment in the neighborhood Youth Corps or other supplementary financial assistance, and referral to evening high schools.

Contact person:
Charles Savitsky, Coordinator
Board of Education

12. There are a number of nursery school or prekindergarten classes operating in New York City, many of which function as part of other programs. Among them are: Prekindergarten classes under the auspices of the Board of Education. An expanded program of prekindergarten classes began in the fall of 1964; 34 schools served some 1,000 four-year-old children with a daily nursery school program conducted in classes of 15 by one teacher and a volunteer assistant. Approximately 7,000 children will be served in 1965–66 in 151 schools. Curriculum guide prepared and now being tested and revised.

Contact person:
Mrs. Rebecca A. Winton, Director
Bureau of Early Childhood
Board of Education

Ten preschool classes are incorporated into the structure of the More Effective Schools Program (q.v.).

Two special four-year-old kindergartens are conducted in conjunction with the Early Childhood Education Division of the Public Schools as a part of Mobilization for Youth's Early Childhood and Pre-School Programs.

Four classes in East Harlem and two on the Lower East Side of Manhattan for four-year-old children are conducted cooperatively by the Early Childhood Education Program of the Division of Elementary Education and the Institute for Developmental Studies at New York Medical College. They utilize a specially developed "therapeutic curriculum," summer school programs, community visits, and parental involvement.

Contact person:
Martin Deutsch,
    Institute for Developmental Studies
Department of Psychiatry
New York Medical College
105th Street and Fifth Avenue
New York, New York

The National Council of Jewish Women conducted 66 preschool classes with trained volunteer personnel under the supervision of the Board of Education during 1965–66.

Contact person:
Mrs. Edna C. Eigen, New York Section
National Council of Jewish Women
Community Services Department
1 West 47th Street, New York, New York

13. A number of programs for pupils suffering from varying kinds and degrees of reading retardation operate in the schools. Among them are:

A new reading program initiated in 10 elementary schools in September of 1965 utilized language resource teachers and other specialized personnel to assist classroom teachers in providing concentrated attention on language skills for some 1,500 severely disadvantaged children in grades K–4. Program emphasizes development of listening and speaking skills and vocabulary through experiences as a basis for reading development and makes use of specialized resource materials.

Contact person:
Helen M. Lloyd, Assistant Superintendent
Board of Education

The Reading Improvement Program (RIP) is conducted in 520 schools through the services of 760 reading improvement teachers who teach reading to regular classes in order to permit the regular classroom teacher to devote a period to reading preparation work. The RIP also provides reading teaching assistance to teachers, especially new teachers, through conferences, demonstrations, and so forth.

The Reading Clinics are servicing the emotionally disturbed, retarded reader in 14 assistant superintendents' districts. Children from grades 2–6, who range from the nonreader to two years retardation for grade, are provided with a clinical and instructional program. The clinics are staffed with full-time psychiatric social workers and psychologists, part-time psychiatrists, and specially trained teachers of reading. The children are given an instructional program in small groups based on diagnosed needs; families are provided with a counseling or treatment program, or both.

The Remedial Reading Program at Boys High School is a special course to enable high school seniors to make up a semester of English by completing certain assignments without having to repeat the course and thus fail to graduate on time.

Contact person:
Anna F. Cohn, English Teacher
Boys High School
832 Marcy Avenue, Brooklyn, New York

About 461 corrective reading teachers provide reading help in special classes to pupils in grades 3–6 who are retarded at least two years in reading. In addition, corrective reading teachers also provide assistance in the teaching of reading to newly appointed teachers and teachers new to a grade.

An After School Study Center Program provides supplementary reading instruction to 5,000 vocational high school pupils in classes of no more than 15, held in school libraries Tuesday through Friday, either before or after school, and on Saturday mornings. Program designed to serve pupils not enrolled in regular school-day remedial reading classes.

Contact person:
Daniel P. Marshall
High School Office (Vocational)
Board of Education

14. The Junior Volunteer Program utilizes the abilities, talents, and time of 600 students from 17 junior high schools neighboring the Day-Care Nurseries, All-Day Neighborhood Schools, After-School Community Centers, and After-School Study Centers in which they serve. Orientation, training, and in-service help are given to the volunteers in games, arts and crafts, kindergarten activities, painting, dance, clay work, sewing, and dramatics for those volunteers in recreational centers. Orientation, training, and inservice help are given on a one-to-one basis to the volunteers in teaching reading and arithmetic and in helping develop library skills. Volunteers function as assistants in recreational activities in All-Day Neighborhood Schools, Day-Care Centers, and After-School Community Centers and provide help to children in reading, arithmetic, and library skills in the After-School Study Centers.

15. Various other programs and practices designed to benefit disadvantaged pupils have been instituted in the New York City schools. Among them are:

A number of assimilative or desegregation practices—an Open Enrollment Program initiated in 1960, the Free-Choice Transfer policy initiated in 1964, and the School-Pairing program which was first put into effect in 1964–65—designed to achieve better racial balance in schools where residential segregation exists and to provide the pupils, Negro, Puerto Rican, and other with an opportunity for education in an ethnically mixed situation.

Based on a number of criteria, of which low reading achievement, median IQ, teacher and pupil mobility, and percentage of non-English-speaking children enrolled, are of primary significance, more than one-third of New York City's elementary and junior high schools have been designated Special Service Schools (299 elementary schools and 64 junior highs in 1964), eligible for extra personnel to permit smaller class size, extra reading and guidance time, additional supervisory personnel, and extra textbooks, supplies, and so forth.

Beginning in 1957–58, Special Service Schools were permitted to employ nonprofessional qualified adults to relieve teachers from lunchroom and related lunch duties. The present program, designated as the School Aides Program, involves such nonprofessional personnel in a variety of nonteaching chores in all elementary schools.

Junior Guidance Classes, which have functioned in New York since 1936, provide a special facility for emotionally disturbed children who cannot be contained within a regular classroom without damaging the functioning of the class.

16. Programs of the National Council of Jewish Women. Preschool programs were initiated by the National Council of Jewish Women in 1962. Since then they have been established by a number of local sections and have often provided impetus to or served as models for Head Start programs in their communities. Some of these preschool programs operate in the public schools. Others have been independently established and are housed in community houses or churches. Each local section receives guidance through the Community Services Department of the national office, including consultation and materials.

The following local sections are working in year-round preschool programs:

Akron, Ohio	Huntington, N. Y.
Baltimore, Md.	Kansas City, Mo.
Brooklyn, N. Y.	Milwaukee, Wis.
Camden County,	Montgomery
N. J.	County, Md.
Central Parkway,	Mobile, Ala.
N. J.	New York, N. Y.
Cincinnati, Ohio	Northern Valley,
Cleveland, Ohio	N. J.
Columbus, Ohio	Northern Virginia,
Evanston-Niles	Va.
Township, Ill.	North Shore, Ill.
Gary, Ind.	Oklahoma City,
Greater New	Okla.
Orleans, La.	Omaha, Neb.
Greensboro, N. C.	Peninsula, N. Y.
Hartford, Conn.	Pittsburgh, Pa.
Hollywood, Fla.	Plainfield, N. J.

Rockaway, N. Y.	Teaneck, N. J.
Roslyn, N. Y.	Utica, N. Y.
San Antonio, Texas	Waco, Texas
St. Louis, Mo.	Westbury, N. J.
St. Paul, Minn.	

Tutoring and cultural enrichment programs have also been set up by local sections under guidelines set by the Community Services Department of the national organization. These programs have functioned in schools, settlement houses, and other premises located by the local sections.

Year-round programs of tutoring and enrichment are conducted by the following Council Sections:

Atlanta, Ga.	Louisville, Ky.
Central Parkway,	Memphis, Tenn.
N. J.	Minneapolis, Minn.
Charleston, W. Va.	Montgomery
Chicago, Ill.	County, Md.
Cincinnati, Ohio	North Broward,
Dallas, Texas	Fla.
Dayton, Ohio	Plainfield, N. J.
Detroit, Mich.	Richmond, Va.
Essex County, N. J.	Rochester, N. Y.
Fort Worth, Texas	Rockland County,
Gary, Ind.	N. Y.
Greater Bridgeport,	San Francisco, Calif.
Conn.	St. Louis, Mo.
Greater Miami, Fla.	South Cook, Ill.
Greater New	Syracuse, N. Y.
Orleans, La.	Tucson, Ariz.
Greater Philadelphia,	Tulsa, Okla.
Pa.	Washington, D. C.
Los Angeles, Calif.	Wilmington, Del.

Newburgh:

Project Springboard, a Project Able program, is a broad-scale attempt to improve the motivation and achievement level of disadvantaged elementary school students and to help deal with their psychological and emotional problems.

Date begun: September 1961

Target population: About 960 pupils from

grades 1–6 in four elementary schools serving a largely lower socioeconomic status Negro population.

Per pupil costs: $52

Sponsoring group: New York State Education Department and local school district.

Staff: Guidance counselor, reading specialist, psychologist, nurse, attendance officer.

Services: Class size held to 25; special slow-learner classes; team teaching; remedial reading; extensive after-school enrichment program including physical education, art, music, dramatics, woodworking, and so forth; group and individual counseling; parent information and consultation through evening home visits; school facilities used as evening and summer community educational, recreational, and cultural centers.

Contact person:
Charles F. Disare, Principal
Montgomery Street School
Newburgh, New York

Niagara Falls:

1. Project Able is an intensified counseling program designed to raise the educational sights of secondary school students.

Date begun: January 1961

Target population: Six hundred pupils of four junior high schools and four elementary schools.

Per pupil costs: $66

Sponsoring group: State Education Department, NDEA, Title v-A funds through Bureau of Guidance. Funded 50 percent through Project Able, 50 percent local funds after September 1965.

Staff: Guidance counselor.

Services: Educational and vocational counseling; after-school tutoring and "how to study" program; field trips; home visitation.

Contact person:
Charles Gambert
Director of Pupil Personnel Services
6th Street and Walnut Avenue
Niagara Falls, New York

2. Re-entry (see New York State)

North Tonawanda:

The Talent Search Program aims to raise the general vocational and educational goals of children who because of their home environment have set much lower goals for themselves.

Date begun: July 1964

Target population: Thirty economically or culturally disadvantaged children in the seventh and ninth grades of one school. All Caucasian.

Per pupil costs: $115

Sponsoring group: NDEA, Title v-A funds through Bureau of Guidance, State Education Department, local school district.

Staff: Program director, counselors (plus regular psychological, health, speech services of school).

Services: General orientation to community possibilities—cultural, vocational, and educational—through field trips, individual and group counseling, parental counseling.

Contact person:
Albert Berbary,
    Director of Pupil Personnel Services
Board of Education
North Tonawanda, New York 14120

Nyack:

The Talent Search Program is designed to raise the level of motivation for school success and reduce dropouts among those students achieving below their ability.

Date begun: February 1964

Target population: Underachievers and students identified as culturally disadvantaged in grades 7 and 8. (Will be extended to grade 9 in 1965–66.)

Per pupil costs: $290

Sponsoring group: NDEA, Title V-A funds through Bureau of Guidance, New York State Education Department, and local school district.

Staff: Guidance counselor, reading specialist, other specialists as needed.

Services: Individual and group guidance; field trips; remedial reading; tutoring; parent orientation.

Contact person:
Robert J. Schild, Assistant Superintendent
Nyack Public Schools
South Highland Avenue, Nyack, New York

2. The Kindergarten Project for experientially deprived children is designed to provide additional perceptual experiences for kindergarten children as a basis for subsequent reading progress.

Date begun: October 1964

Target population: Twenty-four kindergarten children who evidenced informational gaps.

Per pupil costs: Not determined

Sponsoring group: Local school district and Yeshiva University.

Staff: Two graduate interns, university consultant.

Services: Additional hours per week for project children in small groups around school and on field trips; various activities designed to broaden informational background and facilitate verbal expression.

Contact person:
Robert J. Schild, Assistant Superintendent
Nyack Public Schools

3. STEP (see New York State)

Oppenheim-Ephratah (see St. Johnsville)

Parish:

Widening Horizons for Students is largely a counseling program designed to raise the sights of secondary school students in regard to education and vocation.

Date begun: September 1961

Target population: Sixty-five pupils in one junior high school and 65 pupils in one senior high school in a depressed rural area.

Per pupil costs: $12

Sponsoring group: NDEA, Title V-A funds through Bureau of Guidance, State Education Department, local school board.

Staff: Guidance counselor, psychologist, nurse.

Services: Counseling and guidance; guest speakers; field trips to colleges and industries.

Contact person:
Robert W. Galbreath, Director of Guidance
Altmar-Parish-Williamstown Central School
Parish, New York

Rochester:

1. Madison Talent Search Project Mercury was a pilot project designed to establish criteria for the identification of culturally impoverished but talented youth and to discover the requirements for up-grading their vocational and educational goals.

Date begun: September 1960 (concluded June 1964)

Target population: Sixteen lower socio-economic status pupils in the twelfth grade at one high school, over half of whom have IQs above 110.

Per pupil costs: $224

Sponsoring group: NDEA, Title V-A funds through Bureau of Guidance, State Education Department.

Staff: Guidance counselor, reading specialist, psychologist, nurse.

Services: Remedial reading; intensive counseling; tutoring, cultural enrichment; home visits. Pilot was a four year program following students through grades 8–12.

Contact person:
Alfred Stiller, Director of Guidance
City School District
13 Fitzhugh Street South
Rochester, New York 14614

Evaluation: These students graduated June 1964. Five-year follow-up study being conducted.

2. Project Beacon, a Project Able program, is an attempt to change the self-image and identity development of disadvantaged children through a variety of approaches including extensive use of photography and original written materials.

Date begun: September 1965

Target population: Eighteen hundred children, grades K–2 in four inner-city elementary schools.

Per pupil costs: $31

Sponsoring group: New York State Education Department, local school district.

Staff: Director, resource teachers, writer, illustrator-photographer.

Services: Extensive use of special materials, experience charts, photographs, new materials based on children's experiences; enrichment activities including music, art, field trips; teacher training; parental involvement; speech and reading development activities.

Contact person:
Alfred Stiller, Director of Guidance
City School District

3. STEP (see New York State)

Roosevelt:

Project Able is a five year pilot, guidance-oriented program operating in conjunction with varied school services, which aims to increase student self-understanding, to widen student and parent knowledge in vocation and education, and to thereby reduce dropouts and improve school performance.

Date begun: September 1961

Target population: Ninety lower socioeconomic status pupils in one junior-senior high school in a rural area, 50 percent white, 50 percent nonwhite.

Per pupil costs: $50

Sponsoring group: New York State Education Department and local school district.

Staff: Guidance director, school psychologist, guidance counselors, attendance officer, school social worker, remedial reading teacher.

Services: Group and individual guidance and counseling for project students and their parents; extra after-school meetings with teachers; remedial help; special testing and evaluation of project students; extra field trips.

Contact person:
Theodore Alexander
Roosevelt Junior-Senior High School
Roosevelt, New York

St. Johnsville:

Project Able of the Oppenheim-Ephratah Central School is designed to increase the educational and cultural background of students of above-average ability and stimulate their desire to continue their education beyond high school.

Date begun: September 1961

Target population: Pupils in grades 3–8, lower socioeconomic status, white, from culturally limited rural area.

Per pupil costs: $75

Sponsoring group: State Education Department and local school district.

Staff: Remedial reading teacher, psychologist, guidance counselor, school nurse.

Services: Teacher inservice training; remedial reading program and reading encouragement through free reading in classroom; book discussions and book fairs; music and art appreciation programs; educational field trips; auditorium "live" programs; increased parental conferences and programs.

Contact person:
Mrs. Doris J. Skapik,
    Project Able Coordinator
Oppenheim-Ephratah Central School
R.D.2 St. Johnsville, New York 13452

Schenectady:

1. School-Community Project is a Project Able program designed to investigate the needs of disadvantaged children in the community and to develop techniques for fulfilling those needs.

Date begun: September 1962

Target population: About 1,142 pupils from four elementary schools and 323 pupils from one junior high school. Pupils are predominantly lower socioeconomic status and just over one-half are Negro.

Per pupil costs: $2.59

Sponsoring group: New York State Education Department and local school district.

Staff: Classroom teachers, reading specialist, psychologists, guidance counselor, elementary resource teacher, home visitor, nurses, social workers, attendance officer.

Services: Inservice teacher training in understanding the disadvantaged; partial revision of reading and arithmetic curriculum; after-school tutoring and remedial reading; enrichment activities including field trips and cultural events; individual and group parent counseling; involvement of local resource people, social agency representatives, and so forth.

Contact person:
Robert A. Page, Director of Pupil Personnel
Board of Education
108 Union Street, Schenectady, New York

2. Project Re-entry (see New York State)

Shirley:

Talent Search is a program to raise the achievement level and the academic and vocational aspirations of secondary school students.

Date begun: September 1962

Target population: Nineteen predominantly white eighth-grade students of one junior high school in a depressed rural area, 60 percent of whom are above 110 in IQ.

Per pupil costs: $100

Sponsoring group: NDEA, Title V-A funds through Bureau of Guidance, State Education Department.

Staff: Guidance counselor, reading specialist, curriculum coordinator, attendance officer.

Services: Reading and mathematics remedial work and enrichment during and after school; individual and group guidance; cultural enrichment; home visits, parent workshops, guidance-centered field trips.

Contact person:
Fred C. Bockian,
    Director of Instruction, K–12
William Floyd School, Shirley, New York

Evaluation: Available.

South New Berlin:

1. Rural Talent Search is a program designed to provide cultural enrichment and counseling in order to improve the academic achievement of a group of junior high and high school students and to increase the holding power of the schools.

Date begun: November 1960 (county-wide program initiated in 1960 was continued by local school district)

Target population: Thirty seventh-grade pupils of one junior high school and 8 tenth-grade pupils of one high school. Population is of "below average but not impoverished" socioeconomic status and 50 percent presently test above 110 in IQ.

Per pupil costs: $58

Sponsoring group: State Education Department and local school district (prior to September 1965, NDEA, Title V-A funds through Bureau of Guidance, State Education Department).

Staff: Guidance counselor, reading specialist, curriculum coordinator, psychologist, nurse.

Services: Special English classes; remedial help; counseling services; cultural enrichment through field trips to sporting events, musical performances, and New York City.

Contact person:
Mrs. Elizabeth G. Tamsett,
   Guidance Director
South New Berlin Central School
South New Berlin, New York

Evaluation: Informal.

2. STEP (see New York State)

Springfield (see East Springfield)

Suffern (see Hillburn)

Syracuse:

1. The Madison Area Project (MAP), was a broad-spectrum program designed to develop positive educational and vocational aspirations and to increase the educational achievement of disadvantaged youth in a center-city area. It emphasized the development of techniques and attitudes in the school program which could be extended to other schools.

Date begun: September 1962 (incorporated into Crusade for Opportunity—see below—during 1964–65)

Target population: Total school populations of two elementary schools, one junior, and one senior high school, serving predominantly Negro families of lower socioeconomic status.

Per pupil costs: $70 (for sub-Project Able $261)

Sponsoring group: Local school district, Ford Foundation (Youth Development Center and School of Education of Syracuse University—advisory, not financial), and New York State Education Department (for Project Able).

Staff: Reading specialists, instructional specialists, audiovisual coordinator, job-placement coordinator, visiting teachers, guidance counselors, mental health coordinator, psychologists, psychiatrist, psychiatric social worker, physician, nurses, attendance officer, public information coordinator, coordinator of school volunteers.

Services: Team teaching for flexibility in class size and scheduling; ungraded sequences in seventh- and eighth-grades; modified curriculum with new instructional materials and emphasis on development of skills and concepts rather than content; reading clinics; extensive library program; extensive use of volunteers; group guidance; Able program for talented children in each school, utilizing programed instruction; special World of Work curriculum providing half-day school and half-day employment for 15- to 16-year-old potential dropouts; extensive after-school club program for children and adults; demonstration summer school; family involvement —encouragement of family summer activities through project newsletter; Learning Caravan to tell parents what children are doing in school; involvement of community agencies.

Contact persons:
Joseph Bongo and Miss Eleanor Kennedy,
   Codirectors
Madison Area Project
1001 Almond Street, Syracuse, New York

Evaluation: *Laboratory for Change–the Madison Area Project*, 50 cents.

2. Crusade for Opportunity in Syracuse and Onondaga County, Inc., is a community action program involving a wide range of activities for youth and adults in the community. The school program utilizes many of the techniques developed in the MAP project.

Date begun: September 1964

Target population: Eight thousand lower socioeconomic status children, 50 percent Negro, 50 percent Caucasian, in five elementary, three junior high, and three high schools, grades K-12. Four hundred additional pupils attend study and counseling centers in five locations.

Per pupil costs: Not determined

Sponsoring group: President's Committee on Juvenile Delinquency, United States Office of Economic Opportunity, United States Department of Labor.

Staff: Team leaders, instructional specialists, guidance team consisting of guidance counselors, social worker, and psychologist, reading specialists, other supportive school personnel paid for by Crusade but hired by schools involved.

Services: Team teaching organization by grade level in elementary schools, by subject area at junior high and high school levels; corrective reading program; curriculum materials development center to develop special instructional materials; individual and group guidance and counseling at all levels; tutor corps of children from deprived areas who are trained to be tutors; five study and counseling centers, two in rented store fronts, one in a school, one in a community center, and one for juvenile offenders in the County Jail; summer reading camp.

Contact person:
Harry Balmer, Director
Crusade for Opportunity
236 West Genesee Street
Syracuse, New York 13202

3. Project STEP (see New York State)

4. Project Re-entry (see New York State)

Uniondale:

Project Talent Search for Underachievers was a program designed to raise the aspiration levels of underachieving pupils, to increase their self-understanding, and increase their parents' interest and involvement in their education.

Date begun: March 1, 1965 (ended May 02, 1965)

Target population: Twenty-one junior high school pupils.

Per pupil costs: $120

Sponsoring group: NDEA, Title V-A funds through Bureau of Guidance, State Education Department.

Staff: Two counselor educators, graduate students, counselors.

Services: Intensive short-term individual and group counseling; parental involvement; field trips to Hofstra University, and other cultural activities and trips designed to raise pupils' aspirations.

Contact person:
Frank Sawicki, Coordinator,
  Pupil Personnel Services
Uniondale Public Schools
Goodrich Street
Uniondale, New York

Utica:

Potter Project Able is a program designed to improve the academic achievement and raise the aspirations of a group of disadvantaged children.

Date begun: September 1961

Target population: One hundred and twenty-five predominantly lower socioeconomic status Negro pupils in grades 4, 5, and 6 of one elementary school. Expansion through grade 8 in last two years.

Per pupil costs: $40

Sponsoring group: New York State Education Department and local school district.

Staff: Guidance counselor, psychologist, project teacher, home visitor, nurse, attendance officer.

Services: Remedial reading and arithmetic; field trips; extended counseling services; special interest groups; guest speakers.

Contact person:
Francis E. Rodio, Coordinator
Board of Education
Administrative Office, Utica, New York

White Plains:

Project Able is a broad-spectrum program designed to investigate ways of altering the home and school experience of disadvantaged elementary school children in order to bring their academic achievement in line with their aptitude.

Date begun: September 1961 in one elementary school. In September 1964 the organization of elementary schools was changed so that each of the 10 schools had 10 percent to 30 percent Negro children assigned. At this time, Project Able was extended to include all elementary schools.

Target population: Original program serving first- and third-grade children in one elementary school expanded gradually to serve all children (1,000 to 1,100) from disadvantaged backgrounds in 10 elementary schools.

Per pupil costs: $32.25

Sponsoring group: New York State Education Department and local school district.

Staff: Classroom teachers, helping teachers (assist with curriculum and do some remedial work), psychologists, social workers, home-school counselor, physician, nurses, attendance teacher.

Services: Experimentation with flexible class groupings based on heterogeneous homeroom groups; curricular enrichment with emphasis on language development and facilitation of reading and reading readiness; new or original reading and instructional materials; use of volunteers for individualization and enrichment; field trips and guest speakers; guidance and counseling for parents and children; parental involvement through home visits and school meetings; basic education courses for adults; teacher inservice training through faculty meetings, conferences, and weekly information sheet.

Contact person:
Mrs. Marian F. Graves, Director
Pupil Personnel Services
White Plains Public Schools
5 Homeside Lane, White Plains, New York

Evaluation: Longitudinal study of portion of population in progress.

Windsor (see also, Deposit)

Project Able in Windsor is a combined program with a Talent Search Program in Deposit, New York, with the following variations.

Date begun: 1961

Target population: See Deposit, New York.

Per pupil costs: $230

Sponsoring group: New York State Education Department and local school district.

Staff: See Deposit, New York.

Services: See Deposit, New York.

Contact person:
Denis I. Donegan
Alice Freeman Palmer Central High School
Windsor, New York

Wyandanch:

Operation Discovery, a pilot project under the Talent Search Program, is primarily a guidance program designed to elevate educational and vocational aspirations among secondary school students.

Date begun: March 1963

Target population: Thirty junior high and 10 senior high school students with IQs over 90 who come from predominantly lower socioeconomic status families, 75 percent of whom are Negro.

Per pupil costs: $233

Sponsoring group: NDEA, Title V-A funds through Bureau of Guidance, New York State Education Department.

Staff: Three guidance counselors, reading specialist, nurse, classroom teachers for remedial help, attendance officer.

Services: Instruction in study skills; individual and group counseling—both educational and vocational—emphasizing the value of a high school education; field trips to colleges, industrial plants, and cultural events; family counseling.

Contact person:
Allen Layton, Director of Guidance
Wyandanch High School
Wyandanch, New York

Yonkers:

1. Project Able is a program designed to discover the potential of underachieving disadvantaged children and to develop it through a program of enrichment and reading instruction.

Date begun: September 1960

Target population: Fifteen hundred lower socioeconomic status children in grades 3–6 of five elementary schools (one preschool included 1964–65).

Per pupil costs: $45

Sponsoring group: New York State Education Department and local school district.

Staff: Eighty classroom teachers, 10 special Project Able teachers, coordinator, guidance counselor, psychologist, home-school teacher, preschool teacher, speech teacher.

Services: Small-group instruction in reading; use of volunteer teachers and varieties of instructional materials; after-school study groups; parent workshops and home visits; counseling and psychological testing; enrichment through concerts, trips, and so forth.

Contact person:
Noreen Fee, Coordinator
Office of Board of Education
138 South Broadway
Yonkers, New York

2. Project Re-entry (see New York State)

3. Project STEP (see New York State)

North Carolina

Raleigh:

The Comprehensive School Improvement Project is a statewide attempt to develop and implement primary education programs directed toward the improvement of the teaching and learning of reading, writing, and arithmetic for disadvantaged children. (See Winston-Salem for example of specific program.)

Date begun: July 1964

Target population: Priority is given to schools which have a high incidence of culturally disadvantaged children.

Per pupil costs: $60

Sponsoring group: Ford Foundation through the North Carolina Fund and the North Carolina State Board of Education.

Staff: Three teachers per participating school, teacher aide and college consultant for each teaching team. At state level, one researcher and three personnel in curriculum and staff deployment innovation.

Services: Assist in local program design, implementation, and evaluation.

Contact person:
W. B. Sugg, Director
Comprehensive School Improvement Project
North Carolina State Department of Public
 Instruction
Raleigh, North Carolina

Winston-Salem:

1. The North Carolina Advancement School
is an attempt to develop a method, in a residential setting, of educating underachieving
boys of average or above-average potential.

Date begun: November 1964

Target population: Eighth-grade boys, 75
percent Caucasian, 25 percent Negro, who
are working below grade level. Also 200 public school teachers in the state in a program
of inservice education.

Per pupil costs: Not determined

Sponsoring group: United States Office of
Education, North Carolina State Office of
Education, Carnegie Foundation.

Staff: Fifteen teachers, counselors, visiting
teachers, college tutors, specialists, research
staff.

Services: Pupils brought to residential school
for three months; emphasis on developing
basic skills in language arts, mathematics, and
studying, and on altering motivation and
attitudes; teachers from same schools as boys
brought to help with design of instructional
program.

Contact person:
Gordon L. McAndrew, Director
The North Carolina Advancement School
Winston-Salem, North Carolina

Evaluation: In progress. Intensive follow-up
beginning fall 1966; field testing of school-
developed materials in spring 1967.

2. A special preschool and primary program
for culturally disadvantaged children is part
of the Comprehensive School Improvement
Project (see Raleigh). It provides a summer

program to better prepare preschoolers for
school, and follows it with a specially designed three-year program aimed at improving the children's chances for substantial
school achievement in all subjects.

Date begun: July 1964

Target population: Some 540 children selected from three elementary schools, on the
basis of factors which would indicate disadvantaged status; one-half white, one-half
Negro, many of them picked up in summer
before first grade.

Per pupil costs: Not determined

Sponsoring group: Ford Foundation through
the North Carolina Fund and North Carolina
State Board of Education.

Staff: Eighteen teachers, six teachers' aides,
social workers, psychologists, three college
consultants.

Services: Six-week summer readiness program involving teams of one teacher and two
aides per class, for small class work, enrichment experiences, noon meal on request;
regular school program has teams of three
teachers and one teacher aide per team of 90
students; team-teaching organization for ungraded three-year program; extensive use of
technological aids, special materials, and so
forth; home visits and parental counseling
and guidance.

Contact person:
Robert L. Blevins, Assistant Superintendent
Winston-Salem–Forsyth County Schools
Winston-Salem, North Carolina

North Dakota

Fort Totten:

The Preschool Program is designed to provide meaningful social, cultural, and creative
activities for preschool Indian children.

Date begun: 1965

Target population: Sixty Indian children in two classes, predominantly of preschool age.

Per pupil costs: Not determined

Sponsoring group: United States Office of Education.

Staff: Two preschool teachers, teacher aides.

Services: Morning classes involving enrichment of cultural and sensory experiences; mothers employed on rotating basis to prepare lunch; afternoons devoted to individual attention to special needs of children; health care; field trips.

Contact person:
Lewis Goodhouse, Tribal Chairman
Devil's Lake Sioux Tribe
Fort Totten, North Dakota

N.B. The Devil's Lake Sioux Tribal Council expanded its preschool program in 1966 to 120 children and a staff of nine with the aid of United States Office of Economic Opportunity funds.

Ohio

Cincinnati:

1. The Cluster Approach is designed to provide supplementary services to schools in disadvantaged areas by grouping together five schools in close geographical proximity for staffing purposes.

Date begun: January 1965

Target population: Pupils from five elementary schools in a disadvantaged area of the city.

Per pupil costs: Not determined

Sponsoring group: United States Office of Economic Opportunity and local school district.

Staff: Five regular teachers, five remedial reading teachers, supervising teacher, psychologist, visiting teachers, speech therapist, secretary, teacher-librarians in three schools.

Services: Reduced class size; remedial reading program; provision of supplementary supplies and equipment; field trips and other enrichment activities; counseling and speech therapy; inservice teacher education.

Contact person:
Lorena M. O'Donnell, Compensatory
  Education
Cincinnati Public Schools
2355 Iowa Avenue, Cincinnati, Ohio 45206

Evaluation: No formal evaluation.

2. Volunteers in Public Schools (v.i.p.s.) is a program utilizing the services of volunteers to provide one-to-one tutoring during the school day to pupils in need of reading assistance.

Date begun: October 1964

Target population: Two hundred and twenty-four children in three elementary schools (six schools in 1965–66).

Per pupil costs: $4

Sponsoring group: Local school district.

Staff: Sixty-nine volunteers recruited from various women's service groups, one supervising teacher.

Services: Each pupil is tutored once or twice a week during school hours for 30 to 45 minutes; volunteer agencies responsible for recruiting tutors; school responsible for identifying pupils, setting up schedules, training volunteers, and purchasing instructional materials.

Contact person:
Lorena M. O'Donnell, Compensatory
  Education
Cincinnati Public Schools

Evaluation: Informal. Structured evaluation planned for 1965–66.

3. Operation One-to-One is an after-school tutorial program which provides assistance in reading and arithmetic in the elementary

schools and assistance in various subjects in the junior high schools.

Date begun: March 1, 1965

Target population: About 1,793 pupils tutored in 26 elementary and 6 junior high school after-school tutoring centers. (Program expanded to 39 elementary and 7 junior high centers for 1965–66.)

Per pupil costs: Not determined

Sponsoring group: United States Office of Economic Opportunity and local school district.

Staff: Two supervising teachers, 32 center supervisors, 580 volunteer tutors recruited from high schools, colleges, p.t.a.s, churches, and industry.

Services: Pupils tutored once or twice a week after school hours for 40 to 45 minutes; agencies help in recruiting volunteers; schools responsible for identifying pupils and setting up schedules; supervising teachers responsible for recruiting and training volunteers and purchasing instructional materials. Junior high schools are also designated as community centers and will provide, in addition to tutoring and study facilities, recreational and social activities for both pupils and adults.

Contact person:
Lorena M. O'Donnell, Compensatory
    Education
Cincinnati Public Schools

4. Enrichment for Able Pupils is a program designed to provide enrichment activities for elementary school pupils who are able learners but come from culturally deprived backgrounds.

Date begun: September 1965

Target population: Approximately 100 pupils from four elementary schools, selected on the basis of ability.

Per pupil costs: Not determined

Sponsoring group: Local school district.

Staff: One regular teacher.

Services: In-school program involving enrichment during school day through a resource teacher serving four schools who works with able pupils in areas of interest; program provides activities related to children's needs, abilities, and interests.

Contact person:
Lorena M. O'Donnell, Compensatory
    Education
Cincinnati Public Schools

5. Saturday Enrichment is a program that provides an opportunity for teachers and volunteers to work with able learners in order to help them develop an awareness and sensitivity to the world around them.

Date begun: March 1965

Target population: One hundred elementary pupils from four schools selected on the basis of ability.

Per pupil costs: Not determined

Sponsoring group: Local school district and United States Office of Economic Opportunity.

Staff: One coordinator, five teachers, 24 volunteers.

Services: Teachers and volunteers provide a program for fifth- and sixth-grade able learners related to the children's needs and interests.

Contact person:
Lorena M. O'Donnell, Compensatory
    Education
Cincinnati Public Schools

6. In addition to the programs listed above, the Cincinnati schools have instituted a number of other programs and practices to benefit the disadvantaged pupil. Among them are:

An extensive Reading Improvement Program at one elementary school, is designed to provide for early identification and correction of reading difficulties through a concentrated program of remedial reading and the use of new methods and audiovisual equipment.

As in other large communities there are a number of volunteer after-school tutoring programs, organized and staffed by various agencies, to serve one or more schools. The largest of these, the West End Educational Project (WEEP), uses college student tutors, trained by the program sponsor—the United Campus Christian Fellowship of the University of Cincinnati. These programs are presently being directed into the tutorial program organized under the Cincinnati Board of Education.

Contact person:
Lorena M. O'Donnell, Compensatory
  Education
Cincinnati Public Schools

Cleveland:

1. The Hough Community Project, one of the Great Cities School Improvement Programs, was designed to provide orientation for recent in-migrants to the Cleveland School District, to transients, and other culturally limited school-age children, and through work with the homes to improve parent and pupil attitudes.

Date begun: September 1960 (ended August 1964)

Target population: Pupils of six elementary schools (for home visitor program only) and 1,900 pupils of one junior high school, both groups predominantly lower socioeconomic status Negro.

Per pupil costs: $86

Sponsoring group: Ford Foundation and local school district.

Staff: Seventy-four classroom teachers, guidance counselors, reading specialists, home visitors, physician, nurse.

Services: Teacher workshop prior to school

opening; extensive inservice program in reading instruction; college internship program for education majors in junior year; home visitation program to involve parents in school activities and inform them of community welfare services available to them; home visits to parents of elementary school children feeding into project junior high; special counseling at high schools which receive project school graduates; transition classes for seventh-graders unready for traditional secondary school program; dropout prevention classes with block time devoted to "production classes" in home economics for girls and shop for boys; intensified reading instruction including Saturday and summer reading program; augmented health services; field trips, summer camping and day camp excursions; after-school, Saturday, and summer recreation program; adult education program.

Contact person:
Alva R. Dittrick
Deputy Superintendent
Cleveland Public Schools
1380 East 6th Street
Cleveland, Ohio 44114

Evaluation: Evaluation of the Hough Community Project, Cleveland, 1965—available.

2. The Work-Study Program is designed to provide pre-employment training and job placement plus needed remedial academic work to unemployed dropouts.

Date begun: April 1962

Target population: Five hundred unemployed youth, under 21, and out of school for at least six months.

Per pupil costs: Not determined

Sponsoring group: Board of Education and private enterprise.

Staff: Eight teacher-coordinators, assistant supervisor, four teacher-assistants, clerk.

Services: A six-week, three-hour-a-day

orientation course preceding regular program and involving extensive use of visiting lecturers from business and industry precedes each semester; regular program involves school classes in remedial work, work preparation, and four hours per day supervised work experience; weekly review of school and job progress with teacher-coordinator.

Contact person:
William R. Mason, Director Technical-
   Vocational Education
Cleveland Public Schools

3. Community Action for Youth is a broad-scale demonstration program designed to explore various approaches to the prevention and control of juvenile delinquency. The school program has utilized the Hough Community as a laboratory for investigating effective organizational and classroom innovations for teaching disadvantaged populations.

Date begun: July 1963

Target population: Twelve thousand school-age children in the Hough-Addison School District and their parents.

Per pupil costs: Not determined

Sponsoring group: President's Committee on Juvenile Delinquency and Youth Crime, City of Cleveland, County, Board of Education, Welfare Federation, foundations.

Staff: Three hundred teachers and nurses, policemen, specialists, clerical workers, part-time recreation leaders.

Services: Extensive administrative reorganization; establishment of three curriculum centers to develop and disseminate innovative methods and materials; demonstration lessons for classroom teachers by curriculum center resource teachers; preschool family nursery program for three- and four-year-olds with companion parent education program; extensive guidance and counseling for pupils and parents; after-school classes in communications skills emphasizing remedial reading as supplement to regular school program; involvement of junior high home economics classes in baking cookies for preschool snacks; teen-age mothers program providing casework, remedial reading, and arithmetic, and health services to promote continued school attendance; job-training and placement; summer programs of enrichment, monthly community newsletter.

Contact person:
Raphael O. Lewis, Executive Director
Community Action for Youth
1837 East 79th Street, Cleveland, Ohio

Columbus:

1. Columbus City School District Program to Combat Dropouts is a broad-scale program of educational improvement designed to reduce a dropout rate which was 50 percent in 1950.

Date begun: 1955

Target population: All pupils in Columbus City School District senior high schools.

Per pupil costs: Not determined

Sponsoring group: Local school district.

Staff: Classroom teachers, teachers' aides, clinical psychologists.

Services: Classroom reorganizat on with teaching on four ability levels; special teacher selection and education; revised instructional techniques; language laboratories and use of educational radio and TV; work-study program and vocational opportunities for potential dropouts; summer school program; increased guidance; teachers visit homes of students during month before school year begins (personal approach highly successful).

Contact person:
Joseph L. Davis, Assistant Superintendent
Columbus Public Schools
270 East State Street
Columbus, Ohio 43215

Evaluation: Written and available. Dropout rate greatly reduced; 90 percent of students in work-study program graduate.

2. The Enrichment Unit Approach to Effecting Planned Educational Change is a program involving enrichment units in the language arts which provide for freeing human and material resources to improve educational opportunity for disadvantaged children.

Date begun: September 1964

Target population: Approximately 7,440 pupils, 41 percent in first grade, 32 percent in second grade, and 27 percent in third grade in 25 public schools, selected according to median scores on achievement tests, pupil mobility, and conditions of housing.

Per pupil costs: Not determined

Sponsoring group: Local school district.

Staff: Classroom teachers, enrichment teachers, vice principal, Coordinator of Intercultural Education.

Services: Four regular classroom teachers and one enrichment teacher form enrichment unit providing for improved planning to meet needs of children; reduced pupil-teacher ratio; some individual instruction; instructional emphasis on language arts; teacher home visits; inservice teacher education.

Contact person:
Joseph L. Davis, Assistant Superintendent
Columbus Public Schools

Evaluation: Comprehensive evaluation being designed.

Dayton:

The Talent Development Project is a program designed to develop a better educational program for culturally deprived early primary children.

Date begun: Fall 1961

Target population: Children from K–2 in five elementary schools.

Per pupil costs: Not determined

Sponsoring group: Local school district.

Staff: Grade teachers, resource people in art, music, and physical education.

Services: Field trips; reading materials self-created by children; anecdotal records of children's activities maintained; collection of children's stories; extensive involvement in determining what children know, how they think of themselves.

Contact person:
Harold L. Boda
Assistant Superintendent of Schools for
 Instruction
Board of Education
Dayton, Ohio

Evaluation: Interim report, June 1964 (available).

Oklahoma

Oklahoma City:

1. The Cooperative Training or Work-Study program is designed to provide a flexible in-school situation in order to allow pupils to work while continuing their education.

Date begun: 1961

Target population: Pupils at one high school who want to work while still attending school.

Per pupil costs: Not determined

Sponsoring group: Local school district.

Staff: Two classroom teachers, coordinators, girls' counselor, boys' counselor.

Services: Coordinator matches pupils' study schedules with their work schedules and attempts to correlate academic training with their jobs; pupils may attend regular high school, adult day or night school. Extensive use of newspapers, films, guest speakers; extensive counseling.

Contact person:
Bill Horn
Central High School
Oklahoma City, Oklahoma

Evaluation: Follow-up on graduates, and contact with their employers.

2. Other practices: There are two other job-related educational programs in Oklahoma City:

An Adult Institute, for which students pay tuition, functions in the same high school (Central High) as the Cooperative Training program, providing academic courses designated as Job-Related I, II, and III for six credits in three semesters.

Contact person:
Bill Horn
Central High School

A Ford Foundation-sponsored project at Oklahoma State University is a research program aimed at evaluating the most effective methods of providing vocational and academic training to recent high school dropouts.

Contact person:
J. Paschal Twyman, Associate Professor of
    Education
Oklahoma State University
Oklahoma City, Oklahoma

Oregon

Portland:

1. The Jefferson Project is a broad-scale program designed to provide to educationally disadvantaged high school students a variety of compensatory activities intended to enhance their self-concept and improve their motivation and achievement.

Date begun: September 1961

Target population: All students considered slow learners, underachievers, alienated, or otherwise educationally disadvantaged in a single high school serving a middle and lower socioeconomic status 30 percent Negro population. About 45 percent of a total school population of 2,200 are involved.

Per pupil costs: Not determined

Sponsoring group: Local school district.

Staff: Social workers, development reading consultant, special counselor, remedial reading teacher, community agent, secretary, program coordinator, volunteers, entire staff of classes.

Services: Tutoring after school by college students; tutoring during school hours by volunteer adults; reading instruction for adult illiterates; school contact with various community agencies through community agent; parent involvement through home visits, counseling, and parent meetings; reading consultant services by high school teachers to help with reading; communications laboratory with Title I-supported audiovisual equipment to which any child with difficulties including hearing, speaking, writing is assigned for one-to-one remedial help until ready to return to original class; special counseling for actual and potential dropouts; summer-school classes in communications skills; orientation to high school for eighth-graders.

Contact person:
Harold Hansen, Coordinator
Jefferson Project, Jefferson High School
5210 North Kerby Avenue
Portland, Oregon 97217

2. The Sabin Summer School for Children in Disadvantaged Areas was a demonstration summer school conducted as part of a Reed College–Portland Public Schools Institute on the Education of the Disadvantaged.

Date begun: June 15, 1964 (terminated July 10, 1964)

Target population: One hundred and eighty kindergarten and elementary school children, predominantly Negro.

Per pupil costs: Not determined

Sponsoring group: Reed College, local school district.

Staff: Nine teachers, teachers' aides, director, principal, college professors.

Services: Emphasis on raising children's self-esteem through photographs, use of children's names; curriculum based on innovation as needed with focus on developing understanding of the local community; classroom visits by successful members of Negro community.

Contact person:
Clifford W. Williams, Director of Special
  Curriculum Projects
Portland Public Schools, Portland, Oregon

Evaluation: *Reed College–Portland Public Schools Institute on the Education of Disadvantaged Children.* Report, June 15–July 10, 1964.

3. The Model School Program: A Committee on Race and Education appointed by the Portland School Board did an extensive study of the relationship between race and quality of education on which a report was issued January 1965. As a result of this careful study, the district was able to implement the committee's recommendations including the funneling of a greater proportion of the city's resources to schools in severely disadvantaged neighborhoods as a means of equalizing educational opportunity. One of the means of doing this is the Model School Program, a system within a system specifically designed to meet the needs of disadvantaged youth, and operating under the direction of an assistant superintendent. Present plans involve nine elementary schools, five preschools, and an extensive

program, coordinating school, parent, and community activities. Smaller class loads, tutorial programs, and school, parent, and community cooperation are a part of the program. Among currently operating programs are:

A preschool program in the predominantly Negro area of Portland (Albina) involving teacher education as well as preschool classes is being effected.

Volunteer tutoring programs involve both community adults and Lewis and Clark College students in one-to-one tutoring assistance, with adult volunteers providing some classroom assistance as well.

Contact person:
Lloyd W. Colvin, Acting Director
Administrative Research Department
Portland Public Schools

Pennsylvania

Harrisburg:

The Preschool and Primary Education Project is part of a projected long-range statewide program to prevent dropouts which is intended eventually to include pupils from preschool through high school and post-high school levels. The preschool project is designed to improve the performance of disadvantaged children by providing for intervention at age three-and-a-half, with an ultimate goal of attacking the problem of school failure and school dropout.

Date begun: September 1963

Target population: Currently, 320 preschoolers (40 in each of six participating project schools and 80 in another center) who will remain in the program until the third grade. Each year a new group totaling 280 preschoolers will be admitted to the project.

Per pupil costs: $500–$600 per pupil in average daily membership for first year of project, lower in second year.

Sponsoring group: Ford Foundation, Pennsylvania Departments of Public Instruction, Health, and Welfare, local school districts.

Staff: Project teachers, teacher aides (parents), volunteer teacher aides, student teachers, project coordinators, home-school coordinators, social workers.

Services: Preschool summer nursery program followed by school year of work with parents and children at home by same teacher; second summer prekindergarten class with same teacher followed by kindergarten with same teacher; third summer of postkindergarten before first grade; enriched experiences with instructional emphasis on language development, cognitive and perceptual development; improved family services with attempt at parent and pupil attitude reorientation; long-term inservice training for project teachers.

Contact person:
Allan S. Hartman, Associate Director
Department of Public Instruction
Box 911
Harrisburg, Pennsylvania

Evaluation: Pre- and post-testing annually in all projects with reports published each summer.

Philadelphia:

1. The Great Cities School Improvement Program is a broad-scale project including an enriched school program emphasizing language arts, and a wide-range community program. It is designed to raise the achievement and aspirational levels, discover latent abilities among disadvantaged youngsters, and to awaken community responsibility through fostering closer home-school ties.

Date begun: September 1960

Target population: About 1,900 pupils in one junior high school and 5,547 pupils in seven elementary schools. Population is predominantly lower socioeconomic status Negro and Puerto Rican.

Per pupil costs: $37.58

Sponsoring group: Ford Foundation and school district of Philadelphia.

Staff: Two hundred and seventy-six classroom teachers, new teacher consultants, arithmetic consultant, language laboratory teachers, school-community coordinators (including two bilingual coordinators), language arts consultant.

Services: Once-a-week inservice teacher training and workshop experience on school time; summer workshops for staff; consultant teacher help for new teachers; experimental materials and methods in language arts including "culture free" beginning reading and writing system; experimental materials and methods in mathematics; flexible class groupings; extensive use of audiovisual aids; added music materials and books; field trips; after-school instructional and recreational activities; Saturday and summer cultural enrichment trips; special weekly literature enrichment programs for children; school-community coordinator to stimulate community councils, civic associations, parent discussion groups, community interest, understanding, and support; special coordinators for Spanish-speaking parents; homework centers with parent supervision; volunteer tutorial help; "late bloomers" program for slow first-graders.

Contact person:
George Green, Curriculum Office
Room 202, Administration Building
Board of Education
Parkway at 21st Street
Philadelphia, Pennsylvania 19103

Evaluation: Progress report 1960–64 available September 1965 from Curriculum Office.

2. The Experimental Nursery School Program is a multipurpose project designed to train nursery school teachers, to develop a preschool program which will promote the growth of disadvantaged youngsters, and to

involve the parents with the school and the community.

Date begun: July 1963

Target population: One hundred and twenty preschool children, predominantly Negro.

Per pupil costs: Not determined

Sponsoring group: Local school district, Philadelphia Council for Community Advancement, and Temple University.

Staff: Four teachers, four assistant teachers, psychologists, social worker, four home-school coordinators, research assistants, project director, research director.

Services: Eight 4-day-a-week nursery-school classes meet morning or afternoon; fifth day for parent conferences, inservice training; summer teacher-training institute, only first summer.

Contact person:
Gabrielle J. Faddis
College of Education
Temple University
Philadelphia, Pennsylvania

3. Youth Conservation Corps is a multi-faceted approach to combat, prevent, and control juvenile delinquency.

Date begun: August 1959

Target population: Four hundred boys, 100 in the school-work program and 300 in the 10-week summer work program, between age 14 and 17, 70 percent Negro, 25 percent Caucasian, 5 percent Puerto Rican, primarily from depressed areas of city.

Per pupil costs: Not determined

Sponsoring group: Youth Conservation Services, Department of Public Welfare.

Staff: Ten group leaders from September to June, 30 group leaders in summer, director of community services, supervisor.

Services: Summer work program, 40 hours per week in city parks for pay; during school year program becomes part of school-work program of district with dismissal to allow for after-school work, school credit, and cash awards given for work; 1 adult to 10 boys; counseling with boys and their families.

Contact person:
Kavanzo Hyde, Director
Community Services Division
Youth Conservation Services Division
531 City Hall Annex
Philadelphia, Pennsylvania

4. The MDTA Youth Project is a worker education program designed to prepare out-of-school, out-of-work youth for immediate employment.

Date begun: September 1963

Target population: Fifty-four youths 16 to 22 years of age (also 73 heads of households over 22 years of age).

Per pupil costs: Not determined

Sponsoring group: Federal funds through United States Manpower Development and Training Act.

Staff: Twenty-five teachers, 50 shop teachers.

Services: Six hours a day of school for 12 weeks in basic academics and shop; 40-week vocational training program following school program in such subjects as beauty culture, restaurant practice, hospital services, and auto, sheet metal, machine, and electrical shops; subsistence allowance for 52 weeks maximum.

Contact person:
William E. Brunton, Division of Vocational and Industrial Art Education
Board of Education

Pittsburgh:

1. The Compensatory Education program in Pittsburgh is an outgrowth of the pilot Team Teaching Project, one of the Ford Foundation's Great Cities School Improve-

ment Programs. It is a large-scale program to heighten both the desire and the opportunity to learn for disadvantaged pupils in the center-city area of a large metropolis.

Date begun: June 1960 (pilot terminated, July 1964)

Target population: About 1,840 preschoolers in 46 centers, 26,600 elementary school children in 46 schools, and 2,445 junior high school pupils in 3 schools, all drawing from a lower socioeconomic status population.

Per pupil costs: $142.80

Sponsoring group: Local school district, Ford Foundation, United States Office of Economic Opportunity.

Staff: For preschool: coordinator, secretary, teacher, assistant teacher, community aide. For arts program: story tellers, art consultant, eurythmics workshop leader, eurythmics supervisor, eurythmics teachers. For team teaching: team leaders, assistant team leaders, team mothers, special supervisors. For transition rooms: remedial teacher, reading specialist, director. For adjustment classes and mental health: teachers, coordinator, psychiatrists, psychiatric social workers, psychologists, community case aides, secretaries. For family and community work: coordinator, industrial arts teachers, homemaking counselors, physical education instructors, primary teachers, group social workers, itinerant teacher. For teacher workshops: resource speakers and consultants. Also creative dramatics teachers and supervisor, reading specialist, television teacher, kindergarten aides, research assistants.

Services: Team-teaching organization along grade lines in first, second, and third grades; intermediate teams composed of teachers of different subjects and junior high teams organized by subject; team mothers paid to assist team; student interns; remedial work and special programs for teaching reading; nongraded plan for preschool through primary with special transition classes at end of third grade for pupils not ready for regular fourth-grade program; mental health team emphasizing preventive work; adult education program and family guidance; field trips; special TV programs; community involvement in providing personnel and financial assistance for study-halls, tutorial programs, and so forth.

Contact person:
Charles H. Hayes, Director of
   Compensatory Education
Pittsburgh Public Schools
341 South Bellefield Avenue
Pittsburgh, Pennsylvania 15213

2. Other practices: Pittsburgh also has a program at one high school for 16- to 18-year-old boys, predominantly dropped-out students who are given one-half time academic work and one-half time in shop work such as wiring, brick and tile laying, woodworking, and so forth. This is one of the programs growing out of the summer 1963 Dropout Campaign. A full occupational-vocational-technical curriculum is also being developed within the comprehensive high schools, providing various levels of training for variously qualified pupils, and including at the technical level a new curriculum in such areas as computer technology in which training will be continued through the thirteenth and fourteenth grades in a technical institute.

Contact person:
Charles H. Hayes, Director of
   Compensatory Education
Pittsburgh Public Schools

Rhode Island

Providence:

1. The Cooperative Motivation Program is a junior high school project designed primarily to instill college aspirations among talented disadvantaged students.

Date begun: 1962

Target population: Four hundred students from 16 junior high schools, 75 percent of whom score higher than 110 on IQ measurements.

Per pupil costs: $25

Sponsoring group: Carnegie Corporation through Brown University.

Staff: Twenty guidance counselors, directors of guidance, psychologists, college faculty.

Services: Group counseling, visits to colleges.

Contact person:
John A. Finger, Director, Cooperative Motivation Program
130 Angell Street, Providence, Rhode Island

2. The Thomas A. Doyle Jenkins Street Elementary Interim Program is designed to prepare a group of culturally deprived children for a move into a new school in which they will compete with children from a higher socioeconomic status.

Date begun: September 1963

Target population: Thirty-seven children from two prekindergarten programs and 485 children from two elementary schools, predominately lower socioeconomic status Negro population.

Per pupil costs: $63 per month

Sponsoring group: Local school district.

Staff: Twenty-two classroom teachers, reading specialists, general supervisor, principal, psychologist, college student tutors, home visitor, nurse.

Services: Remedial reading, cultural enrichment, numerous field trips, after-school tutoring program including academic and recreational work, prekindergarten program.

Contact person:
Gertrude Coleman, Elementary Supervisor
Department of Public Schools
170 Pond Street
Providence, Rhode Island 02903

South Carolina

Sumter:

Sumter Child Study Project is a long-term program designed to evaluate the effects of various interventions on children's ability to cope with school.

Date begun: January 1963

Target population: One hundred and fifty children for preschool check-up, 25 in summer preschool program, all culturally deprived, 100 percent Caucasian.

Per pupil costs: Not determined

Sponsoring group: National Institute of Mental Health 85 percent, local school district, and State Department of Mental Health.

Staff: Eighteen teachers, teachers' aides, social workers, psychologists, specialized teachers, volunteers, principal investigator.

Services: Evaluation in spring prior to school entry to determine ability to cope with school; summer preschool program for 25 of children including consultation with teachers and parents and special testing and follow-up with children; continuing intervention during early school years by team members and school social workers to improve adaptation to school.

Contact person:
M. R. Newton
Sumter Child Study Project
P. O. Box 1191, Sumter, South Carolina

Evaluation: Continual study of children to determine effectiveness of interventions. *Progress Report 15*, November 1963, Sumter Child Study Project, Box 1191, Sumter, South Carolina.

Tennessee

Murfreesboro:

The Early Training Project is a program designed to provide varying amounts of special experience to preschool children for an extended period before school entrance in order to improve their intellectual functioning and school adjustment. Goal is to determine the minimum intervention which can still affect a child's performance.

Date begun: 1962

Target population: Negro children born in 1958, two groups of 20 plus two control groups. All children identified as culturally deprived on basis of various criteria.

Per pupil costs: Not determined

Sponsoring group: National Institute of Mental Health.

Staff: Project teachers (one per five pupils), director, codirector, consulting psychiatrist.

Services: One experimental group gets three years of summer classes and two years of home visits, the other, two years of summer classes and one year of home visits; classes involve general enrichment, personal attention, and guidance; emphasis upon attitudes toward achievement, aptitudes for achievement, personal-social development, and physical and mental health; numerous trips into community; music, art, group play.

Contact person:
Rupert A. Klaus, Director
Early Training Project
Murfreesboro, Tennessee

Evaluation: Susan Gray and R. A. Klaus, *Interim Report: Early Training Project.* George Peabody College and Murfreesboro Tennessee City Schools, 1963.

Texas

Austin:

1. Project for Children of Migrant Parents is designed to provide migrant children with a regular nine-month school term in six months.

Date begun: November 1963

Target population: First year, 3,000 elementary pupils in five schools and 45 junior high school pupils in two schools whose parents are Mexican-American migrants. Next year, program will serve 9,000 children in 15 schools.

Per pupil costs: $81

Sponsoring group: Texas Education Agency.

Staff: First year, 72 classroom teachers, curriculum coordinators. Next year, 300 teachers.

Services: Basic "instructional" activities with emphasis on oral English usage; children grouped homogeneously at achievement level.

Contact person:
Jack McIntosh, Director
Project for Children of Migrant Parents
Texas Education Agency
Capitol Station, Austin, Texas

Evaluation: Available for pilot project.

2. Preschool Program for Non-English-Speaking Children is a summer program to teach English to Spanish speaking preschoolers. Statewide it utilized 900 teachers to serve 20,000 Mexican-American children in 180 school districts at an average cost of $25 per pupil. (See El Paso for an example of a local program.)

Contact person:
Jack McIntosh, Director

3. University Junior High School's Dropout Research Project is an attempt to alter and enrich the school program in order to improve the holding power of the school for the potential dropout.

Date begun: September 1962

Target population: Each year approximately 25 Spanish-speaking lower socioeconomic status pupils in the seventh grade of one junior high school; 76 students currently in program.

Per pupil costs: $70

Sponsoring group: Hogg Foundation.

Staff: Two classroom teachers, coordinator, bilingual secretary, three summer-school teachers.

Services: Special block-time program with emphasis on reading; enrichment through field trips to museums, businesses, and so forth; supervised study center and tutoring by volunteers; home visits by teacher, principal, and special Latin-American coordinator; paid work on school grounds one hour per day for project pupils; free summer enrichment and language program; inservice teacher training.

Contact person:
Joe R. Stepan, Principal
University Junior High School
1910 Red River Street, Austin, Texas

4. Operation Education is a program designed to provide Saturday tutoring and enrichment for a group of predominantly Spanish-speaking elementary children.

Date begun: September 1963 (to conclude summer, 1966)

Target population: Four hundred and five lower socioeconomic status predominantly Spanish-speaking elementary school children, preschool to sixth grade level.

Per pupil costs: None

Sponsoring group: Palm Elementary School supervises—no extra funds.

Staff: Fifty full-time volunteers, 200 to 300 part-time volunteers, four teacher chaperones.

Services: Saturday-morning sessions at two centers with tutoring in various academic subjects; guest speakers from community; classes in grooming, music, drama, health care, and so forth; field trips.

Contact person:
Louise Campos
2310 Westrock Drive, Austin, Texas

El Paso:

Pre-School Summer Classes for Non-English-Speaking Children is a statewide program designed to prepare non-English-speaking children to enter first grade by giving them a basic vocabulary and classroom experience during the summer prior to their school entry. (See Austin, Texas, for data on total program.)

Date begun: 1960

Target population: Approximately 2,000 pupils, lower socioeconomic status, Mexican-American.

Per pupil costs: $20

Sponsoring group: Texas Education Agency, local school district.

Staff: Sixty-six certified classroom teachers, nurses.

Services: Morning classes taught by certified teachers; oral English and other pre-first-grade preparatory work; milk break at mid-morning; use of special manual for preschool English; parental counseling; home visits.

Contact person:
Carlos Rivera
El Paso Public Schools
P. O. Box 1710
El Paso, Texas 79999

Evaluation: Completed and available.

Fort Worth:

Pilot Program to Reduce Dropouts is a pilot designed to improve the holding power of the school through providing an educational program especially designed for the under-achieving student.

Date begun: September 1964

Target population: Forty pupils in two

classes of 20 each at two junior high schools, all at least 13 years old by grade 7 and two years retarded in reading and mathematics.

Per pupil costs: About $650

Sponsoring group: Local school district, regular state per capita apportionment.

Staff: Two classroom teachers.

Services: Special four-year program in regular three-year junior high; two-hour language arts class by project teacher using special high-interest low-reading level resource materials, mathematics taught at group level, and remaining subjects taken with regular classes; home visits by project teachers; group counseling; educational, cultural, and recreational field trips.

Contact person:
Julius Truelson, Assistant Superintendent
  Junior High Division
Fort Worth Independent School District
Fort Worth, Texas

Houston:

1. The Talent Preservation Project is a program emphasizing curriculum enrichment as a means of improving the holding power of the schools for students who are identified as likely to drop out.

Date begun: September 1961 (preceded by a pilot 1960–61)

Target population: About 2,262 pupils at seventh-, eighth-, or ninth-grade levels in 26 junior high schools and at the tenth-grade level in eight senior high schools, all significantly retarded in school.

Per pupil costs: Not determined

Sponsoring group: Local school district.

Staff: One hundred and twenty project teachers, counselors.

Services: Special four-level curriculum beginning in seventh grade which may culminate in job-training or placement in

regular curriculum; special teacher selection and inservice training; home visits and parental conferences; guidance services; resource speakers; encouragement of extra-curricular activity; community interpretation of program; summer back-to-school drive.

Contact person:
Mrs. Jozie Mock, Supervisor
Talent Preservation Project
Public Schools
Houston, Texas

2. The Houston Multi-Occupational Youth Project is a pilot study providing vocational training and counseling to unemployable secondary school graduates and dropouts.

Date begun: July 1964

Target population: Four hundred and forty-eight youths, predominantly Negro and Latin-American, from 17 through 21 years of age, culturally handicapped, unskilled and unemployable, out of school at least one year.

Per pupil costs: Not determined

Sponsoring group: United States Office of Education, United States Department of Labor through Harris County Department of Education.

Staff: Eighteen teachers, counselors, psychologist, training director.

Services: Vocational trade training in such demand occupations as auto mechanics, shoe repair, cleaning and pressing, meat cutting, office machine repair, for periods from 20 to 52 weeks; weekly training allowance; extensive pupil counseling and guidance.

Contact person:
Paul H. Lewis, Director
Houston Youth Project
409 Civil Courts Building
Houston, Texas 77002

Virginia

Norfolk:

The Berkeley Project is a pilot program designed to improve the school performance of "culturally submerged" children through modification of classroom organization, materials, and teaching techniques, and through alteration of teacher attitudes.

Date begun: September 1963

Target population: Four hundred ninety-five Negro pupils in three elementary schools.

Per pupil costs: $5.95

Sponsoring group: Local school district.

Staff: Eighteen classroom teachers, curriculum coordinator, helping teacher, pre-teaching student assistants, student teachers.

Services: Nongraded primary block; flexible subject-to-subject, classroom-to-classroom groupings; new teaching materials; parent-teacher conferences in lieu of report cards; community involvement in providing funds for field trips.

Contact person:
Mrs. Hortense R. Wells, Coordinator of
  Elementary Instruction
735 Pembroke Avenue, Norfolk, Virginia

2. The Jacox Plan is a secondary school program designed to raise the achievement and aspiration level of disadvantaged students and to improve social and cultural behavior. Modeled after the "Higher Horizons" program.

Date begun: September 1961

Target population: About 1,571 Negro pupils in one junior high school, 75 percent of whom score below 90 on IQ tests.

Per pupil costs: No additional cost

Sponsoring group: Local school board.

Staff: Sixty-five classroom teachers, guidance counselors, subject supervisors, curriculum coordinators, home visitor, psychiatrist, physician, nurse.

Services: Team-teaching; field trips; language laboratory; television classes; remedial reading; group guidance; special assemblies; parental participation; special inservice education in teaching of reading; student and parent guidance.

Contact person:
Margaret L. Gordon, Principal
D. G. Jacox Junior High School
1300 Marshall Avenue
Norfolk, Virginia

3. Other practices: Through the Norfolk Council for the Improvement of Education, supported by five Negro civic organizations and a Negro newspaper there has been a broad-scale attempt to motivate the Negro community and to provide a variety of activities to children and youth of all ages in various areas of the community. In addition to sponsoring remedial and enrichment clinics, summer schools emphasizing upgrading of Negro students recently enrolled in newly integrated schools, individual tutoring programs, city-wide honors and awards day, pupil and parent guidance programs, civic improvement groups, aid to gifted children to encourage higher education, preschool program with block sessions on child development for mothers, the Council has encouraged the establishment in the public schools of additional programs of compensatory education.

Contact person:
Mrs. Vivian Mason, President
Norfolk Council for the Improvement
  of Education, Norfolk, Virginia

Richmond:

The Richmond Human Development Project is a pilot project seeking to raise the academic achievement of disadvantaged pupils and to increase the holding power of the schools.

Date begun: June 1963

Target population: Approximately 4,500 pupils in four elementary and two junior high schools; 74 percent are Negro and all are of lower socioeconomic status.

Per pupil costs: $74

Sponsoring group: Ford Foundation, local school district.

Staff: Reading specialists, 176 classroom teachers, visiting teachers, guidance counselors, psychologists.

Services: Reduced class size; instructional emphasis on language arts with attention to improving reading and developing facility in oral and written communication; inservice teacher reorientation and reading training; before-school study and curricular enrichment; after-school and evening cultural, academic, and recreational activities including adult education; summer school.

Contact person:
James W. Tyler, Director, Research and
   Development
Richmond Public Schools
312 North 9th Street
Richmond, Virginia

West Virginia

Moorefield:

A Community Action Program Project Proposal for a Preschool Program in the Rural Communities of Hardy and Mineral Counties, West Virginia, is a project to provide a school readiness program to the children of low-income families and to help them begin their formal schooling without handicaps.

Date begun: March 1, 1965

Target population: Preschool children in 10 centers; areas selected on basis of various population and socioeconomic factors.

Per pupil costs: Not determined

Sponsoring group: United States Office of Economic Opportunity and local school board.

Staff: Teachers, project directors, teacher aides.

Services: Five-day-a-week, three-hour-a-day preschool classes for nine months a year; program involves development of visual and auditory skills, motor skills, general readiness for school situations; field trips; home visits and once-a-month parent discussion groups; lunch and transportation; follow-through for first three grades of school.

Contact persons:
Floyd J. Dahmer, Superintendent, Hardy
   County Schools
or
Ralph E. Fisher, Editor
Moorefield Examiner
Moorefield, West Virginia

Evaluation: To be made by West Virginia University Appalachian Center for Studies and Development.

Wisconsin

Milwaukee:

1. Orientation Classes for In-migrant and Transient Children (1960–63), was a pilot program which has now been incorporated into the regular program of the Milwaukee schools. It provides special services for in-migrant-transient children in order to better prepare them for success in school.

Date begun: September 1960

Target population: Recent in-migrant pupils from 28 elementary, 4 junior, and 3 senior high schools, most of them Negro or Puerto Rican. Children chosen on basis of recent arrival without records, no English, or transient status within city.

Per pupil costs: Not determined

Sponsoring group: Ford Foundation and

local school district (for pilot). Cost now totally carried by local school board.

Staff: Orientation center teachers, teacher aides, curriculum coordinator, psychologist, school social worker (health and speech therapy services from regular school utilized).

Services: Nine orientation classes serving a number of contributing schools with maximum of 20 pupils per class organized around ungraded classrooms; elementary classes self-contained, secondary classes take academics from orientation center teacher, non-academics with regular students; intensive remedial work and individualized instruction; field trips; ultimate integration into regular school program when and if student ready; monthly teacher workshop sessions; parental approval of participation in program; summer school program for selected pupils (see below).

Contact person:
Clemens C. Zebrowski, Acting Coordinator
Orientation Center Program
Milwaukee Public Schools
5225 West Vliet Street
Milwaukee, Wisconsin 53208

Evaluation: Available: *Orientation Classes for In-Migrant-Transient Children: Final Report*, 1960–63. Milwaukee, Wisconsin, March 1964.

2. The Special Summer School Program is designed to provide supplementary education to disadvantaged elementary pupils in the center-city area.

Date begun: Summer 1964 (repeated summer 1965)

Target population: About 150 to 500 children grades K–6 in three schools in the center-city area.

Per pupil costs: Not determined

Sponsoring group: Local school district.

Staff: Thirty teachers, teacher-interns from local universities.

Services: Complete elementary school program at various grade levels; reading center and special center for in-migrant and transient pupils.

Contact person:
Lillian Paukner, Executive Director
Department of Elementary Curriculum
   and Instruction
Milwaukee Public Schools

3. Secretarial Development Project is an extracurricular program providing both additional classroom training and motivational activities to help prepare business education students for employment.

Date begun: October 1964

Target population: Twenty-three girls from two schools in business education courses.

Per pupil costs: Not determined

Sponsoring group: Local school district, Mortgage Associates, Inc., and Milwaukee Urban League.

Staff: One teacher.

Services: Twice weekly after-school class meetings to upgrade skills in typing, office machine operation, business-English usage, office practices and procedures, and so forth, utilizing materials secured directly from businesses; field trips to offices; visiting speakers on such topics as "money management" and "personal grooming"; parent conferences.

Contact person:
Thomas Cheeks, Coordinator
School-Community Programs
Milwaukee Public Schools

Evaluation: Informal.

4. The Youth Incentive Project is a program designed to widen the vocational horizons of young people, to encourage them to stay in school, and to help develop jobs for them after they are trained.

Date begun: June 1963

Target population: Fifty-six Negro youths from six inner-city high schools.

Per pupil costs: Not determined

Sponsoring group: Urban League and local school district.

Staff: Volunteer teachers, guidance counselors, local volunteers from Urban League.

Services: Group and individual guidance sessions; industrial tours preceded by briefing and provision of information about working conditions, machines, and instruments used by workers, demands of various jobs, and so forth; cultural enrichment programs; guest speakers; summer job placement so pupils can earn money and learn good work habits; parent information programs.

Contact person:
Alfred W. Thurner, Director, Department
  of Guidance
Milwaukee Public Schools

5. In addition to the programs listed above, the Milwaukee Public Schools have instituted a number of other programs and practices which benefit disadvantaged pupils. Among them are:

An ungraded plan of organization operates in the elementary schools—a Primary School arrangement in which pupils work at their own level until they are ready to move into the fourth grade.

A three-day orientation workshop for new teachers is designed to acquaint them not only with the school organization, but with the children they will teach and the community within which they will work.

Extra services are provided to schools serving the disadvantaged: assignment of additional welfare counselors, lay counselor assistants, and an elementary school guidance counselor to work with families and children within the central-city area. Use of a special staffing formula in areas of high population density and mobility provides for improved staff

ratio. Provision of proportionately more special services, guidance, services, recreation programs, and reference books, supplementary readers and other library materials in central-city schools.

Three work-study programs are functioning; one for high school seniors enrolled in business education (q.v.), one for mentally retarded pupils, and a third, for predelinquents, which provides for a half-day in school and a half-day in a sheltered workshop at the Jewish Vocational Service.

University Tutorial Programs are in-school and after-school programs of tutoring carried on by the schools in cooperation with four local universities. Nine secondary schools have "In School During School Time" programs for pupils in need of special help and staffed by School of Education students who thus receive preservice experience. Two junior high schools have after-school study centers where pupils can get help with their studies from college student tutors.

Contact person:
Thomas Cheeks, Coordinator
School-Community Programs
Milwaukee Public Schools

A Reading Improvement Program involves reading centers in all secondary schools, in the in-migrant-transient program (q.v.), and in many elementary schools. An After School Reading Centers program in eight schools provides special low register remedial reading classes for high school pupils judged potential dropouts.

Contact person:
Melvin Yanow, Supervisor for
  Remedial Reading
Milwaukee Public Schools

Guidance programs include: two guidance centers for school dropouts operated since summer 1964, and providing educational and vocational guidance and job placement for high school pupils; establishment of a continuing evening counseling center with follow-up contacts with 18-year-olds who have not returned to school; Swing-Shift In-school Guidance provides evening scheduling of guidance sessions to involve parents in junior high school guidance program; special counselor training.

Contact person:
Alfred W. Thurner, Director, Department
    of Guidance
Milwaukee Public Schools

Racine:

1. The Pilot Kindergarten Project is a program designed to test the hypothesis that a full-day, specially structured kindergarten program for disadvantaged children can help overcome some of their later school problems and to measure the impact of the program upon school achievement.

Date begun: January 1962 (ended 1964)

Target population: Kindergarten children from culturally deprived backgrounds.

Per pupil costs: Not determined

Sponsoring group: Johnson Foundation and Western Foundation.

Staff: Kindergarten teacher, project directors.

Services: Full five-hour school day with extended time utilized for activities designed to compensate specifically for the assumed deficiencies in school readiness of disadvantaged population; extensive use of photographs of children and activities, and of children's own stories; numerous field trips; extensive use of puppetry; attempt to keep parental involvement as a constant.

Contact person:
Richard G. Larson, Stephen Bull School
Racine Public Schools
Racine, Wisconsin

Evaluation: Completed and available July 1965, *Final Report: A Pilot Project for Culturally Deprived Kindergarten Children.*

2. Other practices: The establishment of an Inner-City School Council, including among its members all the principals of the inner-city schools, has resulted in the initiation of a number of practices to improve education in these schools. Among them are:

Improved intraschool, intrateacher communication among the inner-city schools through teacher meetings and newsletters. Teacher education through inservice courses and relevant literature.

Extensive use of lay persons, as volunteer helpers in classrooms, as guest speakers or entertainers, as resource persons to visit classrooms as role models, and so forth.

Distribution of discarded library books and textbooks to disadvantaged children—5,000 distributed by June 1965.